Talking
with
Serial Killers

DEAD MEN TALKING

Born in 1948 in Winchester, Hampshire, Christopher Berry-Dee is descended from Dr John Dee, Court Astrologer to Queen Elizabeth I, and is the founder and former Director of the Criminology Research Institute (CRI), and former publisher and Editor-in-Chief of *The Criminologist*, a highly respected journal on matters concerning all aspects of criminology from law enforcement to forensic psychology.

Christopher has interviewed and interrogated over thirty of the world's most notorious killers – serial, mass and one-off – including Peter Sutcliffe, Ted Bundy, Aileen Wuornos, Dennis Nilsen and Joanne Dennehy. He was co-producer/ interviewer for the acclaimed twelve-part TV documentary series *The Serial Killers*, and has appeared on television as a consultant on serial homicide, and, in the series *Born to Kill?*, on the cases of Fred and Rose West, the 'Moors Murderers' and Dr Harold Shipman. He has also assisted in criminal investigations as far afield as Russia and the United States.

Notable book successes include: *Monster* (the basis for the movie of the same title, about Aileen Wuornos); *Dad Help Me Please*, about the tragic Derek Bentley, hanged for a murder he did not commit (subsequently subject of the film *Let Him Have It*) – and *Talking with Serial Killers*, Christopher's international bestseller, now, with its sequel, *Talking with Serial Killers: World's Most Evil*, required reading at the FBI Behavioral Science Unit Academy at Quantico, Virginia. His *Talking with Psychopaths and Savages: A Journey Into the Evil Mind*, was the UK's bestselling true-crime title of 2017; its successor volume, *Talking with Psychopaths and Savages: Beyond Evil*, was published in the autumn of 2019.

Talking
with
Serial Killers

DEAD MEN TALKING

Death Row's worst killers –
in their own words

Christopher Berry-Dee

JOHN BLAKE

Published by John Blake Publishing,
80–1 Wimpole Street
Marylebone
London W1G 9RE

www.facebook.com/johnblakebooks
twitter.com/jblakebooks

First published, as *Dead Men Talking: The world's worst killers in their own words*,
in hardback in 2009
Paperback edition first published in 2011
This retitled paperback edition first published in 2019

Trade paperback ISBN: 978-1-78946-288-3
Paperback ISBN: 978-1-78946-220-3
Ebook ISBN: 978-1-84358-643-2

British Library Cataloguing-in-Publication Data:

A catalogue record for this book is available from the British Library.

Design by www.envydesign.co.uk

Printed and bound in Great Britain by Clays Ltd, Elcograf S.p.A

1 3 5 7 9 10 8 6 4 2

John Blake Publishing is an imprint of Bonnier Books UK
www.bonnierbooks.co.uk

This book is dedicated my late mother, Mary Dee

CONTENTS

ACKNOWLEDGEMENTS   ix

INTRODUCTION   xiii

1 JOHN EDWARD ROBINSON   1
   The Slavemaster

2 MELANIE LYN MCGUIRE   81
   The Ice Queen

3 PHILLIP CARL JABLONSKI   121
   'I Have No Remorse'

4 KEITH HUNTER JESPERSON   137
   The Happy Face Killer

5 VIVA LEROY NASH   189
   The Oldest Man on Death Row

6 MICHAEL BRUCE ROSS   211
   The Roadside Strangler

SUMMARY   263

ACKNOWLEDGEMENTS

Writing non-fiction is not possible without a collective effort by many people and the study of violent crime on a first-hand basis can be at once rewarding, exciting and distressing; conversely, it also has its lighter moments. But at the end of the road, the time comes to reflect on that journey and to remember all those individuals and organisations who, in their various capacities, helped to make the realisation of a book possible and, hopefully, worthwhile. Now is this time.

First and foremost, I am indebted to my countless readers from around the world. I receive dozens of letters and emails every month from you guys thanking me for my books and how you appreciate the work that I do. Often you are students, studying criminal justice; sometimes police officers, who take on board my no-nonsense approach, at the same time appreciating my black humour when the mood takes me. From whatever walk of life you hail from, you should not thank me, *for I thank you all*. Without you the support would be gone and I would not have the reason, nor the means, to pen another word. An author's public is an author's lifeblood and as we enter the most difficult of financial times, I sincerely appreciate your contribution towards understanding the most evil and twisted minds living within our societies: the serial killers.

Secondly, to my very close friend and publisher, John Blake. John has been supporting me since 2001 and a more generous and fine fellow one could not wish to meet. Also to John's entire team at John Blake Publishing Limited, who have worked tirelessly on all of my publishing projects, to include my commissioning editor, Lucian Randall, John Wordsworth (who wishes to remain nameless), Rosie Ries, Michelle Signore and Joanna Kennedy.

On the bookstore front, thanks to the countless bookstores – whether they be in the UK, USA or otherwise – for promoting and selling my books, especially to Alison Darby at Waterstones. Also a big thank you to the media, from both sides of the pond, for promoting my work where possible.

Although this may seem inappropriate to many readers, I am obliged to thank the principal contributors to this book: LeRoy Nash (the old rascal that he is), Keith Hunter Jesperson, and the other killers featured throughout these pages. They all contributed to the book for their own, oft-times perverse reasons, and without their input the book would have been impossible to write. Oh, I must not forget JR Robinson, who thanks me for exposing him, I don't think. I am also most grateful to Keith Jesperson's daughter, Melissa – a remarkable woman.

Good can come from bad, and my relationship, built up with Mr Jesperson over months and months, has, and will continue to bear fruit in the understanding of how a serial murderer's mind ticks. If he had been executed, which he probably should have been, we would have been denied his 'knowledge'. His writings and thoughts I have passed onto the FBI's Behavioural Science Unit, for further study. They are very grateful.

With the hard core acknowledgements come thanks to very special people.

Unequivocally, and without reservation, the frontrunner has to be Kirstie 'Kiwi' McCallum. Kiwi has selflessly supported me in this writing of this book through very troubled times – because even popular writers feel the pinch sometimes – and it is true to say that no stronger friend can be found.

Then there my friends, 'The Oddball Club', driving me to distraction when a veritable party of serial killers could not: I thank Richard, Craig and Mr Lee; also to Wilf for his devoted friendship and his thoughts on a 'new world order'; Martin 'The Shrink' Balaam, who will one day get weaving and write a book; also to Lizzie, Jim, Dan, Laura, Blake and Tom Stoddard.

Years back my mentor was Robin Odell, one of the finest true crime writers and crime historians of our decade. Under his guidance I was taught 'the trade', so to speak. God bless you Robin.

Then there is Tony, Joyce and Russell Mercier. I have known them since time began. How can one repay a couple who epitomises such selfless kinship for their fellows, who give the world a son whom they must be so proud of? Hey, Tony! You *are* the man; your oil paintings *are* class (with an 'A'); and thank you, all three, for being *you*.

Finally, there is a very, very special debt of gratitude to young Ben Burton, for being himself, and for the 'Green Light Lady' – a should-be-shareholder in Aldo, who, like John Wordsworth, must also remain incognito.

And that's it. 'Period,' as our American friends will say, leaving these Acknowledgements with you desperate to get on with reading what follows - and no nightmares, please!

CHRISTOPHER BERRY-DEE

INTRODUCTION

I have interviewed, face to face, some 30 of the world's most heinous serial killers, spree killers and mass murderers. I have sat with them on death rows throughout the United States, where the stench of cheap disinfectant, human sweat and evil permeates every brick of these correctional cathedrals, the human warehouses that incarcerate those from the legion of the damned.

I have listened to their sickening tales of murder most foul and their boasts of having caused such suffering, which are often beyond the comprehension of normal souls like you and me.

These sexual psychopaths love to play mind games and often are as cunning as hyenas. They are control freaks who attempt to manipulate even a seasoned criminologist like me, prompting the chilling question: what chance did their vulnerable prey have against such twisted characters, who can appear as innocent as the man or woman next door?

With a new millennium, a new generation of monsters has emerged. Long gone are the likes of Ted Bundy, although his story remains morbidly fascinating. Indeed, books are still being written, and TV documentaries are still produced which dredge up the 'oldies' of yesteryear. It seems that not a month goes by without another screening of a programme on Bundy, Arthur Shawcross, Ken Bianchi or Aileen Wuornos. And Ronald DeFeo, a.k.a. 'The Amityville Horror', is still 'hot property' despite the fact that in the big league of mass-murderers he is relatively small potatoes (this continued interest is mainly due to the horror films based very loosely on his case).

This book delves deep into the dysfunctional minds of some of these social outcasts. This time the gloves are off and I have allowed these monsters to say just what they wanted to... and in doing so, they give away more than they intended. In that respect, this book is what newspapers might call a 'worldwide exclusive'.

Over the years, the interviews I have conducted have always been a play off between the two parties – me and the killer in question. The killers do their best to control you and this is frequently on-the-edge-of-the-abyss time. You are so close to them, breathing in the foul air they expel from their often diseased lungs. And, although it may not be quite as direct, the same can be said of spending hundreds of hours corresponding with them. In fact, I have come to the conclusion that, more often than not, what these murderers write in their correspondence is more important to understanding their psychopathology than what they say in the relatively brief face-to-face interviews. In these interviews, you must remember, the killer is on his own ground, you are there at his behest and it is in surroundings that he or she is familiar with.

To truly get inside the heads of these devious social misfits – where is exactly where we need to be if we are understand the true nature of evil – long periods of correspondence are the key. Every word, sentence, paragraph and page of their letters are a clue to the reason behind their homicidal behaviour, making this book a must-read for all professionals and aficionados with an interest in the causation of the unlawful and wanton destruction of human life.

Some of these social strays can read and write, while others struggle with the simplest words. Some have a brain, others half a brain, and still others obviously have a 'To Let' sign planted firmly inside their skulls. A minority are remarkably lucid. And there they sit, in the depths of the prison system, writing away, often reliving their perverted crimes over and over again... in ink this time, not blood.

Each serial murderer and killer is as different as chalk and cheese. There is no common denominator that puts them on the same plate, with the exception of them now peering through cold bars, many of them awaiting execution, or a life term behind razor wire and grim, weather-stained prison walls.

They will never kill again.

Some say a lot, perhaps too much. Others say very little. Some are honest; others indulge themselves in their sickening fantasies. Some deny their crimes, while others admit the whole shebang. But from their words we can all learn something those who commit the ultimate social crime: serial homicide.

CHRISTOPHER BERRY-DEE

CHAPTER 1
JOHN EDWARD ROBINSON
THE SLAVEMASTER

The following account of John 'JR' Robinson's career of crime and murder offers the reader, and student of criminology, a unique and remarkable insight into the warped and perverted mind of a true, blue-chip sociopath and sado-sexual serial killer.

This chapter should also provide psychologists, psychiatrists and law enforcement with food for thought for it clearly illustrates how even the most intransigent of mentally entrenched psychopaths can be easily manipulated into exposing the deepest workings of their clearly dysfunctional minds. And as this chapter draws to a close, you might consider how Robinson will react when he reads this book and discovers that it is he, the master manipulator, who has been hoodwinked. My bet is that he'll hit the roof.

*   *   *

Those unfortunate enough to be invited into John Robinson's world soon found out that it was not one of refined elegance and gentle self-indulgence, as he would have us believe. Instead

1

its epicentre was administered by a liar, scrounger and a cheat on the run for misrepresentation and commercially ritualised fraud. His was a world that deliberately surrounded itself with an impenetrable, pretentious and often plain misleading hypocrisy; his words churned out by a misleading snake-oil salesman who delighted in the obscure and the shadowy, the indistinct and the imprecise.

In search of metaphors even more elaborate, the two faces that this man displayed – the respectable businessman and sado-sexual serial killer – were so close together that they could be accurately described as twin cheeks of the same fat backside. This is a description which will do nothing to endear me to JR at all, for he will view me destroying his gilt-laced reputation as wicked as slaughtering a sacred cow.

Mr Robinson's over-inflated ego always had, and still does have, a front larger than any major high street department store. At face value, the façade is impressive, hinting at an honest deal to be had within. 'Integrity' shouts at one peering through the glass windows, but it is not until one steps through the door, and walks around the displays inside, that the penny drops. John Robinson, the persuasive owner of the store, is the ultimate con-artist. He is the 'quack' of old, peddling phoney medicines and selling goods at over-inflated prices. He is the purveyor of Mickey Mouse, bamboo-spring, 'Rolex' watches, passing them off as the real thing. And if you purchased an item from the JR Robinson store, and complained afterwards, would you get a refund? No way, José!

And, in a kind of warped sort of way, this is why I was attracted to JR, the ultimate I-don't-give-a-fuck merchant, a sort of homicidal Del Boy, whose history, and character, no imaginative screenplay writer could ever invent.

For me, however, the first challenge was to open up a dialogue with this heinous serial killer. He had never cooperated with an author before, or pretty well anyone else for that matter, so realistically I didn't expect him to admit to a single wrongdoing to me either. You see, JR is 'innocent', or so he now says after already admitting to five of at least eight murders that he's committed. If the truth be known, I did not even expect a reply to my initial letter either.

My second task, assuming the first mission was successful, was to discover whether there was any substance to his deep-seated claims supporting his integrity as a decent and honest man. He says he is totally innocent of all of the crimes for which he is incarcerated. He says he has been 'framed' by a crooked prosecutor and a bent judge. He says he never once used the internet to trawl for potential victims, moreover, he categorically states that he was most certainly not into BDSM, or master/slave contracts... God forbid!

Nevertheless, I baited my hook with a cocktail of goodies that this particularly nasty little man might find attractive, then, like the ever-optimistic fisherman, I pulled back my old beachcaster and cast out the line. Then I waited, and waited, and waited some more. I guess that JR sniffed at my lure, swam around it a few times – for a few weeks to be precise – and then sniffed again. The rod tip twitched, the temptation too much for this murderous con man; they say that the easiest person to con is the con man himself. JR took the bait and ran with it... and he ran hard. Then, like any fighting fish, once hooked, he tried to spit the barb from his mouth. The shiny lure was not all that it appeared... all that glittered was not gold.

For a short while, I had landed one of the most twisted serial killers in criminal history. But then, like so many of these cowardly individuals faced with a difficult question or two, he flipped and flopped about, slithering back to the murky water. However, in doing so, he fell into a net from which there could be no escape, and the fascinating results of what happened are published here.

*   *   *

Robinson sweats hatred, the copious secretions dripping out of every pore of his ageing skin. Having pleaded guilty to a number of shocking murders to escape the death penalty, John E Robinson is now demanding $400,000 to prove his innocence. His letters, featured in this chapter, explain that if he is not funded he will use college students to publish his poetry – well, actually other people's poetry which he claims is his - to raise some of the money. The entity that is JR is a damning indictment of a sado-sexual sociopath, a social parasite who exhibits not one iota of remorse for his crimes, insulting his dead victims and their next-of-kin.

> *I want $400,000, although that amount may be adjusted depending on need. My attorney will control all information and distribution of funds.*
> John E Robinson, letter to the author, 20 February 2008.

The bespectacled inmate squinting into the Olathe Police Department booking camera lens is that of a flabby faced, real estate wheeler-dealer lookalike who mortgaged his soul to the Devil. This is John Edward Robinson, a depraved sado-sex sadist who tortured and murdered women then stuffed their corpses into steel drums to rot in their own bodily juices until they were discovered by sick-to-the-stomach police.

An outwardly honest businessman, whose shady dealings and rip-offs took him to prison several times previously, John Robinson has since admitted five murders to escape the death penalty. More recently he has been charged by federal authorities for committing murder across state lines. And, my first question to him was simplicity itself:

John, can you please, please explain to me how the bodies of five women you knew very well ended up in steel barrels, three in your storage locker and two more on your land?

He replied:

I received your 2 January letter. At first I was simply going to forward it to my attorney to place in the file of vultures flying overhead wanting to pick my bones for personal profit.

*   *   *

With several aliases, including 'Anthony Thomas' and 'James Turner', JR (as he was known to the few friends he had) was born on Monday, 27 December 1943 in Cicero, Illinois, a working-class suburb of Chicago. Today, standing 5ft 9in tall, weighing 167lb, with green eyes, he is balding with partially grey hair.

Refusing to discuss even his childhood without receiving large sums of money in return (the aforementioned $400,000 to be precise), we know from official sources that he was one of five children to devout Roman Catholic parents who raised him at 4916 West 32nd Street, two blocks north of Cicero's

Sportsman's Park Race Track. His father, Henry, worked as a machinist for nearby Western Electric's 'Hawthorne Works' manufacturing complex, and, although a nice enough chap, was given to more than the occasional bout of heavy drinking. John's disciplinarian mother, Alberta, was the backbone of the family and ensured that the couple's offspring had a decent upbringing. Little else of her is known.

> He [Robinson] *didn't talk a great deal, but when he did talk, it was to produce an effect that he wanted. He was shrewd. He was aspiring to more than he was capable of, quite frankly.*
>
> Former Eagle Scout public relations officer, Richard Shotke. Kansas City Star, 2005.

At the age of 13, John became an 'Eagle Scout', the highest rank attainable in the programme of the Boy Scouts of America. In 1957, he was chosen as the leader of 120 Scouts who flew to London to appear before Queen Elizabeth II and the Duke of Edinburgh, at a Royal Command Performance at the London Palladium on 18 November. Therefore, I asked JR if he could tell me a little more about this memorable experience. His reply was:

> *I have never discussed this with anyone before, and I will not discuss it with you now. This is very valuable information to me. Your British readers would be very interested in my appearing before the Queen. If you send me $500.00 I will give you the exclusive story, which you can sell to the media and make a lot of money.*

Three days later I downloaded a press cutting of this Royal Command Performance from the internet, posted it to JR and politely declined his generous offer. I already knew that backstage JR had chatted to Judy Garland and had told British actress Gracie Fields that he planned to study for the priesthood.

With that bit of trivia out of the way, it is known that Robinson was a motivated youngster whose ability didn't match his drive. He told his peers that he was planning to become a priest and to someday work in Rome, but no one, probably not even John himself, knows whether this was what he truly wanted to do with his life or this was just his way of getting attention. Anyway, maybe the facts speak for themselves: as a freshman at Quigley Preparatory Seminary, in downtown Chicago, he was a lacklustre student and a discipline problem. He did not return to Quigley for his second year of study and it is believed that he was denied admission as a sophomore, due either to his academic or behavioural shortcomings.

After high school, in 1961, Robinson went to the Morton Junior College, in Cicero. He met Nancy Jo Lynch and they married in 1964. After 41 years of domestic purgatory, they divorced on 25 February 2005, this Latter-Day Saint Monica now aware of her philandering husband's many notable shortcomings, one of which was that he had never done an honest day's work in his life.

Initially, the Robinsons moved to Kansas City, Missouri, where he attended a trade school to learn the radiology profession. True to form, JR never finished his training but this did not prevent him from getting a job at a children's hospital where he papered the walls of his office with fake diplomas and certificates. From his lack of skills with the infant patients his colleagues suspected that he was either a fake or one of the most incompetent technicians ever to practise his craft. Although hospital staff remembered him as being a nice enough young man they knew that no way was he a certified technician. Josephine Bermel, who worked with Robinson, said that he simply couldn't cope with young patients: 'We had to teach him how to do things properly,' she said. This downright incompetence cost him his first job. He was just 21 at the time and his wife had recently given birth to their first child.

Undaunted by this setback, and using his phoney diplomas and certificates, JR soon found work as an X-ray technician at a medical practice in Kansas City. Here, he was employed by retired Brigadier General Dr Wallace Harry Graham, who for many years had been the personal White House physician to no less eminent patients than the former US President Harry S Truman and his wife, Elizabeth. Although, as Dr Graham himself told the *New York Times Magazine* in 1964, 'The Trumans were healthy. I felt like the country's most disemployed doctor.'

In the spring of 1944, as a member of the First Hospital Unit of the First Army, Captain (later Colonel) Wallace Graham had waded ashore at 'Easy Red' Omaha Beach, four days after D-Day. With the battle raging just a few miles ahead, he treated the wounded in the thick of battle and, by nightfall, his tents, with 400 beds, had taken in close to 900 of the wounded. Moving across France and Belgium, then into Germany, his unit saw some of the war's bitterest engagements, including the Battle of the Bulge, where he was wounded. He was awarded the Bronze Star, and other decorations, as well as medals from France, Britain, the Netherlands and Belgium.

While in the White House, where he had a ground floor suite

of offices filled with the latest in medical technology, he also treated some of the senior staffers, and later became a temporary Major General of the Air Force. He continued to look after the Trumans in their hometown of Independence, Missouri. When the 70-year-old President was rushed to Kansas City Hospital for emergency surgery in 1954, it was Dr Graham who removed his gallbladder and appendix. He had earned his medical degree at Harvard Medical School. He developed a lifelong interest in botany and also boxed. It seems that the doctor's only misjudgement throughout his entire, distinguished life was taking on John Robinson.

Quite how Robinson managed to con his way into working for Dr Graham as a lab technician and officer manager is a question for another day, but the doctor was patently no fool. Dr Graham later recalled that he had been impressed with Robinson's achievements as an Eagle Scout and his 'extensive credentials' in radiology. Nevertheless, highly regarded in the community, Dr Graham was a trusting man so he turned out to be an easy mark for a pathological and plausible liar like Robinson.

Soon after taking up his new appointment with Dr Graham, John made a somewhat astute discovery, which developed into an abiding, lifelong attachment to the buoyant pleasures to be had from fleecing almost everyone he came across. The upshot was that he developed the disagreeable technique of making himself wealthy at the expense of others whom he made extremely poor – something the banks have been trying to do for decades. From then on, and to this day, dishonest thoughts occupied every space in John's head; he pushed honesty completely to the back of his mind.

Robinson started his criminal activities in 1967, but he soon came unstuck when he was placed on probation for three years for embezzling $33,000 from 57-year-old Dr Graham. JR started by stealing and taking liberties in the practice's medical office. He boasted to friends and colleagues about a house he had bought. In addition, he engaged in sexual liaisons with both office staff and patients – having sex with one patient in the X-ray lab by pretending his wife was terminally ill and unable to satisfy him sexually.

But how did JR find the money to buy the house? The answer is simple; he drained the practice's bank account to the extent that just six months after he had been taken on, a bewildered and intractably confused Dr Graham was unable to pay Christmas bonuses to his staff. This unexplained loss of revenue prompted an audit of the practice's books and accusatory fingers all pointed towards Robinson being the culprit. JR was arrested and marched away in handcuffs feigning sincerity and remorse, praying that his hand-wringing, accompanied by an 'I'm sorry', would get him nothing more than a slap on the wrist from the criminal justice system. And he was correct.

In 1969 Robinson was convicted of the theft. Because it was his first offence and, pledging restitution, a Jackson County judge exercised leniency, sentencing him to three years probation. Dr Graham never saw a cent of the money JR had stolen from him.

*　　*　　*

JR's next career move was as the manager of a TV rental company. He soon tuned in to stealing merchandise from this employer too. When he was exposed, the company did not prosecute him, but sack him they most certainly did.

Over the next decade Robinson was often in trouble with the police. But despite being on parole for most of this time he still managed to prosper. When asked about his initial meeting with Robinson, one employer said: 'He gave a very good impression, well dressed, nice-looking... seemed to know a lot, very glib and a good speaker. He defrauded tens of thousands of dollars from various companies to help him along the way.'

Robinson? I wouldn't leave him alone in my yard to wash my truck. That sumbitch would steal the car, the hose, the faucet, and carry away as much fuckin' water as he could.
Jeff Tietz, former Kansas City police officer.

Giving credit where credit is due, if John Robinson was anything, he was pathologically persistent and remarkably evasive. For the next twenty years he bounced from job to job, managing to keep out of prison by crossing his fingers and jurisdictional boundaries, and convincing employers not to press charges when he was found out.

In 1977, JR bought a large, waterfront house. It was set in four acres of prime real estate at Pleasant Valley Farms, an affluent and prosperous neighbourhood in Johnson County, Kansas. By now, he and Nancy had four children and it was here, in picturesque, rural surroundings, that the confidence trickster and embezzler formed a company called Hydro-Gro Inc. The firm ostensibly dealt in hydroponics, a method – as any home-grown cannabis enthusiast will know – of growing plants using mineral nutrient solutions, heat and, instead of soil, a hell of a lot of water.

JR's home-grown publicity literature (a glossy, 64-page brochure) portrayed him as a 'sought-after lecturer', 'author' and 'pioneer in hydroponics'. The latter claim would have certainly come as a surprise to the ancients, as the Hanging

Gardens of Babylon, the Aztec's Floating Gardens of Mexico and those of the Chinese are far earlier examples of hydroponic culture. Indeed, Egyptian hieroglyphic records, dating back several hundred years BC, describe the growing of plants in water, so hydroponics is hardly a new method of growing plants. But by the 1970s, it wasn't just scientists and analysts, many of whom worked for NASA, who were involved in hydroponics. The many virtues of hydroponic growing began to attract traditional farmers and eager hobbyists, but John E Robinson was not, and this will come as no surprise, listed among them.

Hydro-Gro Inc was, of course, a bogus set-up, and in its development he swindled a friend out of $25,000. The man had invested because he hoped to get a better investment return to pay for his dying wife's medical care.

With his phoney CV in radiography and hydroponics richly embroidered in merit and distinction, this devious Jack-of-all-trades-and-master-of-none managed to engineer his appointment to the board of governors of a workshop for disabled people. He had held this position for little more than two months when this self-proclaimed philanthropist, with an almost religious desire to help the developmentally disabled, was named 'Man of the Year' for his work with the handicapped.

Amidst the glare of much publicity, the *Kansas City Times* proclaimed Robinson's virtues and, at a special dinner and presentation ceremony, JR was given a grandiose gesture of approbation in the form of a certificate signed by the mayor and a Missouri state senator.

According to Robinson, when he was invited to this dinner he had 'no idea' that they would be honouring him. However, feigning surprise when the winner was announced, he humbly accepted what amounted to a rigged award as members of the organisation's board sat, with their jaws on the floor, in stunned silence. Were the world just, he would have enjoyed universal acclaim, but for various heartbreakingly complicated reasons it was not to be.

A short time later, however, the meritorious award was exposed as having been obtained fraudulently. It had been granted as a result of faked letters of commendation received at City Hall, all written by none other than the 'Man of the Year' himself, John E Robinson Sr.

Thing went from bad to worse for JR when the city fathers, whose names he had forged on the letters of recommendation, read about the event in the local press. One man was outraged because on 'his' letter supporting Robinson, his name had even been spelt incorrectly. The *Kansas City Times*, stung by the scam, took its revenge by exposing him two weeks later as a fraud. His children were ridiculed at school and his wife, who says today that her husband had been unfaithful to her for at least twenty years of their marriage, was reluctant to show her face in public. But how did John react? One might have thought that had he had the right ingredients he would have concocted a potion to make himself invisible. The truth, however, was that JR, a fake as genuine as a hooker's smile, couldn't have cared less.

*　　*　　*

By now the reader will have come to the inescapable conclusion that Mr Robinson is a disagreeable fellow and not a man to trust, least of all the type to enter into any form of agreement with. It came as no surprise to this author when JR penned a letter, dated 20 February 2008, demanding that, 'Before I enter into any further correspondence with you, I want $400,000, although that amount may be adjusted depending on need. My attorney will control all information and distribution of funds. Don't blow smoke! I don't have time for meaningless delays. I will await word from you.'

In 1980 Robinson was given the position of Director of Personnel by another company, and very soon he homed in, like a heat-seeking missile, on his client's chequebook and money, selflessly using the former to direct quite a lot of the latter into his own bank account. After laundering $40,000 into PSA, a paper company he owned, JR yet again found himself placed on probation, this time for five years.

Between 1969 and 1991, John Robinson was convicted four times for embezzlement and theft, earning himself the notable distinction of being barred for life by the Securities and Exchange Commission from engaging in any kind of investment business. Of course, some of his thefts were minor – he lost his job with the Mobil Corporation for pinching $300 in postage stamps – while others were a tad more significant.

He had no real employment, unless you consider figuring out ways of scamming people out of their money to be real employment.
District Attorney Paul Morrison – Robinson's murder trial.

Avoiding financial castration by the skin of his teeth, Robinson soldiered on unfettered and undeterred, founding another firm, Equi-Plus, to add to his impressive portfolio. This newcomer to the Robinson stable specialised in 'management consultancy', and was very soon engaged by Back Care Systems, a company which ran seminars on the treatment of back pain... and give the company a pain, John surely did.

To keep this brief, Equi-Plus, aka John Robinson, was awarded a contract to prepare a package that included a marketing plan, printed publicity material and promotional videos, which advised the public on how to successfully resolve back pain. However, what Equi-Plus actually provided was a string of inflated, in most cases bogus, invoices and little else. Once again, a criminal investigation was started into the business activities of the energetic JR, who responded by producing a series of faked affidavits, all of which attested to the legitimacy of the invoices submitted to Back Care Systems.

While this investigation continued, this slippery eel founded Equi-II, an Overland Park corporation again run by Robinson who, at the time, described himself as a 'consultant in medical, agricultural and charitable ventures'. And it was while he was at the helm of this new outfit that he navigated himself into a sphere of activities far more sinister than embezzlement and fraud.

With some $40,000 of stolen funds neatly stashed away, JR acquired an apartment in Olathe, a city south of Kansas City. Here, in this most agreeable of extra-marital climates, he was able to enjoy sexual affairs with at least two women, one of whom is quoted as saying, 'John kind of swept me off my feet. He treated me like a queen and always had money to take me to nice restaurants and hotels.'

Well done, John, but there is no such thing as a free lunch. Retribution loomed on the horizon for the thieving and libidinous Robinson. The theft of the money resulted in his being convicted and, given his criminal record, this time he faced a possible prison sentence of seven years. However, he escaped with having to spend only a couple of months behind bars and, once more, we find John placed on probation, this time for five years.

> *John Robinson took away from our family our oldest daughter that we all loved so much. After she disappeared, my wife was a changed woman. A big part of her was ripped away.*
> William 'Bill' Godfrey – Paula's father in 2003

In 1984, an attractive, dark-haired young woman, named Paula Godfrey, went to work for JR as a sales rep at Equi-II after graduating from Olathe North High School. She was told by her new boss that she was going to be sent to Texas to attend a training course paid for by the company. Robinson collected Paula from her parents' home in Overland Park to drive her to the airport. Her family never saw her again.

Having heard nothing from their daughter for several days, Paula's parents became anxious and, eventually, they contacted the Overland PD to report her missing. The police questioned Robinson, but when he professed ignorance of Paula's whereabouts they went away satisfied with what he had told them.

Not long afterwards, the police located a letter bearing Paula Godfrey's signature which began: 'By the time you read this I'll be long gone. I haven't decided on Cleveland, Chicago or Denver, oh well.' In the rest of the letter, Paula seemed to be saying that she was perfectly fine but didn't want to remain in touch with her family. This neatly folded letter had been found in the bottom of a briefcase belonging to one Irving 'Irv' Blattner, an ex-con associate of Robinson, who had been arrested on an entirely unrelated matter. The one-pager was a photocopy and accompanied an original letter from JR addressed to Blattner in an Equi-II business envelope.

After reading the letter, the police closed their investigation, however, Paula Godfrey was to become JR's first murder victim; the truth of what happened to her would not come out until 2003.

It seems that Paula, an excellent ice skater, had got into some kind of boyfriend trouble, with Robinson assisting by loaning her money. For his part, Irving Blattner helped her find places to stay in Belton, on the Missouri side of the state line, where her boyfriend couldn't find her. One night, Robinson drove to a Belton motel where the young woman was staying and, for reasons known only to the tight-lipped JR, he hit her in the head with a lamp while Blattner blocked the doorway so she couldn't escape. Her body has never been found.

Notwithstanding this, in pursuit of his new vocation as a philanthropic helper of young women, JR approached the Truman Medical Center in Independence, a small city in Montgomery County. Here, he spoke to social workers, telling them that he, together with some other local businessmen, had formed 'Kansas City Outreach'. This, he explained while patronisingly peering over the top of his glasses, was a charitable organisation, which would provide young unmarried mothers with housing and career training, along with a babysitting service. The Truman Medical Center smelled a rat. They refused to help this Patron Saint of Lost Causes, so this 'Saint Jude' pitched the same story to Birthright, an organisation which gave help to young pregnant women, who, in turn, pointed him in the direction of Hope House, a refuge for single mums.

According to the writer David McClintick, JR told both organisations that Kansas City Outreach was likely to receive 'funding from Xerox, IBM and other major corporations', which would have been news to them. In any event, the great philanthropist asked the social workers to submit candidates whom they felt would be suitable for the KC Outreach programme and, in early January 1985, he was contacted by the Hope House shelter, and put in touch with Lisa Stasi.

At this stage it is worth hitting the pause button and briefly examine JR's modus operandi around this time. Here we have a pathological liar, convicted fraudster, embezzler, and priapic womaniser who cheated on his wife. Here is a man who has no conscience. A person who will stop at nothing to achieve his own ends; if this meant stealing from the mentally ill and deceiving decent members of the public, then so be it. Now we find him, once again, using bogus organisations to make contact with vulnerable women. He could trawl, with impunity, for young females, and any gullible single mother agencies would unwittingly provide him with his prey.

*   *   *

Poor, uneducated and unworldly, nineteen-year-old Lisa Stasi was as pretty as a picture and real cute, with long, dark hair, and trusting eyes. With a four-month daughter called Tiffany Lynn, Lisa was homeless and living at the Hope House shelter for single women. Sadly, her marriage to Carl Stasi had fallen apart and he'd left his wife and baby to rejoin the US Navy, at the Great Lakes Naval Base outside Chicago.

Carl later testified that he'd met his wife through a friend. They had married in Huntsville, Alabama, in August 1984, where Lisa had been raised. Lisa was eight months pregnant at the time. 'We were going to stay there and start our lives there,' Carl Stasi testified in court, adding, 'but I didn't have no insurance and the baby was due and so we came back here [to Kansas].'

Tiffany Lynn was born a few weeks later at the Truman Medical Center, a hospital well known for its care of the indigent. Nevertheless, broke and without a home, the Stasis' marriage quickly fell apart. 'It was shaky,' Carl explained. 'I was irresponsible and I wasn't working at the time. It was going downhill from there.' He and Lisa separated in mid-December, with him returning to the Navy a few days after Christmas.

John Robinson, using the alias 'John Osborne', now arrived on the scene. Using his phoney credentials, he offered Lisa free accommodation and career training. He explained to her that this involved helping her to gain her High School Equivalency Diploma, after which he would arrange for her to go to Texas to train as a silkscreen printer. When she had completed her training, he said, there would be job opportunities for her in Chicago, Denver or Kansas City. In the meantime, her new mentor told her, he would not only pay for her accommodation and living expenses but also give her a monthly stipend of $800.

It was an offer she couldn't refuse. The kindly benefactor took Lisa and Tiffany from the refuge to install them in Room 131, at a Rodeway Inn, a motel in Overland Park, telling her that she and the baby would be travelling to Chicago within a few days.

When JR left the motel, Lisa went to see her sister-in-law, Betty Klinginsmith, to discuss matters with her; she stayed the night. 'I fed her [Lisa] and the baby. She slept a long time, she took a bubble bath,' Klinginsmith recalled at Robinson's trial. The following morning, Wednesday, 9 January 1985, Lisa telephoned the front desk at the Rodeway Inn to learn that an irate 'Mr Osborne' was looking for her. She left a message for Osborne with the clerk asking him to call her at Klinginsmith's home. A few minutes later the phone rang and Betty gave Osborne directions to her house.

He [Robinson] *came to my door about 25 minutes later, rang the doorbell. I went down to the door with my son, who was five. [...] Lisa put on her coat. He didn't waste any time on pleasantries. He didn't say anything to me. He just stood there and looked at me.*

After expressing anger that she had checked out of the motel, Robinson insisted that Lisa and her daughter leave with him immediately. There was a heavy snowstorm when Lisa carried Tiffany to his car, which was parked down the street. She left her own damaged yellow Toyota Corolla and many of her belongings behind. Like Paula Godfrey, Lisa Stasi was never seen again by her family.

Back at the motel, later the same day, Mr Osborne produced four sheets of bank notepaper, which he asked Lisa to sign. He also asked for the addresses of her immediate family, saying that as she would be too busy to write letters when she got to Chicago, he would write them for her, just to let her relatives know her whereabouts. Perhaps she resisted, but we do know that she telephoned Betty Klinginsmith.

'I took it for granted she was at her motel,' Betty would tell investigators. 'She was crying real hard, hysterical. She was telling me that "they" said that they was going to take her baby from her, that she was an unfit mom. They wanted her to sign four sheets of blank paper. I said, "Don't sign nothing,

Lisa. Don't put your name in anything."' According to Betty, the last words Lisa said were: 'Here they come,' before the phone was disconnected.

According to testimony given years later by JR's wife, Nancy, he had brought the baby home that night. She recalled that it was, 'snowing heavily' and that, 'the infant was not very clean and smelt badly. There was dirt under the child's fingernails. Apart from some spare nappies, the baby had only the clothes she was wearing, and some baby food.'

The next morning, the 10th, Betty Klinginsmith telephone the Rodeway Inn, only to discover that Lisa and Tiffany had checked out and that the bill had been settled by a John Robinson, not John Osborne. She reported him to the Overland Park PD and the FBI.

That evening, JR's brother Don and his wife Helen, who lived in metropolitan Chicago, received an unexpected telephone call from John Robinson. The childless couple had been trying to adopt a baby through traditional placement services for some years, and JR had previously told his brother that he had a contact with a Missouri attorney who handled private adoptions; that for an upfront consultancy fee, of $2,000, he could act as a liaison for Don and Helen. The trusting couple soon handed over the cash, which JR back-pocketed.

That was way back in 1983 and for the next two years Robinson put into place a plan to procure a child for his brother. If the scam was successful, he probably intended to expand it to 'help' other childless families realise their dream of adoption. Nevertheless, several times during the following months, Robinson put Don and Helen on notice that an adoption was imminent, but a child never materialised.

John's crooked scheme required locating pregnant, single

women and he knew exactly where to find them. Putting on his civic philanthropist façade, he approached local pregnancy programmes and social workers to alert them to a new programme, Kansas City Outreach, that he and several fanciful leading businessmen 'from the East Coast' had created to help single mothers.

Karen Gaddis was a social worker at the Truman Medical Center in the City of Independence, the county seat of Montgomery County, and she had previously met Robinson when he had been seeking referrals in 1984. He was looking for young mothers, preferably white women, who had no close ties to family members. He even showed Gaddis an apartment which he maintained on Troost Avenue, Overland Park. It was a place, he said, where the women would stay.

Gaddis knew Caucasian babies were valued on the adoption black market and, because Robinson couldn't provide her with any paperwork about the programme, she didn't refer any women to him. 'I think he thought we were a real fertile ground for young women that nobody would be looking for,' Gaddis told NBC's Dateline when the Robinson story broke. Within days, however, Robinson was at Hope House, where he picked up Lisa Stasi.

A day later John Robinson explained to his brother that a new mother had committed suicide at a woman's shelter and, for a further cash sum of $3,000 (payable to the imaginary lawyer) and their signatures on a adoption certificate (which was bogus), JR could hand the baby over to them.

On Thursday, 10 January 1985, Don and Helen Robinson flew down to visit Robinson at his Missouri home, where they handed over the $3,000, and were given extremely convincing adoption papers with the forged signatures of a notary, two lawyers and a judge. They were delighted with their new child, whom they named Heather. By now, of course, Lisa had been murdered, probably brutally raped, and it would be fifteen years before Heather's true identity was revealed, and then in the most shocking circumstances; the man she knew as 'Uncle John' would stand in court accused of killing her mother.

Several weeks after Lisa vanished, Betty received the first of the letters that JR had faked. It was dated the day of Lisa's disappearance, and it immediately raised concerns because she knew that Lisa couldn't type:

Betty,

Thank you for all your help I really do appreciate it! I have decided to leave Kansas City and try and make a new life for myself and Tiffany. I wrote to Marty and told him to let the bank take the car back, the payments are so far behind that they either want the money or the car. I don't have the money to pay the bank all the back payments and the car needs a lot of work. When I wrote to Marty about the car I forgot to tell him about the lock box with all my papers in the trunk. Since the accident I couldn't get the trunk opened. Please tell him to force the trunk and get that box of papers out before the bank gets the car.

Thanks for all your help, but I really need to get away and start a new life for me and Tiffany. She deserves a real mother who takes care of her who works. The people at Hope House and Outreach were really helpful, but I couldn't keep taking charity from them.

I feel I have to get out on my own and prove that I can handle it myself.

Marty wanted me to go to Alabama to take care of Aunt

Evelyn but I can't. She is so opinionated and hard to get along with right now. I just can't deal with her. Marty and I fought about it and I know he will try and force me to go to Alabama. I am just not going there.

I will let you know from time to time how I am and what I am doing. Tell Carl that I will write him and let him know where he can get in touch with me.

The second letter typed out by Robinson was posted to Cathy Stackpole at Hope House:

Dear Cathy,

I want to thank you for all your help. I have decided to get away from this area and try to make a life for me and Tiffany. Marty my brother wants me to take care of my aunt but I don't want to. He is trying to take over my life and I just am not going to let him. I borrowed some money from a friend and Tiffany and I are leaving Kansas City. The people you referred me to were really nice and helped me with everything. I am grateful for everyone's help.

I wrote to the outreach [sic] people, Carl's mother and my brother telling them all that I had made the decision to get a fresh start in life. If I stay here they will try and run my life more and more like they are trying to do. I finally realised that I have a baby to take care of and she is my first responsibility. I asked my brother to tell the bank to pick up the car because the tags have expired and I am so far behind with the payments that I could never get them up to date, and with no job the bank wants the car or the money. I will be fine. I know what I want and I am going to go after it. Again thanks for your help and Hope House and thanks for telling me about outreach [sic]. *Everyone has been so helpful I owe you a great deal.*

At the time that Lisa and Tiffany disappeared, Ann Smith, an employee of Birthright, had somewhat belatedly began to check up on the details that Robinson had provided concerning Kansas City Outreach. They were false. Deeply concerned, she contacted two FBI agents, Thomas Lavin and Jeffery Dancer, who were assigned to investigate JR and they teamed up with his probation officer, Stephen Haymes.

During this period, information emerged that showed that JR was being investigated by Johnson County's district attorney. Under the glass was Equi-II, in connection with strong allegations that the company had defrauded its client, Back Care Systems. Not only that, but JR and fellow ex-convict, Irvin Blattner (now deceased), were being investigated by the US Secret Service for forgery involving a government cheque. None of this, however, was connected to the disappearance of Paula Godfrey, Lisa Stasi and baby Tiffany, so the trail in this direction was in danger of going cold.

Although everything seemed to point to JR having abducted and murdered two women, despite their own strong suspicions the two FBI investigators and Haymes could do little. Nevertheless, Haymes decided to call Robinson in for a meeting during which the plausible crook confirmed that he was involved in a group called Kansas City Outreach, but as might be expected, he declined to provide Haymes with a list of his 'colleagues'.

In a second, subsequent interview, Robinson admitted to Haymes that he knew Lisa Stasi, and that he had put her up at the Rodeway Inn, in Overland Park, with her baby. He also said that, 'she had come to my office on 10 January 1985 with a young man named Bill and told me that she was going off to Colorado to start a new life'.

In a third interview, in March 1985, Robinson told yet another story to Haymes. He claimed that Lisa and the baby had been found in the Kansas City area. Lisa had been babysitting for a young woman, and the woman had contacted his office to see if he had an address for Lisa so she could hire her again. Haymes pounced on this information and demanded the woman's name and address. JR stormed out of the interview protesting that he was being harangued over the matter; however, a few days later, in the knowledge that his parole could be revoked if he pissed Haymes off, he came up with the details.

The woman, a prostitute called Theresa Williams, made a statement to Haymes claiming that she had, indeed, hired Lisa Stasi as a babysitter, however, when FBI Agent Lavin questioned her more closely, she said that Robinson had made her go along with this false story because she owed him money and he had photographed her nude in order to promote her services as a prostitute.

With the FBI suspecting a violation of the Federal Mann Act (also known colloquially as the 'White Slave Act'), for possibly transporting Lisa and Tiffany Stasi across state lines, authorities in Missouri and Kansas started looking into JR's activities on a local level, connected to the disappearance of Paula Godfrey.

With Haymes now suspecting that the embezzler had now turned to abduction and murder, he dug deeper and learned through the prostitute, whom Robinson had photographed naked, that he might be involved in the Kansas City underground sex industry and probably ran a string of hookers specialising in domination and submission sex practices.

With this new angle to pursue, the FBI arranged for a female agent to pose as a prostitute and approach JR on the pretext of looking for work.

According to author David McClintick it was around this time that Robinson developed a taste for sadomasochistic sex, but he also saw its potential to make a lot of money, and very soon he was running a thriving business exploiting this lucrative sector of the sex market. He organised a string of prostitutes to cater for customers who enjoyed S&M. To look after his own carnal appetites, JR employed a male stripper, nicknamed M&M, to find suitable women for him.

The female FBI agent was wired to record any conversation and arranged to meet JR at a restaurant in Overland Park. During lunch, he explained to her that, working as a prostitute for him, she could earn up to $3,000 for a weekend travelling to Denver or Dallas to service wealthy clients. She could also make $1,000 a night just working the Kansas City area. His clients, he said, were drawn mainly from the ranks of doctors, lawyers and judges.

JR went on to explain that, as an S&M prostitute, the young woman would have to allow herself to be subjected to painful treatment, such as having her nipples manipulated with pliers. When they heard this part of the recording of the conversation, the FBI investigation team decided to end the undercover operation out of fear for their agent's safety, and it is doubtful that the female agent would have been enthusiastic to continue after hearing about that aspect of the job either.

JR had installed the attractive 21-year-old Theresa Williams in his Troost Avenue apartment in April 1985. She had been introduced to JR by M&M as a suitable candidate for prostitution, and having worked at various odd jobs around

Kansas City, Theresa jumped at the chance. After photographing her nude and 'test-driving' his new acquisition in a motel room, JR initially offered her a position as his mistress. This involved her being given an apartment with all her expenses paid, and for her there was an added attraction; he would keep her well provided with amphetamines and marijuana. She would also be expected to provide sexual services for others, for which she would receive prostitution fees. Theresa took the job, moved into the apartment and, in doing so, became a candidate for JR's next murder victim.

Haymes's suspicions that Robinson was running a string of streetwise hookers proved unfounded. And, in hindsight, although a cunning and devious individual, he wasn't well connected enough to be able to pull off such an unpredictable enterprise. JR liked to be in control of his nefarious schemes. His preference was to be in charge, and a stable of prostitutes, all as equally cunning and more streetwise than the portly 'businessman', would have run rings around him. Nevertheless, life for Theresa was not to be a bed of roses.

To start with, he began using her to discredit ex-convict pal, Irvin Blattner, who was cooperating with the authorities over the Back Care Systems and a postal scam. JR ordered Theresa to begin writing a 'diary', which he dictated, implicating Blattner in a number of other schemes. He also had her sign blank papers and a draft letter to his attorney giving the lawyer the authority to recover the diary from a safety deposit box in the event she disappeared. Indeed, the last entry in the diary was meant to be the same day that Robinson and Theresa were leaving for the Bahamas – a trip police suspected he was never going to make with her.

Rewinding a little, one night towards the end of April, after being given $1,200 and a new outfit by JR, Theresa was taken, blindfolded in a limousine, to a mansion. There she was introduced to a distinguished-looking man of about 60, who led her down to a basement which was fitted out as a medieval torture chamber. Her host instructed her to remove all her clothes and moments later she found herself being stretched on a rack. Theresa panicked and demanded to be allowed to leave. Blindfolded again, she was driven back to the Troost Avenue apartment. JR reacted angrily to this betrayal, and a few days later she had to refund him the $1,200.

On another occasion, JR took her to task for entertaining a boyfriend at the apartment. However, the worst was yet to come. In late May, he paid her a visit during which he did something that caused her more fear she had ever known in her life. She was asleep when he let himself into the apartment. He burst into the bedroom, dragged her out of bed by her hair and spanked her until she began to scream. After throwing her onto the floor, JR drew a revolver, put it to her head and pulled the trigger. Instead of an explosion, there was only a click – the chamber was empty. By now, Theresa was whimpering with fear, but she went rigid with terror as JR slid the barrel slowly into her vagina. He left it there for several terrifying seconds before withdrawing it, replacing it in its holster and, without another word, stormed out of the apartment.

About a week after the incident with the gun, FBI agents Lavin and Dancer called unannounced at Theresa's apartment. Having been told that they were investigating the disappearance of two women and that JR was the prime suspect, she decided to reveal the truth. This, of course, involved telling them about the drugs that JR was supplying to her as well as the incident with the gun. When the Feds learned that Theresa had been asked by JR to sign several blank sheets of notepaper, they felt they had reason to believe that her life was in danger, and moved her to a secret location.

Together with Stephen Haymes, the FBI agents filed a report with the Missouri courts outlining details that confirmed Robinson had violated his probation conditions by carrying a firearm and supplying drugs to Theresa Williams. They asked a Judge to revoke JR's probation and put him where he belonged: behind bars.

In 1987 Robinson started a prison term for his parole violation. He was held until the appeals court overturned the probation revocation order on a technicality: his attorney successfully argued that, because he had not been allowed to confront his accuser, Williams, his constitutional rights had been violated. However his real estate fraud case, in Johnson County, ended with him being sentenced to serve between six and 19 years. He would stay locked up until 1991.

*　　*　　*

Around the time that JR was about to enter the correctional system for the first time, police were searching for 27-year-old Catherine Clampitt. Born in Korea, but adopted and raised by the Bales family in Texas, Catherine was a one-time drug user now seeking rehabilitation. JR hired her to work for him at Equi-II in early 1987, but the arrangement fell through. She vanished a few months later. Despite the fact that in various quarters, suspicion of murder once again fell on Robinson, no further action was taken against him.

Much later, in 2003, it emerged that Catherine had lived at several different locations in Cass County, and had started visiting Robinson once or twice a week, usually receiving money in return for sexual favours. Nevertheless, in May or June 1987, she called Robinson and invited him to her apartment. There were two other people at the place when JR turned up, including a person identified only as 'GT', and Clampitt demanded money from JR, who started arguing with her. He grabbed a lead-filled baton known as a tyre thumper, and beat her in the head. Robinson instructed 'GT' on how to dispose of the body, and the deed was done.

Strangely, like so many so-called 'intelligent' serial murderers, JR took to the prison regime at the Hutchinson Correctional Facility like a duck takes to water. Like John Wayne Gacy and Arthur Shawcross, he was the model inmate, making such a good impression on the prison authorities that the parole board set him free. Robertson walked out of prison in January 1991 having served just four years.

However, he still had to go to jail in Missouri for having violated the terms of his probation resulting from the $40,000 fraud he had perpetuated more than a decade earlier. He went back behind bars, serving time at two facilities for a further two years.

It is interesting to read Stephen Haymes's assessment of Robinson, from a memo that he wrote to a colleague in 1991:

I believe him [Robinson] *to be a con man out of control. He leaves in his wake many unanswered questions and missing persons...I have observed Robinson's sociopathic tendencies, habitual criminal behaviour, inability to tell the truth and scheming to cover his own actions at the expense of others. I was not surprised to see he had a good institution adjustment in Kansas considering that he is personable and friendly to those around him.*

While in jail at the Western Missouri Correctional Facility, JR forged a friendship with the prison doctor, William Bonner. He also developed an extra-curricular relationship with Bonner's vivacious 49-year-old wife, Beverly. She was the prison librarian and JR very soon found that he had a job looking after not only Beverly but also her books.

For her part, Nancy Robinson had found the going tough without her husband's income. After selling their palatial home at Pleasant Valley Farms, she had to take a job to keep body and soul together. She was fortunate in getting one that provided accommodation: she became the manager of a mobile-home development in Belton. It was to these modest quarters that JR went when he was paroled from prison early in 1993. By now, the two older children had grown up and left home and the twins were at college, so JR and Nancy had the place to themselves. They rented local storage lockers to house their surplus belongings.

Almost as soon as he'd stepped through the door, JR went about restoring the family fortunes. Of course, there was never any real likelihood that he would stay on the straight and narrow for very long and he was soon back to his unctuous ways.

The completely besotted Beverly Jean Bonner had since left her husband and began diverse proceedings. Naturally, she conveniently forgot to mention that, for months on end, she had spent a considerable amount of time lying on her back with her legs akimbo.

The adulteress told William that she was moving abroad and would set up a post office box number where he could send her the alimony cheques. A few months later she moved to Kansas City, where she went to work with JR, who appointed her a director of his company Hydro-Gro. Not long after this grand appointment, Beverly's alimony cheques were finding their way into an Olathe post office box number used by Robinson.

Beverly Bonner was not seen or heard from again after January 1994. Robinson placed her belongings into the storage locker in Belton, and later, when he was asked about Beverly by the storage facility staff, he said that the woman, whom he described as his sister, was in now Australia. He told them that she was enjoying herself so much that, 'she'll probably never come back'.

No one could have ever guessed that Mrs Bonner was actually rotting inside a steel barrel in a locker (E2), next to two other 55-gallon barrels containing the remains of Sheila Dale Faith and her daughter, Debbie, whose government cheques also continued to supplement Robinson's income.

Subsequently, two of Beverly's brothers received several letters from her beginning in January 1994. The first one was handwritten. In it, the recently divorced and even-more-recently dead Beverly wrote that she had taken a new job in the human resources department of a large international corporation and would be training in Chicago and then travelling to Europe. In subsequent letters, all typewritten, the deceased woman said her new job was 'wonderful', and that she was working with her boss, Jim Redmond.

*   *   *

Sheila was interested in BDSM and used the internet and personal ads to meet men. She would start talk about BDSM, and I said, 'I don't want to hear it. It's not my thing.'
Nancy Guerrero, close friend of Sheila Faith, 1994.

One of three sisters, 45-year-old Sheila Dale Faith was a widow. Her husband John died of cancer in 1993 and she was left to raise Debbie, their fifteen-year-old daughter. Debbie had been born with spina bifida, had cerebral palsy and she spent her life in a wheelchair, with barely enough strength to manipulate the chair's joystick controller. Since the death of the patriarch, mother and daughter had lived a lonely life in Fullerton, California. Looking to 'start over', they upped sticks and moved to Pueblo, Colorado, in a beat-up white van.

As with so many thousands of lonely women, Sheila began trying to meet a man on the internet and she made a number of bad choices before making the fatal choice of John E Robinson. Sheila told family and friends that she had met her 'dream man', John, who had promised to take her on a cruise. He portrayed himself as a wealthy man who would support her, give her a job and pay for Debbie's therapy.

One night in the summer of 1994, without prior warning, Sheila's 'dream man' called at her home and she and Debbie were whisked away to live in the Kansas City area. As was the case with other women who were befriended by JR, the Faiths were never seen alive again. When they did eventually turn up, they were corpses in barrels.

Both of Sheila's sisters later received typewritten letters from Sheila and her daughter after their disappearance. 'She always hand-wrote letters,' said her sister, Kathy Norman, who received correspondence postmarked Canada and the Netherlands. 'This isn't Sheila,' said another sister, Michelle Fox. 'It was a happy letter and Sheila wasn't a happy person.'

The fatal fiscal attraction for JR was that Sheila had been receiving disability benefits from the Social Security Administration (SSA) for herself and Debbie. Now these payments were being directed to a mail centre in Olathe, where JR collected them.

In the autumn of 1994, according to court documents, Robinson filed a medical report to the SAA. In it, not to be diverted from his scheme by the mere technicality of a morbid deception, he wrote that Debbie was totally disabled and would require care for the rest of her life. Under the circumstances, it was not strictly true: she was already dead. The report bore the forged signature of William Bonner, the doctor that JR had befriended in prison and who had, until recently, been Beverly's husband. When he was eventually questioned on the matter, Dr Bonner categorically denied ever having met Sheila or Debbie Faith, and had certainly never treated them. In any event, JR would continue to collect the Faiths' disability cheques for almost six years. In July 2000, Cass County prosecutors alleged that, between 1994 and 1997, Robinson defrauded the US government of more than $29,000 in Social Security and disability payments by forging documents to suggest that Sheila and Debbie Faith were alive.

It was also later proven that JR received more than $14,000 in alimony cheques that should have gone to Beverly Bonner. Colleen Davis, the owner of the mail centre from which Robinson retrieved the cheques, told police that she knew JR as James Turner.

If we are to give John any credit, we would have to say that, at the very least, JR was going through a lifetime of psycho-pathologically determined trangressional retro-development with great consistence. In other words – words that John would understand – he was an out-of-control sado-sexual sociopath and spiralling downhill fast. Indeed, at the time of writing he still hasn't bottomed out, as the following extract from one of his diatribes to the author proves:

You will have seen all the tripe published or on the internet. Eighty percent of which is grossly incorrect, exaggerated fiction with small tid bits of fact thrown in. For example, the moniker given – internet slave master – hype provided by a prosecutor looking for votes and carried through to sell books and enhance TV ratings. According to reports I was an internet stalker who waited in 'chat rooms' to locate victims. Great for publicity but factually incorrect and both the police and prosecutors knew it was a fabrication.

John E. Robinson, letter to the author, 10 January 2008.

For the record, JR's interest in sadomasochistic sex had continued to flourish and he upped the ante by starting to place adverts in the personal columns of the Kansas City newspaper *Pitch Weekly*. He met and had relationships with a number of women before he fell in with Chloe Elizabeth, who described herself as a 'businesswoman' from Topeka, Kansas. She claimed that JR sent her a wealth of publicity material selected to show him in a good light. He included newspaper clippings describing his appearance before the Queen when he was a Boy Scout, his hydroponics brochure, details of his 'Man of the Year' award, and a Kansas University brochure containing pictures of two of his children. It was altogether an odd portfolio for someone wishing to engage in a BDSM encounter – the term widely used to describe relationships involving bondage and sadomasochism. Unsurprisingly, JR's lengthy and distinguished criminal record received no mention whatsoever.

In later years, Chloe Elizabeth described an event that took place during the afternoon of Wednesday, 25 October 1995: 'I was to meet him at the door of my house wearing only a sheer robe, black mesh thong panties, a matching demi-cup bra, stockings and black high heels. My eyes were to be made up dark and lips red. I was to kneel before him,' she recounted.

Some red-blooded male readers would find nothing wrong with JR's request at this point... indeed, there might be thousands of men who would applaud John for his imagination. However, as events would later prove, things would turn sour, for upon his arrival JR took a leather-studded collar from his pocket, placed it around Chloe's neck and attached a long leash to the collar. After a drink and some small talk, he made her remove all her clothes except for her stockings, and then took from another pocket a 'Contract for Slavery' in which she consented to let him use her as a sexual toy in any way he saw fit (it was a template contract he had downloaded from the internet).

'I read the contract and signed it,' said Chloe Elizabeth. 'He asked if I was sure. I said, "yes, very sure".'

With her signature on the dotted line, he promptly tied her to the bed, whipped her and carried out a variety of imaginative acts on her breasts with ropes and nipple clamps; JR was in his element. Sweating profusely, he concluded their first date by making her perform oral sex on him. The submissive Chloe Elizabeth, it seems, was delighted with her 'Dom Slave Master' and he was pretty much delighted with her.

'That was the first date,' she later told the judge at Robinson's trial. 'It was sensational! [...] He had the ability to command, control, to corral someone as strong and aggressive and spirited as I am.'

In any event, before the perspiring and head-to-toe-trembling JR left the house that evening, he told his new slave that she had been stupid for allowing him to do everything he had done to her. 'I could have killed you,' he said, with a smirk on his face.

For JR, this master-slave contract with the amply proportioned Chloe Elizabeth had to be about as good as it could get; however, she was not as naïve as he may have thought. Without his knowledge, she had taken the precaution of having a male friend stationed in another room of her house, listening vigilantly, upturned tumbler to the wall, for any sound of excessive behaviour – as if the aforementioned was not excessive enough.

The relationship between JR and Chloe Elizabeth blossomed and they were meeting at least twice a week before it waned as she started to find out that Robinson was not all he claimed to be.

Although this author has no personal experience in such matters, I am reliably informed that it is not unusual in BDSM relationships for the dominant partner to take control of the submissive partner's assets (as in financial affairs), an arrangement that is sometimes included in the contract drawn up between slave and master. For Chloe Elizabeth's part, she was required to sign over power of attorney to JR. In return for sex he promised to get her a job in the 'entertainment industry', for which he needed publicity photographs and, this will come as no surprise, he demanded her Social Security number. As an obedient submissive, she should have followed his orders explicitly, but she refused, correctly suspecting that he was after her money.

So, if JR had imagined that Chloe Elizabeth's submissiveness extended beyond her sexual inclinations, he was badly mistaken; she was an intelligent and successful businesswoman, not an ill-educated teenage mother desperate for help and support. Moreover, their relationship was now moving in the wrong direction as she found out more and more about him, and she started to voice her concerns to JR.

Realising that he was coming unstuck, he told her that he was going to Australia and would be away for some time – perhaps a very long time. However, she soon discovered that he had not even left Kansas. When she telephoned his office, the phone was answered but remained utterly silent. About an hour afterwards, her own phone rang and she found herself being berated by a furious JR. He accused her of checking up on him and warned her, in very unpleasant tones, against that sort of behaviour.

The final straw for Chloe Elizabeth was when she found out about JR's criminal record, and, in February 1996, she ended their relationship.

*   *   *

It wasn't long until another woman (her name is omitted for legal reasons) entered into a master-slave contract and struck a deal for financial support with Robinson. She didn't learn until years later how close she had also come to ending up in a barrel alongside Sheila and Debbie Faith and Beverly Bonner.

JR told this woman that he was divorcing his wife and that's why he could never stay the night. However, he showered this 'Ms X' with gifts and clothes, but she soon noticed that most of the clothes he presented to her appeared unwashed and well worn. When she asked about this, ever the cheapskate Robinson said they were left behind at his office by former employees. Given that most of the clothes were raunchy undergarments leaves us begging the question, what in God's name was going through her mind?

This notwithstanding, the relationship was going fine until one day Robinson told her to get ready to travel with him. He was going to take her to London on an extended business trip. He told her that she should leave her job and advise friends that she would be gone for some time. She gave up her apartment and Robinson moved her into a local motel. Like those before her, she was told she would be so busy that she should take the time to write letters to her family straight away, as there would be no time while travelling. Robinson said that he would take care of her passport application, as he had friends in the US State Department.

The woman thought it was rather strange as the day came for the pair to leave and JR turned up at the motel with his truck and a trailer loaded with clothing. What further concerned her was that he said that he was going to spend the night in the motel with her.

Nevertheless, excited at the thought of the trip, the woman awoke the next morning at 5am, and roused Robinson. 'He was like a man possessed,' she said later. 'He jumped out of bed yelling at me and barely stopped berating me as he showered and dressed.' Still angry, JR said that he was going to check her out of the motel and that he had errands to run. He told her that he would meet her at a nearby restaurant, but he never turned up. Confused, and very disappointed, she tried to call him. He refused to take her calls. She persisted. When she finally connected with JR, he said that he was unable to trust her and that the relationship was over. For some reason, he had got cold feet. It wasn't until Robinson was arrested for murder that the woman realised how close she had come to being killed that day. It is thought that JR had brought his trailer as a means of removing her corpse from the motel and, by rising before he did, she thwarted his plans; the motel had been busy with guests and he would have preferred a quick and silent kill while the woman slumbered.

* * *

In pursuit of his sexual preferences, JR had left the personal ads behind him by now and had enthusiastically embraced the internet. In that same year the Robinsons left the mobile-home park and went to live near Olathe, on the Kansas side of the boarder. The upmarket mobile-home development that they moved to was called Santa Barbara Estates, where once again Nancy worked as estate manager.

Their new address was an immaculate grey-and-white mobile home at 36 Monterey Lane, and here they certainly didn't opt for inconspicuous anonymity. They erected a statue of St Francis of Assisi in the yard at the front of their home, hung wind chimes over their front door and, at Christmas, earned quite a reputation for their spectacular display of decorations.

As well as their home, which came as part of the perks of Nancy's job on the Santa Barbara Estates, JR and his wife somehow managed to lease farmland near the small town of La Cygne, south of Olathe. They had about 16 acres that also contained a fishing pond to which JR invited his few friends from time to time. The couple improved the place by parking a mobile home and erecting a shed on the site.

And, it was at 36 Monterey Lane, using no less than five computers and the handle 'Slavemaster' – while at once trying to set up a legit wheeling and dealing web site business – he spent a lot of time browsing BDSM websites. Ultimately it would be two of his internet contacts who were instrumental in bringing his world crashing around his ears, but in 1996 that crash was still some years ahead.

* * *

In 1997 Robinson encountered a young Polish-born undergraduate on the internet. Her name was Izabela Lewicka, and the perky lass was studying the fine arts at Purdue University, in West Lafayette, Indiana.

Izabela's parents became very concerned when, in the spring of 1997, she told them she was moving to Kansas, having been offered an internship. She wasn't forthcoming with the details, doing nothing to allay her parents' misgivings other than leaving an email and a contact address on Metcalf Avenue in Overland Park.

Her parents, Andrew and Danuta, attempted to talk Izabela, who had just finished her freshman year, out of leaving home. 'She was past eighteen,' explained Danuta. 'She's protected by law. We could not stop her.' In June, Izabela packed up her 1987 Pontiac Bonneville with books, clothes and several of her paintings, then left Purdue for Kansas City. Her parents would never see her again.

In August, when it was time for school to start, and after receiving no reply to their letters, the Lewickis grew extremely anxious about their daughter's welfare, so they drove to Kansas to find out what was the matter. They arrived to find that the address on Metcalf Avenue was simply a mailbox; their daughter didn't live there. When they asked the manager of the place for Izabela's forwarding address, he refused to divulge the information. Despite their anxiety, Izabela's parents did not bother to contact the police but returned to Indiana. Shortly after this Andrew received an email from his daughter:'What the hell do you want? I will not tolerate your harassment.' The message went on to insist that in the future they contact her at another address. When he later testified at Robinson's trial, Andrew said, 'We exchanged email messages every couple of weeks. In most cases, it was her response to my email messages.'

Izabela was still alive at that time and living a life far removed from the one she had known in Indiana. And she had good reason to keep it a secret from her parents, for her new friend, JR, had provided her with an apartment in south Kansas City, where they enjoyed a BDSM relationship. They even had a slave contract, one which contained more than 100 clauses governing their conduct – she as the slave, he as her master.

In return for her submission, JR maintained Izabela financially, paying all her bills. When she wasn't engaged in sexual activity with him, Izabela enjoyed the life of a lady of leisure. Her main interest was reading gothic and vampire novels bought from a specialist bookstore, one that she visited frequently in Overland Park. But she didn't abandon her studies completely, for in the autumn of 1998, using the name Lewicka-Robinson, she enrolled at Johnson County Community College. Her adoption of JR's name lends weight to reports which concluded that the young woman believed they were going to marry – he being 58 and she 18.

Around Thanksgiving in 1997, Andrew emailed his daughter in Polish saying, 'I write in Polish because I'm not 100 per cent positive that your letters are coming from you. [...] As you know anyone could create an email account and sign it as you. If you would telephone, I would feel much, much better.'

Izabela purportedly replied, insisting that all further contact be in English.' I have told you I'm happy,' she wrote. 'I'm well. I have a wonderful job and a wonderful man in my life who loves me. I want to be left alone. I don't know how I can make it any clearer.'

At JR's subsequent trial for Izabela's murder, a friend of the dead girl testified that Izabela had confided in her that she was going to do secretarial work for an international publishing agent named 'John', who was also going to train her to be an S&M dominatrix. Jennifer Hayes also told the court that Izabela was going to begin her sex education as a slave.

In January 1999, JR moved Izabela into another apartment, this one in Olathe. It was closer to his own home, which may account for his sometimes describing her as a graphic designer employed by his new internet company 'Speciality Publications'. On occasion, however, he is known to have referred to her as his adopted daughter, while at other times he described her as his niece.

Then in August, Izabela Lewicka disappeared and was never heard from again. Police believe that she was killed and disposed of around that time. However, her parents continued to receive emails purportedly from their daughter up until Robinson's arrest. In the final months, John said that she was always travelling in some exotic land. In one of her last ever emails, she claimed to have just returned from China.

We all finally find what we want and need and I found mine.
Suzette Trouten's last email to her friend, 2000.

*   *   *

'The Slavemaster' soon returned to the world of sadomasochistic chatrooms. He made contact with Suzette Trouten, a bored 27-year-old licensed nurse from Newport, Michigan, who lived a double life; nurse by day, submissive slave by night. A substantially built young woman with a mass of bubbly brown hair, Suzette, whose non-sexual interests were collecting teapots and doting on her two Pekinese, pursued a highly active BDSM lifestyle, carrying on relationships with as many as four dominants at once.

Suzette had pierced not only her nipples and navel but also five places in and around her genitalia, all to accommodate rings and over devices used in BDSM rituals. A photograph of Suzette, with nails driven through her breasts, had been circulated on the internet and it must have acted like a magnet to JR. Quite understandably, a relationship soon developed. In fact, JR was so enamoured of his new submissive friend that he concocted a very attractive job offer to entice her to fly down from Michigan for an interview. He paid for her flight and when she arrived in Kansas City there was a limousine waiting at the airport to meet her.

The job, JR told her, involved being a companion and nurse to his very rich, elderly father, who travelled a lot but needed constant care. He went on to say that his father did most of his travelling on a yacht and that her duties would involve her sailing with them between California and Hawaii. For this, she would be paid a salary of $60,000 and be provided with an apartment and a car. JR neglected, however, to mention that the only way to have contact with his father would be through the use of an Ouija board or a medium, as the old man had been dead for some ten years. But as we have already established, JR was not a man to let such trivial details inhibit his grand design, so he gave Suzette to understand that the interview had gone well and the job was hers. She returned to Michigan and began putting her affairs in order before relocating to Kansas.

While she was making ready to move, Suzette spoke to her mother, Carolyn, to whom she was very close, telling her all about her new job. In fact she also gave her mother JR's telephone numbers – giving police a lead to follow when she later disappeared in March. She also discussed the job offer with Lore Remington, an eastern Canadian friend. The two women had met in a chatroom and shared an interest in BDSM. Later Suzette introduced Lore to JR on the internet, and they too developed a long-distance, dominant-submissive, cyber-sex relationship.

In February 2000, Suzette rented a truck, loaded it with her belongings and headed off to her new life in Kansas City. Along with her clothes, books, a collection of teapots, and the two Pekinese, she took with her an array of BDSM accessories, including whips, paddles, handcuffs, various lengths of chains, numerous items made from rubber, and just about anything else that a self-respecting, bona-fide BDSM enthusiast might care to invent. And, on John's insistence, and although he had no interest in the game, she also purchased two golf balls (brand name undetermined) and a length of elastic, but more this later.

Lenexa is a busy suburb of Kansas City, lying west of Overland Park and north of Olathe, and it was there that Robinson took Suzette when she arrived on Monday, 14 February 2000. He had reserved accommodation for her, specifically Room 216 at the Guesthouse Suites, an extended stay hotel. Claiming that they didn't allow pets at the hotel, he told her that he had generously arranged for her dogs, Peka and Harry, to be boarded at the kennels of the Ridgeview Animal Hospital in Olathe.

As soon as Suzette had settled in, JR told her to get herself a passport as they would be leaving in a fortnight. He also produced a master/slave contract covering their BDSM activities, which she duly signed. Then, ominously, he got her to attach her signature to 30 sheets of blank paper and to address more than 40 envelopes to relatives and some of her friends. Just as he had done with other women, he told Suzette that he would take care of her correspondence while they were travelling, as she would be too busy to do so herself.

Suzette was the youngest of a family of five children and, according to her mother, Carolyn, 'was a kind of mama's girl'. While she was in Kansas, she phoned her mother every day, keeping her informed of how things were going and, although Mom had at first worried that she would be homesick, she seemed to be in good spirits and was certainly happy with her employer, John Robinson. Evidently, he was happy with her too.

On 1 March, Carolyn spoke to her daughter, who was looking forward to her impending yacht cruise with her wealthy boss and his father, and Suzette promised to phone Carolyn regularly before she disappeared. After not having spoken with her daughter for some time, Carolyn made a few discreet enquiries, then she picked up the telephone and called the police.

Detective David Brown began an immediate and thorough investigation of the man he saw as the prime suspect, John Robinson. He obtained JR's criminal antecedents then contacted the Overland Park Police. The 'rap sheet' acquainted him with the reports of other missing women and soon he saw a potential connection. After he had spoken to two other detectives and Stephen Haymes, Robinson's probation officer in Missouri, it became clear that he could possibly be investigating a serial killer, and a somewhat clumsy one at that.

David Brown instructed the Trouten family and a few of JR's acquaintances to tape their telephone conversations with him and to give the police copies of any emails that they received from him.

For several weeks after 1 March, Robinson spent time contacting Suzette's submissive friends and some of her relatives by email, pretending to be her. Most weren't fooled by the subterfuge. He soon dropped the act and set his sights on Suzette's Canadian friend, Lore.

Lore and another Canadian woman began their own amateur investigation of the man they believed was named 'JR Turner'. Robinson moved quickly after Lore told him she was interested in finding a dominant master for a friend. The emails and chat sessions turned to telephone calls, which were picked up by the police wire taps now in place. The Lenexa PD contacted Lore and told her they were investigating Robinson. They did not explain the extent of the probe, but asked her to continue the relationship.

'The police didn't tell me to get John Robinson to lure me to Kansas City,' Lore said later at Robinson's trial. 'I was willing to help.'

Robinson made vague offers to Lore about meeting in her person. 'He offered nothing other than I would be financially taken care of and never have to work,' she said.

At the time that Suzette had been preparing to move to Kansas, the sexually insatiable JR, using the name James Turner, had established two more BDSM friendships on the internet. The first woman, Vicki, was a psychologist from Texas who had placed an advert on a BDSM site. She had recently lost her job and when JR became aware of this he promised to help her find work in the Kansas City area.

Vicki arrived in Lenexa on 6 April and, while staying at the Guesthouse Suites, spent five days getting to know JR. During this time she signed a slave contract in which she consented to, 'give my body to him in any way he sees fit'. They also discussed her working for Hydro-Gro before he told her to return home and prepare to move to Kansas City. She was, in many ways, and obvious choice for Robinson... that is to say, she was vulnerable. She suffered from depression and a lack of meaningful companionship and was eager to change her life; she fell completely for Robinson's 'bull'. She returned to Kansas City for another long weekend in late April, and it was then that she found that JR was eager to pursue more severe and violent forms of bondage sex than she wanted, but as she believed he was going to find work for her she consented to his demands, allowing him to brutalise her far beyond the limits she had intended.

Vicki later testified that he took photographs of her bound and nude and he hit her hard across the face. 'I had never been slapped that hard by anybody before', she later told the court. She also stressed that the photographs were taken against her wishes and despite her protests.

Fortunately for Vicki, the promised move to Kansas never took place. When she demanded the return of her sex toys, worth more than $500, JR chivalrously refused. Moreover, he threatened to publicly reveal the slave contract and the explicit, compromising photographs.

Vicki's response was to report the matter to the police, and was astonished to learn that all of her phone conversations with JR had been tape-recorded from the outset.

A woman called Jeanne was the second of the two women, and she turned out to be the last one to fall foul of 'the Slavemaster'. She was an accountant and, after some weeks of preamble on the internet, agreed to become Robinson's sex slave. In mid-May, she journeyed to Kansas for a few days with JR and was installed in an apartment at the Guesthouse Suites, who, by now, regarded Robinson as an excellent customer.

Later, Jeanne recalled that on Friday, 19 May, she received a phone call from Robinson telling her that he would be coming round to see her. During the call he instructed her that when he arrived she was to be kneeling in the corner of the room completely naked with her hair tied back.

Submissive Jeanne was ready, as instructed, when JR arrived. Yet she wasn't prepared for what would actually happen. He walked into the room, grabbed her by her hair and flogged her brutally across her breasts and back. Like Vicki before her, Jeanne was discovering that JR was interested in a much rougher relationship than she had anticipated. She, too, didn't like being photographed during sex, but he insisted on doing so; he seemed excited by recording the marks his beatings made on her body. However, Jeanne's genuine distaste for that level of treatment must have spoiled his enjoyment, because he told her he didn't like her attitude and wanted to end their relationship. Her body burning and bruised from the flogging, Jeanne became hysterical to the extent that after JR had left she dressed and made her way in tears to the reception desk. There she asked for the registration card and it was then that she discovered that her host's name was not James Turner, but one John Robinson. Worried and distraught, she called the Lenexa PD, who, on hearing that JR was involved, gave her complaint the utmost priority.

The detective who arrived at the hotel in response to Jeanne's call was David Brown, who had been investigating Robinson since the disappearance of Suzette Trouten for more than two months. Convinced that JR was a killer, Brown was not going to risk leaving another woman in the position of becoming a potential victim. When he heard Jeanne's tearful story, he got her to collect her belongings together and moved her to another hotel.

The next day, Jeanne gave a full statement to Detective Brown. She explained how she had met 'James Turner' via the internet, and how she had been invited to Kansas to embark on a master and slave relationship. She told him that Robinson had beaten her with a violence far beyond her desires, explaining that she didn't go in for pain and punishment or marks on her skin. 'I'm a submissive, not a masochist,' she said.

The statements made by Vicki and Jeanne gave police the means to justify the arrest of the man who had been the subject of their investigation into the unexplained disappearances of several women.

*   *   *

For decades, JR had been baiting traps for other people, killing eight of his victims. But on Friday, 2 June 2000, the traps he had set for his prey ultimately became his own trap. It snapped shut when nine police cars drove up to 36 Monterey Avenue, Santa Barbara Estates, and officers got out, surrounded the building and pounded on his door.

Detectives arrested John E Robinson and charged him with aggravated sexual battery and felony theft; by the end of the following few days he would have willingly have settled for such simple charges. Visibly shocked, JR was handcuffed and driven away to the red brick edifice which is the Johnson County Jail in Olathe, where he was detained on a $5 million bond. At the same time, police and detectives from a number of agencies, including the FBI, spilled from eight other vehicles and began to execute a search warrant for the Robinson home.

Inside, as well as seizing all five of JR's computers and fax machines, police found a blank sheet of paper which had been signed by Lisa Stasi in January 1985, some fifteen years earlier.

Along with this were receipts from the Rodeway Inn, Overland Park, which showed that JR had checked Lisa out on 10 January of that year, the day after she had last been seen alive by the inn's manager and her mother-in-law. However, those first scraps of evidence were only the tip of a gigantic iceberg of evidence; far more would come to light over the next few days and it would mortify those who found it.

Although somewhat belated, the police investigation had been thorough and revealed all of the property owned or rented by Robinson. Consequently, a second search warrant had been obtained for that morning and, as JR was being driven to jail, detectives were busy rummaging through his storage locker in Olathe. Here, they unearthed a cornucopia of items connecting him to two of the missing women, Izabela Lewicka and Suzette Trouten. They found Trouten's birth certificate, her Social Security card, several sheets of blank notepaper signed, 'Love ya, Suzette', and a slave contract signed by her. Along with Suzette's things, they located Izabela's driving licence, some photographs of her, nude and in bondage, a slave contract and several BDSM sex implements. They also located a stun gun and a pillowcase.

The following day, Saturday, 3 June, another search warrant was issued. This time, cops descended on the smallholding that the Robinsons owned near La Cygne. They found two 55-gallon metal barrels near a shed and opened one. Inside was the body of a naked woman, head down and immersed in the fluid produced by decomposition.

After prising the lid off the first barrel, crime scene investigator Harold Hughes turned his attention to the second barrel and opened the lid of that one. Inside he found a pillowcase, which he removed to reveal another body. Again, it was that of a woman, but this one was clothed. Like the first body, it was immersed in the fluid resulting from its own decomposition. Hughes completed the nose-pinching procedures of photographing and fingerprinting the barrels before resealing them and marking them: 'Unknown 1' and 'Unknown 2'.

Later that same day, Stephen Haymes, Robinson's former probation officer, was told of the discovery of the bodies. After so many years of suspicion, his judgement of JR was vindicated. He later told writer David McClintick, 'It confirmed what I had always believed, but the move from theory to reality was chilling.'

At the time Haymes was learning of JR's arrest, the District Attorney for Johnson County, Paul Morrison, was contacting his counterpart in Cass County, across the state line in Missouri, in order to negotiate the issue of yet another search warrant. Detectives had discovered that Robinson maintained a locker at the Stor-Mor-For-Less depot in Raymore, a Missouri suburb of Kansas City. DA Morrison was an influential figure and was given total cooperation in cutting through the red tape inevitable in jurisdictional issues negotiated between two states. Early the next morning, as a result of his discussion, he and a group of detectives from Johnson County arrived at the office of Cass County's Deputy Prosecutor, Mark Tracy. They carried with them the longest affidavit, in support of a search warrant, that Tracy had ever seen. It asserted that Robinson was believed to have killed several women and that it was suspected that evidence connected with the murders was hidden in the storage locker in Raymore; he had paid to rent his locker with a company cheque, in order to conceal his identity.

We started removing boxes from the front [of Locker E2].
After less than 10 minutes there was a very foul odor that
with my past experience I associated with a dead body.
Douglas Borcherding, Overland PD officer.

Shortly after 8am on the Monday, Mark Tracy served the search warrant on the storage depot and the Johnson County detectives were led to Robinson's locker – effectively a small garage with a brown, lift-up shutter door. Inside was a lot of clutter and the task force spent more than half an hour sifting through it before they saw, hidden at the back, three barrels. Wafting from the barrels emanated the nauseating, unmistakable stench of decomposing flesh.

As it was virtually certain that the barrels contained dead bodies, Tracy summoned his boss, Chris Koster, and the state of Missouri assumed immediate control of the crime scene. A new team of police investigators arrived and the locker was emptied of all its contents, save for the three barrels, which were standing on piles of cat litter; obviously a futile attempt by JR to reduce the smell coming from them.

The first barrel, a black one with the words 'rendered pork fat' on the label, was opened by senior criminalist Kevin Winer. The contents revealed a body wrapped in blue-grey duct tape, and a light brown sheet. There was a pair of spectacles and a shoe. When the crime scene technician had removed the sheet, he took hold of the shoe, only to find that the foot was still attached to a leg. On the assumption that the storage depot wasn't perhaps the best place to investigate the barrels and their contents, it was decided to reseal them and take them to the medical examiner's office in Kansas City. However, this was not as simple a procedure as it seemed. There was a very real fear that the bottoms of the barrels were corroded and might give way, so a police officer was sent to a nearby Wal-Mart to buy three children's plastic paddling pools and these were slipped underneath the barrels before they were loaded on to a truck.

Back at the medical examiner's office, the barrels were opened and, as expected, each contained a severely decomposed female body. Dr Thomas Young determined that they had all been beaten to death with a blunt instrument, probably a hammer, and had been dead for some six years. The body of Sheila Faith also had a fracture on her right forearm that was consistent with a defensive injury.

The first body was fully clothed. The second was wearing only a T-shirt, and in its mouth was a denture which was broken in two. Body three was that of a teenager wearing green trousers and a silver-grey beret. Identification was not immediately possible and would take some days to complete.

Over in Kansas, in Topeka, the two bodies found on the Robinson smallholding were identified by a forensic odontologist as those of Izabela Lewicka and Suzette Trouten.

A few days later, with the help of another forensic odontologist, two of the bodies that had been found at the storage depot were identified. One was Beverly Bonner; the other was Sheila Faith. Soon afterwards, Sheila's disabled daughter, Debbie, was identified by means of a spinal X-ray, the technology of which, in past years, Robinson had been briefly acquainted with.

The case against Robinson was beginning to assume a structure, although there was the problem of jurisdiction in relation to which state, Kansas or Missouri, would be responsible for each murder. Eventually it was resolved that Robinson would be tried first in Kansas; the date being slated for 14 January 2002, before being postponed until September of the same year.

> *I was represented by court-appointed attorneys who did NO INVESTIGATION, hired no experts, tested nothing and admitted in open court a day prior to my trial they had not read the discovery.*
>
> John E Robinson, letter to the author, 24 January 2008.

> *I resent the fact that people are now claiming that Mr Robinson, either directly or indirectly, is a serial killer. As each day has passed, the surreal events have built into a narrative that is almost beyond comprehension. While we do not discount the information that has, and continues to come to light, we do not know the person whom we have read and heard about on TV. The John Robinson we know has always been a loving and caring father.*
>
> Byron Cerrillo, public defender for Robinson at his trial.

In suggesting that five decomposing bodies found in barrels on two premises rented by his client could never indicate that John was a serial killer, Byron Cerrillo seemed to have watched too many episodes of *The Practice* – an American legal drama based on the partners and associates at a Boston law firm. Still, with elements of kinky sex and infidelity, the trial was guaranteed to become a sordid affair.

Carolyn Trouten was forced to come to terms with her daughter's bizarre sex life on the stand and, on 14 October 2002, jurors were subjected to a 40-minute videotape of Trouten and Robinson engaging in sadomasochistic sex. Early in the video, Trouten sat on the bed, looked into the camera, and said to Robinson: 'This is what you wanted me to tell you...I'm your slave...everything is yours.' While several jurors covered their eyes, others winced as Robinson was seen to say: 'The most important thing in life is that you are my slave.'

The jurors were confronted with solid evidence that could only point to JR's guilt. In counter-argument, the defence team could only say that there was no physical evidence, except a few fingerprints, to link Robinson with anything connected to the bodies.

Indeed, although JR grumbles and complains about the 'negligence' of his trial attorneys, he was as guilty as sin. The court heard from Don Robinson who testified about how Tiffany was delivered to him by his brother JR, as well as from the notary public, the judge and two lawyers who said that their signatures on the adoption papers had been forged.

DNA tests linked saliva on the seals of letters sent to Carolyn Trouten by Robinson, to JR. A criminalist gave evidence that Izabela Lewicka's blood was found in Robinson's trailer in La Cygne, and on a roll of duct tape of the same type used to bind some of the bodies.

Suzette Trouten's hair was also found in JR's trailer, and maids at the motel where she had been staying testified that the amount of blood on the bed sheets in her room was much more than they had ever encountered when cleaning before.

Even Suzette's prized Pekinese became evidence when a veterinarian testified that Robinson had dropped the two dogs off for boarding. The animals were later abandoned in the mobile home park where JR lived. Dog lovers among the readers will be delighted to learn that 'Peka' and 'Harry' were later adopted from the humane society.

The pillowcase found in a barrel also formed a solid link

between Izabela Lewicka and Robinson. Her mother had given her daughter some distinctive bed linen with a pattern, identical in every single respect to the pillowcase that ended up in the drum containing Izabela's body. A former lover of Robinson recalled that JR had given her similar sheets, but she didn't recall there being any pillowcases.

Nancy Robinson talked of her husband's philandering and how several times she wanted to divorce him, only reconsidering because of the children. Although, at the penalty phase of the trial, JR's family asked the court to spare his life, when the jury had reached a decision about his punishment the Robinson family put a lot of air under their car's tyres and were nowhere to be seen.

Nancy divorced her husband on 25 February 2005, and wants nothing more to do with him, further exposing Robinson as a pathological liar. In a letter to the author dated 10 January 2008, he writes: 'My family worked for two years to put together a team which included every possible requirement from data-base set-up to forensic testing, most volunteers. Unfortunately the actual cost budget put together was $2.5 million dollars, an impossible amount.'

*   *   *

In January 2003, Judge John Anderson III sentenced Robinson to death twice and handed down a life sentence for the killing of Lisa Stasi.

With John Robinson now on Death Row in Kansas, the state of Missouri were still pursuing the three murders that had been committed within their jurisdiction. For his part, JR was more worried about being extradited to stand trial in Missouri, because that state was much more aggressive in using capital punishment than Kansas. However, in point of fact, Kansas has not executed anyone since the reinstatement of the death penalty in 1976, so JR's fears were groundless.

Despite Robinson's argument that his attorneys were all but useless, they had negotiated tirelessly with Chris Koster, the Missouri prosecutor, who stood firm against their offers and tried to get Robinson to lead investigators to the bodies of Lisa Stasi, Paula Godfrey and Catherine Clampitt.

Either because he could not, or would not reveal where he had dumped the bodies, Robinson demurred until Koster and his team became convinced the women's remains would never be found. Only then did Koster, with the permission of the victims' families, agree to accept the guilty pleas in return for life without parole sentences. JR would never be executed in Missouri.

In mid-October 2003, JR, looking much older than his 59 years, stood before a Missouri judge and, in a carefully scripted plea, acknowledged that the prosecutor had enough evidence to convict him of capital murder for the deaths of Godfrey, Clampitt, Bonner and the Faiths. He demanded the unusual plea agreement because an admission of guilt in Missouri might have been used against him in Kansas – Kansas prosecutor Paul Morrison said he wasn't convinced the murders actually occurred in Koster's jurisdiction – and nothing he said in Cass County, Missouri, resembled anything like a confession of guilt.

This was classic John Robinson. The guy was a gamesman to the end.

DA Paul Morrison, speaking to the *Kansas City Star*.

Once again, JR gave no statement or even a hint of what prompted his homicidal acts. As the victims' next of kin shared their feelings of anger and pain before his sentencing to life in prison in Missouri, he ignored them and stared straight ahead, oblivious to the hurt he had wrought. His mind unable to empathise with them, Robinson appeared bored with the entire process. In this, the final time he was ever likely to appear in public, it was clear that the depth of their emotions were something he had never experienced, and cared not a jot about.

Amazingly, some good news followed: on 6 July 2000, authorities located Lisa Stasi's daughter, Tiffany, alive and living with Robinson's older brother, Don, in Hammond, Indiana. Unaware that the adoption was not legal or that the girl's mother had disappeared and presumably been murdered by Robinson, whom the child knew as 'Uncle John', Don and his wife raised the little girl in a normal, loving fashion. At the time of writing, Tiffany is 23. She has been made aware of the true identity and fate of her mother and has since met her biological father.

* * *

The deal I offered JR was that he could write what he wanted to say in this chapter, in fact my brief was that he could have his own book if he agreed. This was his chance, perhaps his one and only chance, to come clean, to atone for his dreadful crimes and, more importantly, put the minds of his victims' families to rest and give them some form of closure.

I also offered JR the opportunity to be interviewed by one of the UK's leading top end television producers of documentaries, on camera, to say what he needed to say, to clear the slate as he saw fit.

I have tried this approach more than fifteen times over the years, and have succeeded with thirteen of America's most notorious serial murders. In doing so, I have cleared up a number of homicides and other serious related offences. My books *Talking with Serial Killers I* and *II* testify to this success, as does my TV documentary series, *The Serial Killers*, which is still being screened, over two decades after the series first appeared on our TV screens.

My offer to JR, however, included a proviso: I would not edit a word that he sent to me, providing that he told the truth and was up front. He broke this agreement from the outset, so, in the absence of any worthwhile input from JR himself for the reader to assimilate, it now falls upon me to provide a psychological profile, if you will, of this man. Let's visit the dysfunctional mind of John Edward Robinson.

JR has always imagined that he is more intelligent than anyone else. It is an ego thing, a state of mind not uncommon among the more learned, and 'intelligent' of the serial murderer breed. One might imagine that an 'intelligent' person might learn from previous errors of judgement but, alas, the true sociopath does not.

JR is a true sociopath. He understands the difference between right and wrong, yet he carried on committing his antisocial offences regardless of the pain and suffering he caused as the result. Sociopaths – once labelled psychopaths – just simply don't feel remorse for their actions. They don't care.

Like so many sado-sexual serial killers, John, the man with several identities and many faces, trawled for his victims. In a few instances he selected vulnerable women from places where women felt safe – in one case at least, a hostel for women in danger.

John the flim-flam man, conned men and women, even his own family.

John the sadist, abducted, used and horrifically sexually abused women.

John the serial killer, bludgeoned these terrified women to death.

John the garbage man, disposed of the bodies, leaving them to decompose and rot in their own bodily fluids.

That's how this lowlife disposed of his victims. Some of the deceased have never been found, while other intended victims escaped by the skin of their teeth, their lives mercifully intact. If the truth were known, if law enforcement had not been on their toes when JR first appeared on their radar as a potential homicidal maniac, many more women would have been murdered as a result.

Despite his pathetic protests that he didn't use the internet to entrap prey, JR was the first serial killer in criminal history to use the internet. He hung out in S&M chatrooms, like a deadly spider waiting to ensnare a victim.

But where did all this start?

Unlike the majority of those who graduate into the serial taking of human life, John did not suffer from an abusive childhood. His folks were decent, hard-working and of strong Catholic faith. There is no evidence whatsoever that he was inclined towards criminal activity during his teens. Then one day, in his twenties, he embarked on a series of frauds, becoming a plausible liar and a serial swindler who embezzled his employers and friends, even his own brother, out of considerable sums of money. He had suddenly metamorphosed into a real life Dr Jekyll and Mr Hyde, and it was all about money, and lots of it.

Simply put, John mutated. But it wasn't just a sudden change in a single gene, the whole genetic package of his makeup underwent a complete deviation into evil personified. The motive for his first murder was not sexual deviancy. JR needed cash, even if it meant deceiving his own brother, Don, over the adoption of baby Tiffany. Here was a quick way to earn $5,000, and the disposal of the baby's mother, Lisa, was merely a side issue. But there can be no doubt that having this young, attractive mother begging him for mercy turned him on. I think that the very act of control over Lisa gave him sexual pleasure. This control freak was then, psychologically, pressed on to commit the most violent sexual acts on any woman who fell into his clutches. And, as most psychiatrists and psychologists might agree, once the pleasure/reward switch for certain actions has been flicked on in the human brain, it is almost impossible to switch off. This state of mind is called addiction. Combine sexual addiction with a sociopathic mind and disaster is as sure to follow as night does day.

Whatever the case, to satisfy his perverted cravings, JR soon graduated into trawling for sex by exploiting women who were lonely and dissatisfied with the hum-drum dreariness of their day-to-day existence. He could smell them a mile off, and was able to hone in on them with unerring accuracy.

Your unwarranted accusation of attempted manipulation and flim-flam pretty much says it all.
> John Robinson, letter to the author, 4 March 2008.

John Robinson portrayed himself as a respectable businessman, a high achiever, the well-dressed 'man of the year'. Using blatantly false credentials, he even fooled the distinguished former physician to President Truman. What chance did vulnerable women have when confronted with the philanthropic generosity and charms of a man like John E Robinson, a pillar of the community? The answer is, of course, none.

John's history is adequately covered throughout the previous pages, and the reader may look into his psychopathology as they see fit, but where do we go from here, bearing in mind that John is now locked up and will remain so until he dies?

One might have thought that this man could, one day, tell us the whole truth of what happened and how he managed to earn himself the accolade of one of the most heinous serial killers in recent history. God only knows how JR feels about having deceived his loving wife of so many years. Regarding his doting children, is there any sorrow and regret? No.

Does this man feel any remorse for his homicidal activities? I think not, and it is at this point that we return, once again, to his correspondence with the author.

'Don't blow smoke!' JR demands in one of his letters. 'I don't have time for meaningless delays. I don't have the time or the funds to play games,' he rants, while at once stating that it will take at least a year before he could even discuss his childhood, and that is after his attorney – no name or address given in his letters – is placed in funds to the not-insubstantial tune of almost half a million dollars.

While demanding that the author and a TV production company digs deep to follow his every whim (and bear in mind he has already pleaded guilty to each murder), he adds:

Next we will proceed to the expert phase. First to examine and evaluate documents, photos and testing. Then to complete the necessary testing that has never been done. Each step of the way, we will evaluate and adjust our investigation or approach as required. The proposed budget

is fairly simple at this point but may have to be adjusted depending on need:
Database: $100,000
Investigator: $150,000
Travel: $20,000
Experts: $60,000
Attorney: $50,000
Communication, copies, supplies: $10,000
Equipment: $8,000
Misc. $2,000

Total: $400,000

My attorney would control all information and distribution of funds. Nothing will begin until there is a firm written agreement in place!

My first letter was clear about the possibilities available to you. Yet you responded with a request for information about my formative years, assuming it would be no threat to my present or future legal status. Unfortunately, that is not the case. When I win a new trial, it will be necessary to prepare a "mitigation case" containing the very information you now seek. My attorneys did not investigate or provide any mitigation evidence at my first trial.

I did offer you a smidgen of palpable researchable material right there in England. In November of 1957, I was a 13-year-old Boy Scout who traveled to London to appear in the Command Performance for the Queen. No one has of yet recovered the newspaper articles of that trip. As you see, everything is tied together.

John goes on to say:

> *I offered you the opportunity to do a real life true crime book and documentary. One that would expose blatant police and prosecutorial misconduct, fairly present the real evidence including complete details of the lives of the victims, and perhaps unveil the real killer. You could of course simply go for titillating, sensationalized products based on the fiction already out there. That decision, of course, is yours.*

The titillating and sensationalised products John refers to are the official trial records!

John E. Robinson is very much like John Wayne Gacy – another businessman/sado-sexual serial killer who also had all the apparent trappings of integrity. Both men used their human hunting skills to trawl and entrap their prey, but whereas bisexual Gacy tortured and murdered young lads, in many instances male prostitutes, only JR actively searched for prey in the S&M internet chatrooms.

I would use the analogy of JR being very similar to one of the Cornish wreckers of old who used lanterns to lure ships on to the rocks, and then plundered the cargoes that spilled from the wrecks. This predator and human parasite, Robinson, sent out attractive signals that were intended to lure the vulnerable toward him... like an insect where one genus fools another into approaching using a flashing code. This, the intended prey does; it approaches and is summarily eaten. So it was with John Edward Robinson.

If anything, John is a determined man, and he says that for the past five years he has been 'tireless [in his] attempts to locate individuals, companies, or organizations willing to assist in the completion of the necessary investigation, testing, etc., required to fully disclose the real story'. Blah, blah, blah.

Determined to either prove my innocence or die trying I began writing letters to anyone and everyone I could think of for both the UK portion of my case as well as those who might possibly help on this side of the pond. I wrote to Alan Hayling – head of producing documentaries at the BBC, in March 2007, and received not even a courtesy reply. I recently wrote to Mr Felix Dennis, owner of Maxim *magazine who lives in Stratford-upon-Avon, and have no word yet.*

My basic offer has been very simple. If they would provide funding [the $400,000] *for the investigation and testing, along with some equipment necessary, I would give them access to the results no matter the outcome as long as everyone agreed that nothing would be made public until my attorney authorized release.*

John E Robertson, letter to the author.

No doubt that the BBC and *Maxim* were bowled over by the generosity and business opportunity offered them by JR, and the reason they haven't replied is because they haven't, as yet, recovered their composure!

Moving up a gear, JR gets into full swing. Working up quite a lather, he wrote to me, saying:

The cost of putting all discovery information onto a searchable interactive data base, investigating, testing, travel and equipment will be about $400K and will require *at least twelve months to complete. The investigator will need some specialized equipment – video and digital recorders capable of two concurrent recordings. All funds would be disbursed by an attorney. I would receive nothing but an allocation to cover supplies and postage.*

But now, and completely carried away, JR almost bursts into song:

We are starting from scratch with a thorough methodical investigation of everything. Every document, every photo, every video, every witness, testing every item and utilizing acknowledged experts to evaluate to calculate every person or object.

'Ah, yes, John, that sounds fine,' I replied, 'but what about the five decomposing bodies found in barrels on your property and in your unit at the storage depot?'

To facilitate this investigation we have obtained every page of material connected to my case, some 300,000 more or less. Here is how we anticipate proceedings:

A) A data base will be designed with unlimited search capabilities. All documents will be scanned, cross-referenced with new documents added as developed.

B) A full time investigator will be hired under the supervision of my attorney. He/she will complete the legwork required to secure records and documents previously ignored, and conduct video interviews with all witnesses.

'John…'

I may be able to up the ante for you. For several years I have been in contact with a person who befriended Dennis Rader, the confessed BTK serial killer of 10. This person visited him in jail and corresponded with him regularly. This individual claims to have details and information never before revealed and has been working on a book. This person has the information, wants to do a book but has no industry name. The two of you should be able to do a great 'insider' true crime book and a documentary about BTK. You and your publisher could end up getting two for the price of one. I will await word from you.

'For God's sake JR, what about the bodies!'

I was embezzled out of over two hundred thousand pounds over a three-year period. To that end I have received preliminary word that a non-profit organization – Reprieve – operated by an attorney Clive Stafford-Smith OBE has agreed to help. My attorney has replied to a letter I received from them, by email, and we are still awaiting a reply… Finally I must tell you that I am working with a group of college students to publish a book of my poetry and short stories. An attempt to raise the money for the required investigation. No credit would be given – no author named. The book will, if published, simply be written by A Condemned on Kansas Death Row. I will receive nothing.

'John… the five bodies in barrels…'

For the record, I will explain exactly how the Kansas Department of Corrections mail system works. When a letter is received it is automatically date stamped on the outside of the envelope. Then the letter is opened by the censors, date and time stamped, read and all the letters to the inmates in segregation copied...

And so he goes on, and on, and on for ten pages of excruciating drivel, so it was at this point in our relationship that JR told me never to write to him again: 'You, Berry-Dee, have wasted my valuable time,' he spouted from his Special Housing Unit cell, where he lives in solitary confinement because the other inmates would kill him. 'I have never asked you for $400,000. I have never asked anyone for $400,000. I didn't say that I was going to use students, and if you print this I might sue you. I fucking told you that I never used the internet, and I was never into BDSM and I was never into kinky sex. FUCK OFF!'

And, that was it: end of story. Clearly, I'd pissed him off. If John Robinson wasn't such a deadly serious man, one could read his letters and have a rib-tickling good laugh.

But was this really the end of my work with JR? Has this sick psychopath learned any lessons from his previous behaviour? I'm afraid not. You see, while I am truly and genuinely sympathetic towards this nut ball who lives in a world where elephants fly, lead balls bounce and fairies reign supreme, I am also mindful that JR, when he can afford the stamps, is trawling for gullible people to send him donations so that he can start up yet another nefarious scheme. He is asking people to send in their poetry so he can claim it as his own, and then get the stuff printed and sold, through a friend, to raise funds. I am mindful, too, that this scumbag still hasn't revealed the locations of several of his victims' bodies, thereby denying closure to their families. So, I designed a honey trap by entering into the equation a woman who has been writing to scores of serial killers for over a decade. If anyone could get inside the head of John Edward Robinson it would be Annabel Leigh. With her degree in Criminal Justice, I asked her to study his life and crimes, and she presented him with bait which he could never have resisted. Together, we set John Robinson up. We turned the tables on this man who has, for decades, been turning the tables on just about everyone he came into contact with. The results were disturbing yet electrifying. And, when JR reads this book, he will flip.

In trying to get inside the heads of serial killers, any attempt to appeal to the better side of a psychopath's better nature will be judged by these master manipulators as a sign of weakness, for conscience is something they do not possess, and one's efforts will fail. While every case is different, in some instances the only key to success is recognising their own perversions and needs, for these people never learn from their own mistakes.

Christopher, you should be using their own 'victimology' against them. It is the strongest weapon of all. You would have achieved much greater success with the serial sex-killer, homosexual John Wayne Gacy, had you presented yourself as an attractive young man when you wrote to him - falsify a 'pretty' photo if needed be – so that Gacy could have sexually identified with you; in his subconscious you becoming a possible victim, and a photographic image that he could masturbate over while locked up in his prison cell.

You, like so many criminologists and psychologists, miss the obvious. With respect, you guys fail to think outside of the box. If you are writing to a female killer, you should use a multi-sensory approach: the written word which has to appeal to the inmate's way of thinking; photographic visual stimuli that will conform to their victim type and, finally smell - the latter being most important. A spray of expensive cologne will linger in her cell long after the written word has been absorbed, making your letter stand out, and bring back memories of better days long past. The same approach works even better with men. A sexy photo, a splash of perfume, and they have to reply, and this is why I adopted this approach with JR Robinson.

While this may seem very unprofessional from me, I think that your thousands of dedicated readers will appreciate my no-nonsense statement, being: Mr Robinson's thought-processing system seems, for the better part of his life, to have been hung between his legs. For my part, I see no reason why nothing much would have changed today. Therefore, I hope that you, and your readers, will find the results of my correspondence with JR of some interest.

Annabel Leigh, to the author.

Annabel's plan was simplicity itself. She would write to John Robinson posing as someone interested in him as a person, saying that she was not interested in his criminal offences, and she enclosed, with her first letter, a photograph. She also told him that she was fascinated by BDSM. Considering that JR had blown me out, one would have thought that he would have been very careful about who he wrote to next. He wasn't:

Annabel,

I received your letter. First of all let me explain that I have some simple rules for anyone that I write. You must realize that all kinds of people write. It usually happens when some story is run on TV. All claim to want to 'be my friend' when actually all they want is to receive a letter from a death row inmate. My attorney even located a blog that tells people how to write me to receive a response. If that was your goal, here you are...

I laughed when you said you were into true crime, if you have read either of the books written about me, you just read a media created fairytale. 85% of the material is false, but people like to read crap so that's what they write. The DA who prosecuted me had his wife, who owns a media company; create quite an evil persona of me.

OK, the rules – first, if you really want to communicate with me you MUST sent me a photocopy of your driver's license and a photo ID that shows who you are, your birth date, address. Second, don't ask me about my case. I have maintained my innocence from the beginning. My case is on appeal and I don't need to discuss it. Third, if I detect any phony BS I won't respond again. Fourth, you must guarantee me that anything we write will remain completely confidential!

If you write to me here is a way to do it. On the front of each page write a very normal letter. If you want to write other information about your experiences, fantasies, etc, write them on the back of the page like a separate letter.

Your list of lifestyle interests looks like you copied it from the alt.com website questionnaire [the website where he found Suzette Trouten]. *If you are seeking, tell me but understand I am very demanding!*

I am enclosing information that tells you what can and cannot be sent in... actually it's a list of don'ts. Look good at the information about photos' 'sexually obscene material or nudity'. Yes, I want you to send pictures but they have to get past the censors so use your head.

I'm also enclosing you information about how you can help out financially. I live in solitary confinement, I don't work (they won't allow it) and I have very limited funds. If you want to help out with postage and supplies you need to follow the directions.

You say you have two degrees, in what, from where and when?

How involved do you want to get? Are you interested in helping if I need typing complete, computer searches, light investigation? Tell me about your computer literacy, etc. I will give you the opportunity to tell me all about yourself and I want you to be very frank about what you're looking for! I need someone who will be committed to helping me. If I'm ever going to prove my innocence I need a person on the outside I can really trust.

So, there you have it. The beginning, where we go from here is up to you! You know all about me, I need to learn everything about you.... I mean everything!!!

'What kind of animals do you have? How long a sub in the lifestyle? Are you willing to take this to whatever level?'

There may come a time when I need to ask a favor, are you willing to help?

'Thanks for the letter and the picture. I hope it's just the

first..... Oh, last rule – if we're going to do that you have to commit to write at least once a week!

JR

P.S If you have experience is setting up websites or blogs, let me know!

From here on, Robinson didn't waste any time in returning to his controlling ways. He said that he was in a 'foul' mood because someone was 'attempting to sell an envelope' supposedly written by him on the internet for $40. 'I hate that kind of crap, and that's why I'm careful about writing to people,' he whinged. 'They use me and I hate it!! Your first assignment is to go online and see if you can find out who it is for me.'

Despite being told by Annabel that she wasn't interested in his case, JR then wrote that his, 'conviction was more than a miscarriage'.

I was framed, and that is what I have to prove. My appeal, when filed, will result in a new trial. But, when that happens I have to have everything necessary to prove my innocence. Your degree might come in handy if you are to work with me...help me investigate what needs to be done, etc. In time I will reveal what has to be done...I do have attorneys provided by the state for my appeal. One is a young woman who I trust. She tells me I will get some relief either a new trial or convictions reversed. If not, there are more appeals and whatever the case it will require heavy investigative efforts. This is not a game!!! We believe

we know who set me up, why it was done and how. Now
we have to prove it.

Ever the authority on BDSM – although he categorically denied it
to me – JR goes on to say, 'Submission has to be a total
commitment without reservation.' Then, completely contradicting
himself, he adds, 'Obedience is voluntary and must be given,
accepting the Dom as her master, following his instructions. Tell
me about any fantasies you have, how, why, what. I also need to
know what you think I can offer you.'

Returning to funding and empire building. JR, he asks:

Check out how difficult it is to set up a website. I've had
an idea… for a long time now to set up a non-profit
organization specifically to help death row inmates with
$s for investigators, lawyers, etc. Yes, there are a lot of
anti-death groups out there, but none actually help the
inmates. They protect, hold vigils and raise fund to pay
big salaries. Hell, with your smarts we might just do…Of
course you would probably have to move here [to Kansas
from California] *when it really got going. So, the website*
would have to be really professional, able to accept
donations, tax free, etc. I've been working up the idea for
awhile. Interested?

Then, in the same paragraph, he hit's overdrive, changing
direction in a heartbeat, with: 'I like my submissive shaved and
able to complete simple tasks…like masturbation. I want her to
be able to begin, get just to the point of release and stop. Wait
a moment, begin just until she is ready and stop again,
repeating this four times, it takes practice, then on the fifth time

feeling the massive release...Do it. Write about it. How did it make you feel?'

Reading down through JR's correspondence to Annabel, one gets the idea that he is about to break into song and dance. 'You say you like poetry. Do you write it? What kind?' he asks. 'Send me something you have written. I too like poetry and would like to do a book of it but not identify the author of a book of poetry and short stories from an anonymous death row inmate. Hell, with self-publishing it should be easy! Just need someone to type up my poems, locate pictures on the internet to go with them and go. You must type it out for me.'

Changing tack again, he boasts: 'I just finished a two-year project and wrote a disertation [sic] on the history of the death penalty in Kansas. From territorial days to today. A reference librarian at the Kansas Historical Society got me the research information. It's pretty good...needs to be typed also, so you can do it as well! Can't send it out, no money!'

And, almost immediately, and without drawing breath, he suggests: 'One letter a week, photos that will please me. Now, in your next letter at the end of it under your name, I want you to put something make-up color on your erect left nipple and make a print of it. A nice, small, round print, and you'll enjoy it.'

As far as I can ascertain, John's only hobby, other than fleecing and murdering people, was fishing in the pond on his rented La Cygne property, however, it seems that he does have a passing interest in golf, as he suggests: 'Also next time you're out shopping, pick up a package of golf balls. 3 balls in a package, and locate some very small tiny rubber bands. Insert them into your vagina when you next go dancing. You will find that I am demanding but reasonable. I want you to be all you can be and still commit. You'll understand more about that later.'

No doubt there are some golfers who will have something to say about that!

With him being a self-professed pioneer in hydroponics, we should not be surprised that John then moved on to horticulture, not that he'll be doing any of it for some time to come: 'I am into gardening and growing things,' he claims, then instantly changing the subject:

As we progress I will of course ask you to help with things. Looking up people on the internet, locating them, perhaps even doing some investigative work, Nothing dangerous, but it will be important...I don't have much support. In fact, sometimes I think I can count the number of people in the world who think I'm innocent on my penis!!! I need some help to keep going. I want you to figure out if you can afford something each month...I am seeking at least $400,000. You tell me! Can't promise a return, but if together we can prove my innocence it will be one hell of a story.

Dream on, John! But hard on the heels of that letter came one where he explained, most astutely in fact, that he was, 'not the most popular person in the world', and that he lives in a 6x10ft concrete cell 24-hours a day. 'This is called "segregation,"' he informed Annabel, 'a kind word for solitary confinement.'

Always the most charitable of guys, John says that he draws sarcastic cartoons about politics, his case and prison. 'My attorney keeps the originals but I have sent some signed copies to certain individuals. One [copy] was sold with my permission by a local battered women's shelter for $750. When I found out that a guard's ex-wife bought it I had a great laugh. I do hate it when people write to me and con me and then sell envelopes, etc, for personal gain.'

When I asked the Kansas Department of Corrections to confirm whether Mr Robinson was, indeed, such a popular and accomplished cartoonist, a spokesperson eventually replied:

'It is a policy of the KDOC not to comment on an inmate's specific custodial details, so I am afraid I cannot answer your question. I can tell you that this inmate does not attend any art-related activity because of his security status combined with his inability to draw a straight line.'

So, ever the pushy bullshitter, JR finishes off another letter, with:

I AM expecting one letter a week from you. I want to know everything about you and your body measurements. How it reacts to my directions to what turns you on, how intense your reactions and release. What kind of experiences have you had, your most memorable that left you completely quaking and exhausted. Do you enjoy prolonged play, multiple responses...explain your oral technique...do you enjoy doing it and why? How complete do you envision your submission to be? Where did you grow up. What kind of brothers, sisters...what was your first experience with sex? Were you abused? Do you really understand what total commitment means and are you ready? Now that I guess that you're a bit moist you may have some work to do! You might look for some padded tapestry hangers...PS: Perhaps the 'imprints' [nipple] should be in something light...now do the right one...Lemon juice?

So, John Robinson, you have become unstuck. The padded tapestry hangers, what the hell is all that about, you old rascal? Perhaps we will never know. As John Steinbeck wrote: 'There are some of us who live in rooms of experience that we can never enter or understand,' and I suggest that the room inside John E Robinson's head is one of them!

CHAPTER 2
MELANIE LYN MCGUIRE
THE ICE QUEEN

How do you do that? A beautiful young mother of two adorable kids shoots her husband, chops him into three large pieces, stuffs the remains into suitcases, then slings them into the Chesapeake Bay. And these are the actions of a highly educated and attractive lady.

'Motive' is always the buzz word in domestic crimes such as this. Double-indemnity insurance pay-out, jealousy, greed salted with a bucket-full of avarice, even. But try as I could, one will never find the motive in Mel McGuire.

The jury had her 'bang-to-rights'. She was 'the Scarlet Woman' and 'the Ice Queen' all rolled into one, who 'iced' her husband, after shooting him. But where did she commit the crime...where did she power-saw his body up? Not a speck of flesh, not a drop of blood was ever found, and no one has ever figured out how this petite little nurse managed to haul her grim baggage to a high bridge across a busy highway and heave the load into the swirling waters beneath.

This is what fascinated me, and I set out to try and find out,

'How did she do that?' I am still as puzzled as I was from the outset, and I leave it to the reader to figure out.

Where does discontent start? You are warm enough, but you shiver. You are fed, yet hunger knaws you. You have been loved, but your yearning wanders into new fields. And to prod all these there's time, the Bastard Time.

John Steinbeck.

As a brown-eyed, brown-haired nurse, she was known for her kind and generous nature. As a wife and mother she seemed to have a perfect life. In fact she and her husband had just realised their perfect dream – buying their own home. But behind that perfect picture were secrets and soon they would surface, revealing a murder, chilling in its calculation and its cruelty:

- 1 count of murder – life
- 1 count of disturbing/desecrating human remains – ten years
- 1 count of perjury: false statement – five years
- 1 count possession of firearm for unlawful purposes – life

Millions of years ago a melting ice age carved itself into the memory of Virginia. Early Americans called the area Chesapeake, or 'Great Water'. Even today the vast area is still a haven for wild life, and where, on occasions, the broken come to rest.

It all started in the spring of 2004, the season in the Chesapeakes for trophy fishing for bluefish, perch and striped bass. Chris Hankle and Don Conner thought they might get lucky with a catch or two in the bay that early May, then they spotted a black fabric suitcase, bobbing in the water near the bridge tunnel of a road bridge.

'It was right there, so I'm thinking immediately that it probably had blown off somebody's luggage rack of a car coming down the road,' said Conner, 'or, something like that.'

The men and the very excited 12-year-old son of Conner's pulled the suitcase onto the boat, thinking it was a real life treasure chest, and quickly opened it to find crumpled black, plastic garbage bags and a pair of decomposing legs severed at the knees. The lad recoiled in horror. His father comforted him and the police were called.

A week later, another gruesome find turned up in the bay. Virginia Beach crime scene supervisor Beth Dutton was already processing the first suitcase when police hauled in the second case. It contained a 5lb weight, black trash bags and more human remains – this time a man's head and torso.

Gunshot wounds told the cause of death, but when and where the man had been killed was still a mystery. 'He had some hair slippage, some decomposition – much greater than the legs,' reported Beth Dutton.

The third and final suitcase surfaced on 16 May, this time holding the man's hips and thighs, but who was the man? Virginia Beach PD launched an intensive investigation to identify the victim.

Events led to the corpse being 34-year-old William T. McGuire, a computer programmer at the New Jersey Institute of Technology, in Newark. The killer, his younger wife, a fertility nurse and a real-life femme fatale.

Melanie McGuire's own fate was settled in 2007 after more than thirteen hours of deliberation by the nine-woman, three-man jury. They had listened wide-eyed to 76 witnesses and had patiently reviewed over 1,200 exhibits during the course of the seven-week trial. When the verdict was announced, by Superior Court Judge Frederick De Vesa, Melanie burst into tears – she would stay in prison for the rest of her life.

Followers of this, one of the most notorious trials in New Jersey's history, referred to the 5ft 3in, 121lb woman as an 'Ice Queen', because she was so cold and emotionless through the entire proceedings. Perhaps if she had expressed her feelings to the jury, even though she refused to testify, they may have been more likely to acquit.

During deliberation the jury asked to view footage from a parking lot surveillance camera that formed part of the evidence. The jury also requested to view emails that were sent between Melanie McGuire and her friend from nursing school, James Finn. There were also wire-tapped conversations between these two submitted into evidence. It was sordid stuff, indeed!

Perhaps the saddest part of this tragic story is, that by murdering her husband the couple's two sons are left without any parents to raise them.

This is a defendant who puts on a face and shows the people before her whatever it is she wants to show. I don't know who the real Melanie McGuire is.

Assistant State's Attorney Patricia Prezioso at Melanie McGuire's trial.

With a younger brother, Christopher, Melanie was born a Libra, Sunday, 8 October 1972, at Ridgewood, New Jersey, to Robert and Linda Slate. Her parents divorced when she was just five years old. Today, she is serving a natural life sentence at the Edna Mahan Correctional Facility, Hunterdon County, Clinton,

New Jersey (the Garden State) for murdering her husband William 'Bill' McGuire.

Bill McGuire was last seen alive on Thursday, 29 April 2004, the day the couple had closed the sale on a $500,000 up market house in Ashbury, Warren County, New Jersey.

Shortly after Bill disappeared, over a period of days three black suitcases bobbed up in Chesapeake Bay. They contained his dismembered remains which were wrapped in black plastic garbage bags.

In a case, built entirely on circumstantial evidence, prosecutors theorised that Melanie McGuire served her husband a celebratory glass of wine spiked with a sedative then shot him to death. Investigators found the murder weapon, and in a phone conversation with a friend she claimed that she had purchased the gun just two days before her husband disappeared.

Police claimed that Melanie cut Bill up into four pieces in the shower using a saw, though investigators were unable – using all the forensic techniques available to modern law enforcement – to link the man's death to his home, or his wife to his remains.

Lawyers for Melanie McGuire would later aggressively contest these allegations, arguing that their client had no motive to kill her husband, whom they claimed was, like Melanie, also involved in an extramarital relationship.

Melanie told police that the last she saw of her husband was on the morning of 29 April after an argument over their new home. She said he drove off in his car and was never seen again. Indeed, at her subsequent trial, it was suggested that his death may have been related to gambling debts; a letter, from an unknown but alleged mobster from a major organised crime family in New Jersey, surfaced. The writer claimed that Bill

McGuire owed a $90,000 debt to a Mafia family and this is why he was fed to the fishes, in true Cosa Nostra style.

* * *

Beauty is only skin deep, and Melanie McGuire is undeniably pretty when the camera catches her right: with her lustrous dark hair, pixie-like profile, almost vulnerable features, she is certainly not unattractive. However, in her prison mug-shot she appears all washed out. When one views her all made-up she is confident and self-assured, a real femme fatale; when otherwise, a self-serving and manipulative woman playing upon the heartbreak that has been 'forced' upon her.

When I put it to her that she must have lots of people writing to her, and that she was a femme fatale, she responded: 'Lots of guys write me, but, femme fatale, REALLY?'

That singular statement from Melanie McGuire says everything about the woman who has been convicted of murdering her husband, who was claimed by the defence to be a hard-drinking, womanising, gambling, wife-beating man who threatened to take his wife's doting children away from her – or so she claims.

There is that old saying: 'one shouldn't judge a book by its cover'. Although Melanie McGuire used to be a pretty, a magazine-cover-glossy, classy act, it also transpires that this woman has a personality, which manifests itself through her letters, that is seductively enigmatic. When I asked her about her favourite food, she responded in her beautiful penmanship, with: 'Asian (be it Japanese, Chinese), French (No, you just can't get decent foie gras in prison). Seafood (hey, I'm from the shore). I fail to cite Italian as that is my 'ordinary' food.'

When I asked Melanie about her favourite colour and hair

products, she answered: 'If I had to choose one, it would be the grey/blue/green of my younger son's eyes – but, yes, and it is indeed on the list, but I'll spare you the hair-care products – you've suffered quite enough – Oh, I was joking about the color.'

*   *   *

After Melanie's parents divorced, Linda Slate remarried Michael Cappasaro. Melanie writes: 'My biological father and I had sporadic contact before he died on 26 February 1987, when I was fourteen.'

From eleven years onward, Melanie's lived in Middleton, New Jersey, where she graduated from Middleton High School South in the top 50 per cent of her class. She went to Rutgers College, then Rutgers University, where she was a 'pretty average student'. She admits that as this was her first time away from home, she was far more interested in immersing herself in 'collegiate lifestyle academics'. She adds, one senses with a wry smile: 'Yes, and this incarcerant can write, too.'

Melanie graduated with a baccalaureate degree in statistics, in 1994, a few months after she had met Bill McGuire, while they both waited tables at a nearby town to earn some spare cash. 'I was attending the Rutgers School of Pharmacy at the time,' she writes, 'ironically housed in the same building as the Stats Dept.' She had been less than enthusiastic about the major she had chosen, even taking a number of psychological and education courses, so, the 22-year-old woman made a decision to enrol in the Charles E. Gregory School of Nursing, in the Autumn of 1994.

It is here that Melanie McGuire finally hit her stride, excelling in her classes, she graduated second in her class in 1997. And, it was also here that she befriended James 'Jim'

Finn, who would soon become a famous American football fullback. They had what she calls 'a bit of an on and off relationship', but they kept in touch. Finn became a witness in her subsequent trial.

While at the nursing school, Melanie responded to an advertisement for ovum donors. By the time she graduated, she had undergone three egg donations, 'treatment cycles which were anonymous at the St Barnabas Medical Center'. She says that: 'In talking to the staff and head nurse there, they knew that my licensure exam wasn't far off, and they offered me a position as an "ovum donor nurse coordinator".'

Bill and Melanie were still very much an item, and he encouraged her to accept the job offer. They became engaged in 1998, after she had completed two more ovum donations – this time solely for research purposes. The couple married on Sunday, 6 June 1999. She was 27, he was 34, and a week before the wedding she learned that she was pregnant with their first child.

Melanie was thrilled:

I'd suffered a very early miscarriage about six months before that, I was thrilled, but nervous. Later that year, the physician I worked with left St Barnabas to form Reproduction Medicine Associates (RMA), and I left with them. I would eventually come to meet and work with Dr Bradley T Miller there, and he still runs a successful practice in Morristown today.

Brad would soon become Melanie's lover.

Reflecting back on her formative years, I asked Melanie if she thought that the break-up of her parents' marriage, while she was just five, may have had any negative impact on her. She replied:

> *I wouldn't necessarily say that my parents divorce troubled me – I barely have a recollection of it, and I consider myself infinitely fortunate that my mother subsequently remarried to a wonderful man, who I truly consider to be my 'real' father. However, I can and do acknowledge some pervasive abandonment issues – it would be disingenuous of me to say I wasn't affected by my natural father's absence (and occasional re-entry) into my life. I am reluctant to reflect on that and assign blame – I am an educated woman, and if it has power over me, it's because I allow it to.*

Melanie says that she is currently steeped in an environment where she is 'almost incessantly bombarded with people who seem to relinquish responsibility for their lives and blame any deficits in themselves on their upbringing, or lack of it, as it were'. She suggests an example of this typical inmate thinking: '"I robbed an old lady at gunpoint and beat her within an inch of her life because my mother was mean to me," and that sort of thing.'

Using verbal skills that any psychotherapist would be proud of, Melanie McGuire is also clear on another point:

> *I don't mean to intimate that one's earliest experiences (or the perception of them) don't impact our psychological development – but if I have issues related to my rearing, they are just that – my issues. As adults, we bear the charge of choosing how we allow these things to impact or dictate*

our own choices. Did I have a 'bad' marriage? Yes. Was my husband abusive, be it emotionally, and/or physically? Yes. But I am responsible for staying and for bending to his will on issues that I should have remained firm on. So, while I think things like a 'battered woman's syndrome' do, indeed, exist and are appropriate affirmative defenses in some cases, I do place some degree of accountability on the 'victim', albeit limited. In my criminal case, I never waged an affirmative defense – my defense was always that of actual innocence.

Melanie McGuire admits that she allowed many of her choices to be fashioned, or impacted, by 'the tenor of the relationship', but she adds:

I won't sit here [in prison] and cry that my biological father's absence explains it all away. It may be useful in coming to understand some of my choices and my rationale for not walking away from my husband sooner. My husband's abuse does not absolve me of my poor choices, but it lends a somewhat mitigating context for the situation and the perfect storm of circumstantial evidence that has put me here.

Melanie finishes this issue with her usual dry humour:

I'm not certain if I'm being clear, or if this is going to read like a flight of ideas from Plath, [Sylvia Plath, the American novelist and poet] *or something. Somewhere, several hundred miles away, I sense my appellate attorney developing an unsightly facial tic, so I'll stop for now.*

I also put it to her that she must be proud of her academic achievements, and Melanie McGuire responded in her typically humble fashion:

> *Chris, dear Chris, my academic achievements are anything but interesting. But I'll run through them if you like. When I was in the second grade, someone thought it would be helpful to test my IQ. As a result, I was placed into what was called a 'Gifted & Talented' programme (how politically incorrect). I was in this programme throughout grammar/middle/high school, where I excelled even in a fairly competitive school system. I was a member of a both the Spanish Honor Society (I like the word, honor) and the national Honor Society, and a drama club. I was selected as an Edward J. Bloustein Distinguished Scholar* [intended to recognise the highest achieving graduating high school students in or from New Jersey and to reward them with awards that are granted regardless of need]. *Then I went to Rutgers University, and got a 1.0 GPA my first semester to the acute distress of my parents. I discovered unchecked freedom – and parties. I think I pulled a 3.0 or better each semester after that: Statistics major, Psyche minor, Religion mini, but my initial fall from academic grace doomed me to mediocrity. I decided in my senior year that I wanted to pursue nursing, but didn't have the credentials to switch majors at that point, so I completed my BA first at my parents' insistence.*

Although Melanie and footballer Finn had a short relationship, she says she is not the football type – being more of the 'conspiracy theory/science fiction type'.

Melanie McGuire admits that by anyone's standards her marriage was far from happy. 'Jim had a few problems – drink, gambling, and women on occasions,' but she is quick to point out that she is 'not entitled to any righteous indignation about this last, as I, too, was unfaithful'.

So, Melanie Lyn McGuire has her feet firmly placed on Mother Earth. A highly intelligent and self-effacing woman, she certainly likes her books, too. Her favourite authors are Stephen King, Janet Evanovich (selected works), P.G. Wodehouse, Martin Amis, Haruki Murakami, Hugh Laurie, and Matt Beaumont, whom she describes as 'hilarious'. She intends to read *Duma Key* by Stephen King, *The War against Cliché* by Martin Amis, and *The Gnostic Faustus* by Ramona Fraden. 'That's quite a queue I know,' she admits.

Melanie McGuire finished by saying: 'Alas, time for group therapy, so I'll close for now (and before, somewhere in DC, my appellate attorney has a grand mal seizure). Let the healing begin (yes, that's sarcasm you smell). This should all be duplicative anyway, as I've channelled to your mailman all I wanted to say (the poor bastard).'

*   *   *

The depravity of this murder simply shocks the conscience of this court. One who callously destroys a family to accomplish her own selfish ends must face the most severe consequences that the law can provide.

Superior Court Judge Frederick De Vesa – sentencing
Melanie McGuire.

On Thursday, 19 July 2007, Superior Court Judge Frederick De Vesa rejected Melanie McGuire's claims of innocence and sentenced her to life in prison. She was visibly shattered as she listened to the judge. Her lawyers had asked for the minimum sentence of 30 years for the murder count. She had been convicted on Tuesday, 23 April 2007, of four counts, including first-degree murder. She also received 10 years for desecrating human remains, to be served concurrently, and an additional five years on one count of perjury for lying to a family court judge regarding the whereabouts of her husband, Jim. In an agreement among the lawyers, Judge De Vesa merged one count of unlawful possession of a weapon with the murder count.

Melanie McGuire will be eligible for parole after serving 85 per cent of her sentence, or when she is 100 years old, and that is after the judge gave great weight to 'the cruel and heinous nature of the crime', in determining the sentence after hearing pre-sentencing witness impact statements from William McGuire's family.

Clutching a tissue, Laura Ligosh told the judge that her memory of her 'Uncle Jim' was marred by the image of his bloated limbs after they were pulled from the Chesapeake Bay. 'She [McGuire] has stolen our smiles, our laughter, our joy,' she said through sobs. 'She has also taken from us something deeper from us all – our innocence, our faith in humanity.'

The motive for the murder was claimed to be that Melanie McGuire killed her husband so that she could start a new life with her boss without a messy divorce, and during the seven-week trial the prosecutors relied on evidence of the affair and testimony from a forensic expert who said the garbage bags containing the victim's remains were consistent with bags from the couple's home.

While McGuire's attorney, Joseph Tacopina, maintained her innocence, stressing: 'She didn't do this,' the prosecutor,

Assistant State Attorney Patricia Prezioso said that McGuire's 'meticulous nature was what almost enabled her to get away with murder', and urged the judge to hand her the maximum sentence.

'This is a defendant who puts on a face and shows the people before her whatever it is she wants to show,' Prezioso said. 'I don't know who the real Melanie McGuire is.'

*   *   *

Way back in 2004, John and Susan Rice had been hearing about the bizarre story of suitcases containing a dismembered body turning up in Chesapeake Bay, Virginia, but by then there were engrossed in another bizarre tale – this one involved their favourite couple, the McGuires. The Rices had just heard about the beautiful new home their friends had bought in New Jersey, and a few days later Melanie phoned the Rices to say that she and Bill had had a terrible argument about their dream home just hours after signing on the dotted line. Melanie said that John had got physical with her and stormed out of their apartment.

It didn't add up. Bill loved the boys, and having just signed up for the house, John Rice, who knew Bill from their US Navy days together, was suspicious. But Melanie insisted that he had left her and he had hit her. She had even got a restraining order in case Bill decided to come crawling home, she told the Rices.

She told the family court judge: 'He [Bill] told me I was stupid, and slapped me, uh.' The judge asked: 'Where did he slap you, ma'am?', to which Melanie replied: 'In the face.'

While the Rices were stunned, others were not, and they lived closer to the McGuires, in New Jersey. Selene Travis' had known Melanie almost all of her life: 'I don't think Jim was a good husband,' she said. 'I don't think he was a good father, either. For years I feel that Bill was stressed by all his responsibilities and he was quick to anger.' And, the light-hearted repartee between husband and wife, the banter the Rices had so enjoyed? Selene said it had become 'a one-way tongue lashing. She was no longer fighting back, no more arguing back and forth.' Selene thought that Melanie was better off without Bill.

But, where was Bill?

Selena and another friend called Alison McCaulsey said that Melanie later confided in them about Bill's other problem – gambling. Maybe he had fled to glitzy Atlantic City...gone on a bender...met up with the wrong people?

'Melanie knew all about Atlantic City,' said Alison, 'she always knew that Atlantic City was a monkey on Bill's back, and she also wasn't sure to what extent he was involved with gambling, or if he owed heavy debts.'

On the other hand, the Rices would say this was all nonsense. Bill did not have a gambling problem, and did not hang around with unsavoury characters. But, they did think it possible that their dear missing friend was in Atlantic City. And, of course, most adults only travel to Atlantic City to gamble in the many casinos.

'We actually started calling hotels in Atlantic City, just to check for ourselves whether Bill had checked in,' Susan Rice said. And, when one week turned into the next, with no sign of Bill, her concern became tangible fear.

But now Susan started paying attention to that other strange story she had been hearing – the one about the suitcases and the unidentified man inside them. The TV was on, and the reporter said that the police had released a sketch of the dead man, so Susan draped a towel around herself and came out of the bathroom:

'I looked at the picture, and something about the military-style haircut looked familiar, so I compared it to a photo I had of Bill,' she recalled. 'I just remember that my heart just sank to my stomach, so I told my husband and then called the Virginia Beach Police on their hotline: 1-888-LOCK-U-UP.'

When the Rices learned the truth they went into shock and were physically sick. Virginia Beach Detective Ray Picalle was the officer who broke the tragic news, and now that he had the victim's name he could now try to find out who had hated Bill so much as to saw him into thirds. The sleuth was especially interested in speaking to the victim's wife, Melanie McGuire – he needed her help most of all. Little did he know how much help she would be, and he soon formed the opinion that she was 'a lousy actress'.

The possibility that Bill had been the victim of a gangland killing, perhaps over a large unpaid gambling debt, was soon ruled out. The almost surgical dissection of the body was the work of someone with medical knowledge, and not that of a thug off the streets. And, crime technicians found something else, a hospital blanket inside one of the cases. Picalle did a little checking and soon found out that Bill McGuire's wife was a nurse. She worked at a doctor's office and the same type of blanket was used by her boss for his patients.

Roughly a week later, the detective was interviewing the 'grieving' widow in her attorney's office and asking a few questions.

Had she owned black matching luggage, now missing?

'No', she replied, but she did tell the detective that her husband's missing car might be in Atlantic City, New Jersey.

And that's just where the police found the blue 2002 Nissan Maxima. After crime technicians had thoroughly examined the vehicle, they handed over to Detective Picalle a phial of white liquid, which they had found with a syringe in the glove box. This, and the blanket were very significant finds indeed.

Picalle also searched the McGuire's home because it was the last place Bill had been seen alive. It was spotless, no sign of a struggle there. In fact the property was empty for Melanie had already moved out.

When the detective asked to see the victim's clothes, she told him she had given them to a friend. Picalle soon found them still in the bags Melanie had packed. They were black plastic bags, just like those containing Bill McGuire's remains.

And that luggage? The day after Melanie's interview she told the detective she had just suddenly remembered something; that she had, in fact, owned a matching set of Kenneth Cole luggage.

'I showed her a picture of one piece of luggage recovered from the Chesapeake Bay,' said Picalle, 'and she identified it as a family piece of luggage.'

A changing story, hard-to-believe coincidences, but still nothing to firmly tie Melanie McGuire to the murder of her husband. So, Picalle left Virginia certain of only one thing: Bill McGuire's body may have been dumped in Virginia, but had been killed in New Jersey, so it was in the Garden State's jurisdiction and, therefore, their problem to solve.

*　　*　　*

At the end of the day it was a horrible, gruesome murder.
Detective David Dalrymple - New Jersey State Police

As lead investigator, Detective Dalrymple started by taking a fresh look at the case. He searched gun registration records and cold-called at gunshops, looking for anyone within Bill's circle of friends who might have been armed, and he got a hit. On 26 April, just a few days before the murder, Melanie had purchased a .38 calibre special handgun at a small gunshop in eastern Pennsylvania.

Then police tracked down James Finn, the on and off again boyfriend of Melanie's. Finn was a gun enthusiast. Weeks before he killing, she had emailed him, saying, 'There has been a lot of weird stuff going on at home,' and she wanted advice about buying a gun for protection because she was worried about Bill's growing paranoia.

Finn told her that she could buy a gun in Pennsylvania in only one day. Now the police wanted to know where the gun was, and they persuaded Finn to call Melanie – the conversation would be taped:

> Finn: *Throw me a bone...where's the gun?*
> McGuire: *The gun was in the lock box when he* [Bill] *first left...I put it into the storage unit. Of course, I went later and looked and it's not there.*

A missing gun that couldn't be tested as a possible murder weapon – how convenient for Mrs McGuire!

But what was the motive for killing her husband? To try and answer that question, the police contacted Dr Bradley Miller, Melanie's boss at the RMA fertility clinic. Here they learned that Miller had been involved in an extra-marital affair with Melanie for three years. And the doctor told the cops a lot more, too. He told the investigators Melanie had admitted a crazy story; how after the fight with Bill, after getting that protection order against him, she had driven two hours to Atlantic City. Once there, she had somehow managed to find his Nissan car and, out of spite, moved it to the out-of-the-way Flamingo Motel, at 3101 Pacific Avenue. 'A security camera may have caught me doing it,' she had told her lover. She explained that, exhausted she had taken a taxi ride back home. The next day she took another cab back to Atlantic City to retrieve her own car.

The detective thought that this story was 'incredible'. He even checked with every cab company in Melanie's area. None had receipts for a taxi drive that would have cost hundreds of dollars, besides, if she was so exhausted, why didn't she simply book into an Atlantic City hotel that night. It just didn't add up at all.

Moreover, Melanie also told Miller that she had been shopping for furniture in Delaware, not far from the Chesapeake Bay, the day before the first suitcase surfaced.

Detective Dalrymple convinced the good doctor to confront his lover in secretly taped telephone conversation:

Miller: *The trip to Delaware. They* [the police] *want to know what you were going down there for and what furniture stores you were looking for there and seem to believe that you went with your father.*

McGuire: *There was nobody else in that fucking car with me… I think that they're… when it comes to, like, the mythical second person. I think they're talking shit.*

Miller: *I think they're either gonna come down on me or come down on your father. That it was, you know, the one that helped you, uh, do the murder.*

The evidence police had, circumstantial though it was, looked damning all the same: a missing gun, trash bags, strange trips, bullets, and a blanket – what exactly did it all add up to, and would it all end in an arrest?

The evidence presented to you in this case presents an absolutely crystal-clear picture of this defendant's participation in her husband's death.

Prosecutor Patti Prezioso's opening speech to the jury at McGuire's trial.

Thursday, 2 June 2005; it had been almost a year since Bill's shocking murder, and Melanie McGuire was getting back to her old routine. She dropped her two kids off at the Kinder Kastle day care centre and was in a rush to get to work, to see her patients. But on that particular morning, New Jersey had other plans for Widow McGuire; state police finally had made their move and she was arrested in the Middlesex County borough of Metuchen. She was charged with murdering her husband and she pleaded not guilty. There was no direct evidence, no eyewitnesses, but certainly the investigators had amassed a great deal of circumstances that pointed to one person – her.

Nearly two years after Melanie's arrest, during which time she was free on bail, prosecutor Patti Prezioso prepared to convince a jury that all those circumstances pointed to Melanie McGuire's guilt. The picture she painted was while her husband slept; she shot him, dismembered him, dumped his remains like garbage into the bay, and then ditched his car at an out-of-the-way motel to distract police.

'When Bill was engrossed in purchasing the house, and all the fine details involved with closing the deal,' Prezioso said, 'the defendant was planning his death.'

Pacing slowly around the courtroom, the prosecutor carefully explained: 'Starting with the gun. She bought the .38 special just two days before her husband's murder. She only told friends about the pistol after Bill's death, and even then shifting stories. She told some friends that it was Bill who wanted the gun, but she told Mr Finn that she wanted it for her protection against her husband.'

Then the black, plastic bags. Forensic scientist, Tom Lesniak, used a laser pointer to show the jury the visual similarities between the rubbish bags that were found with the victim, and the ones she used to give away her husband's clothes in. His conclusion? They were all manufactured on the same production line and on the same extrusion run.

But what the prosecution found most suspicious was what Lesniak didn't find when he and his team meticulously searched the McGuire's apartment, including its bathroom. They hadn't been able to find a speck of blood, no DNA material whatsoever, no trace at all, in fact, that the McGuires had ever lived there.

'Who scrubs a bathroom that well when they're leaving an apartment?' asked the prosecutor.

However, the forensic expert went on to say that Melanie might not have covered her tracks as well as she thought she had, because he found traces of the crime scene somewhere else.

'I found particles that to me looked like, um, it could be human tissue,' Lesniak told the court. Indeed, he had found particles of Bill McGuire's human tissue in the vacuuming taken from the floor of Bill's car. It was another significant find, and we remember that Melanie had already admitted moving the Nissan to the parking lot at the Flamingo Motel that night.

Prosecutor Prezioso said that it all added up. Melanie had probably picked up traces of Bill's tissue on the soles of her shoes when he had been cut up, that she had transferred that tissue to his car when she had driven it to Atlantic City.

Next, the prosecutor explained about other important evidence that showed that the murder had been carefully planned – all of it captured on the McGuires' home computer.

A forensic computer expert told the jury about incriminating internet searches that had been made during the days before Bill's death.

'There were several searches,' she testified. 'They involved things like names of chemicals and poisons. There were searches that involved guns (one of which was www.nvastore.com), gun laws and things like that.'

The expert told how someone browsed the internet for advice on how to commit murder, and then there was a Google search for chloral hydrate – a powerful but uncommon sedative. There was also a search for a nearby Walgreens pharmacy.

Hooking it all up to the computer, the searches led police to Walgreens and a very significant prescription in the name of an RMA patient – RMA, as in the clinic where Melanie worked. The prescription was for chloral hydrate, and it was filed at the pharmacy just a mile from the day care centre where Melanie always dropped off her children.

There was something else about that prescription too. It featured the signature of Dr Bradley Miller – Melanie's boss and former lover. He was also the state's star witness. Under examination:

Prezioso: *Sir, did you write the prescription?*
Miller: *No, I did not.*

Prezioso: *Are you familiar with the handwriting on the prescription?*

Miller: *Yes.*

Prezioso: *And, whose handwriting do you believe it to be?*

Miller: *It appears to be Melanie's.*

Melanie McGuire glared at her former lover. Her face crumpled up and the corners of her mouth dropped.

Certainly Melanie had written prescriptions for Dr Miller in the past, and she would be familiar with doing that, and had access to the pads. And then the prescription had been picked up on 28 April – just hours before Bill disappeared. A phial of the very same chloral hydrate had been found in the deceased man's car by police.

The prosecutor said that Melanie had used the sedative to knock him out before shooting him, but the jury must have been privately asking themselves, what had motivated the defendant to commit such a brutal, such a calculated crime?

Dr Miller said, 'Melanie and I were hoping to be together in the future and to have kids together,' future plans that Melanie felt would never come true while Bill was still alive.

In her summing up, Patti Prezioso told the jury:

All of this evidence together leaves you no doubt that she participated in his murder. While drinking wine to celebrate his new home, Bill had no idea that the drink was laced with chloral hydrate, and his wife wanted to grow old with her lover, and not him. The next day, the kids out of the way and at the day care centre, she shot the still sleeping man, a pillow muffling the noise. The dead man is cut up in the bathroom, stuffed into bags and suitcases. She drives to the Chesapeake Bay Bridge and tossed the suitcases in the air and into the water.

Melanie McGuire had murdered her husband, and the evidence seemed overwhelming. It might have looked like a convincing case against her, but it rested on circumstantial evidence – there was no direct evidence and no smoking gun.

The prosecution's case is circumstantial at best, yet utterly unconvincing.

Joseph Tacopina, McGuire's attorney.

Desperate whispered words: 'I didn't fucking do anything. I didn't fucking do anything,' she told James 'Jim' Finn over the phone. 'Then why are they all over you?' he asked. 'Hello, because I bought a gun…because I had an affair,' she replied.

But could it all be so simple?

For five weeks the prosecutor had depicted this petite young mother, a woman whose vocation since college was nursing, as a ruthless, determined killer. But her attorney, Joe Tacopina, said the investigators had got it all wrong; that they had zoomed in on Melanie from the start, focusing on evidence that incriminated her while disregarding other leads.

'Was there any forensic proof that she had committed this crime?' he asked the jury. 'No! And, no eyewitness, absolutely no motive whatsoever.' At least that's the way Tacopina saw it.

Tacopina's strategy was to tear down the prosecution's witnesses on cross-examination, and convert them into witnesses for the defence. Case in point: the forensic scientist who searched the McGuires' apartment four times for evidence of the crime and found nothing.

> Tacopina: *Well, you looked hard, didn't you?*
> Lesniak: *Yes, I believe we did. Yes.*

The prosecution had argued that there was no evidence because Melanie had carefully scrubbed away all traces of her crime. Was it possible to commit such a brutal murder and cut Bill up in the apartment and not have left any sign? 'It's impossible,' said Tacopina. 'Absolutely impossible.'

The defence said there was a much simpler explanation as to why there were no traces of blood in the apartment – the murder never happened there.

But what about the particles of skin in the victim's car? The prosecutor claimed that the killer likely stepped in Bill's remains, transferring the human tissue into his car and Melanie had admitted being in Bill's car.

The defence attorney made another plea for common sense, although a weak one at that: 'Why wouldn't traces of Bill's own skin be found in his own car?' And, in cross-examination of Lesniak, the expert conceded that there was no proof that the tissues had come from a dead body. But what was the defence's explanation for Melanie being in her husband's car at all after he had disappeared?

Tacopina said that she was just turning the tables on her husband – playing a little trick Bill had previously played on her after an argument. Bill had moved her car so that she didn't know where it was, or so she said.

Then the defence grilled Dr Bradley Miller, Melanie's boss and former lover, and the man, the prosecution claimed, embodied her motive for murder. Miller had previously testified that they had been having an affair for three years; they wanted to be together and have children. Joe Tacopina pounced, and now somehow Dr Miller's story sounded different.

Tacopina: *Dr Miller. Never once, not before or after the death of her husband did Mrs McGuire ever ask you to leave your wife?*

Miller: *No.*

Tacopina: *Nor did she ever insinuate to you, doctor, either directly, or indirectly, that, 'Hey, look I'm available now, wanna get together?' She didn't, did she?*

Miller: *No, she did not.*

Joe Tacopina also revealed to the jury that even though Dr Miller had told police he would secretly tape his telephone conversations with Melanie for them, he hadn't told the investigators that he was still sleeping with the woman. This brought a hushed gasp from the public gallery. This man who says he loves this woman so much is secretly recording their telephone chats and sharing the same bed?

But, Tacopina believed that Dr Miller did Melanie a favour, for not only did she not incriminate herself she was saying things that screamed out innocence:

Miller: *You swear you had nothing to do with this* [the murder]?

McGuire: *Yes.*

Miller: *On your children's lives, 'cause I'm standing by you.*

McGuire: *Yes.*

The defence also tackled a critical piece of evidence – the gun. The prosecutor had claimed that it was highly suspicious why Melanie couldn't get her story straight on why she'd bought the weapon. But Tacopina countered that she couldn't tell people the real reason was because Bill was a convicted felon who could not legally purchase a firearm for himself.

'Melanie was really committing a crime by purchasing the gun under her name with the intention of letting somebody else use it,' the immaculately turned-out Tacopina told the jury. Indeed, one of Bill's closest friends even testified that buying a gun had been very much on Bill's mind in the weeks leading up to his vanishing act.

The defence now called its own professional witnesses to knock down the remainder of the state's case. A computer expert suggested there was just as much evidence to show that Bill had made the online incriminating searches as Melanie. For example: a search for data of undetectable poisons had been made a mere twenty seconds after a search for information on gambling – Bill's pastime.

A plastics expert thought that the prosecution's analysis of the rubbish bags from the victim, and the bags that had Bill's clothes in them from the apartment, were not from the same extrusion run, and no match whatsoever.

And, finally came the 'Melanie experts', friends who said that she was no killer. Technically character witnesses, and as they were called by the defence, they depicted Melanie in glowing colours.

'It's like watching your next-door neighbour. It's just so surreal,' said Jennifer Collese. 'There's no way, not the Melanie I know...absolutely not.' She went on to say that as she was trying to get pregnant in early 2005, she made her nurse,

Melanie, promise her something: 'I want you to promise me that you'll not leave this clinic until I am done,' to which Melanie replied: "Don't worry, they won't drag me out until I am 85", and I said "okay".'

Linda Smith weighed in with: 'Melanie's dedication and commitment to bringing life into this world makes her the last person capable of murder…Someone who is in the position of giving life and helping people achieve life, there's no way you can take life so carelessly.'

Melanie's old friend, Alison McCausley, went a step further. She said the very idea that Melanie could dismember her husband defied common sense. 'His whole torso, essentially, in one of those suitcases had to weigh 150lb, or more. She's going to throw that in a car, drive down to the Chesapeake Bay Bridge…and how big is Melanie? I think Melanie was slightly over 100lb , if that.'

But, if her staunch supporters weren't buying the prosecution's scenario, the Rices, her former friends, were. By now John and Susan Rice were convinced Melanie had murdered their friend, Bill, and they could recall a time when Melanie had fought strong waves to save John, who was drowning.

'I hear that this petite little person couldn't do something like Bill's size and be able to carry the suitcases and dump them in the Chesapeake Bay – absolutely she could. I am that confident.' said Susan Rice.

After deliberating for four days, the jury foreman announced they had reached a verdict. McGuire was guilty of six of the ten counts.

'Melanie began pulling me on my arm and my lapel,' remembers Joe Tacopina. 'She was saying and sobbing: "I didn't do it, I didn't do it....my babies, my babies," meaning her two sons.'

Melanie McGuire was sentenced to 30 years to life with no parole. Unless her appeal is successful, she will die in jail.

Even Bill's friend, John Rice, felt a pang of something as he watched Melanie almost collapse when the sentence was read to her. But his feelings were tempered by the outrage at what she had done. 'I really thought I'd be happy,' he said afterwards. 'There was no win in this at all.'

Clutching John's arm, Susan Rice stood firm: 'Bill loved those boys. They were his crowning achievement, and maybe one day he would have brought them to Chesapeake Bar, so blue and so peaceful. Melanie could have filed for a divorce, but I think that's the choice she is going to have to ponder now.'

People say that Bill McGuire had loved Virginia ever since his days as a young man in the Navy. They even say he wanted to return and live there. Instead, he drifted back, lost and broken on the waters, his shattered body in need of a place to rest. Chesapeake Bay – ever accepting – gave that to William T. McGuire, if only for a moment, may his soul rest in peace.

*　　*　　*

Does Melanie Lyn McGuire really deserve being dubbed 'The Ice Queen'? It seems to this author that for 99.9 per cent of her life – all but a week of it – we find a dedicated nurse who cared desperately about her patients who wanted to bring children into this world. I do not think we can fault her for that.

Melanie was unhappy with her marriage and, as we have seen from her own letters, she admits that she should have left Bill way back. However, she also admits that she placed her children first, she adored her two young sons...that she wanted to bring them up not losing their father at such early ages, just as she, herself, had done, aged five.

Melanie had been having a long-term affair with her lover, Dr Miller, who was cheating on his wife. So, it would be fair to say that what both lacked at home, Dr Miller and nurse McGuire found in each other's arms. No terrible sin here either; at least not unless one spends their life living a puritanical existence, the real world a million miles away. And Bill was unfaithful himself.

Of Melanie McGuire's guilt? This chapter does not judge Mrs McGuire's guilt, for a jury of her peers have already done so. The state of New Jersey says she has committed a most heinous crime, and, although she is appealing the conviction, this is the way it stands at the time of writing. And there are a number of questions that raised themselves while I researched this chapter on Melanie McGuire.

The first being that the defence argued that within twenty seconds, either Melanie, or Bill, searched the internet on their home computer for information on gambling in Atlantic City, followed by a search for poisons. Tick tock, watch your clock. Twenty seconds...it had to be the same internet user.

It makes little sense that Bill McGuire would make a search for gambling venues in Atlantic City – he was already as at home there as a duck on a pond. But, it does make a lot of sense that Melanie, a nurse, might be looking for some form of drug to knock her husband out after briefly doing a little research on where Bill might gamble in Atlantic City – indeed, perhaps she was looking for a specific venue; an address from where she could allegedly take his car and move it elsewhere – although he was already a dead man walking in advance.

The second matter is, of course, the purchase of the gun.

Melanie has given two conflicting accounts as to why the weapon was purchased, the first being to James Finn: that she needed a gun to protect herself from Bill's growing paranoia. The other reason, that she gave to friends, was that Bill wanted a gun, but he couldn't legally purchase one because he had a criminal conviction. And, it is the word 'paranoia' that catches the eye. Bill had already allegedly told a buddy that he was interested in purchasing a firearm, but for what purpose? Did Bill believe that he may become the target of a hit man over unpaid gambling debts, and wanted to be able to protect himself? Or, was he secretly worried that his wife might want him out of the way? But thousands of US citizens want to own a gun, and talk about it to others, so the significance of him talking to a buddy about getting hold of one may mean nothing at all.

What we do know is that Melanie McGuire made enquiries about purchasing a gun, and Pennsylvania state gun law, through James Finn – a self-acknowledged gun enthusiast – weeks before a search was made by either husband, or wife, on the McGuires' home computer, and that Bill suffered fatal gunshot wounds to the head, just two days after the weapon was purchased. Conveniently, it seems for Mrs McGuire, the weapon went missing from her storage locker, a secure box to which Melanie had sole access.

Criminal history affirms that there are thousands of individuals who carefully, even meticulously plan the 'perfect murder'. However, they fail, to their cost, to plan the perfect getaway, for the Devil is in the detail.

Mrs McGuire was too careful, yet plumb-dumb stupid at the same time. She was lacking common sense. She left a trail of circumstantial clues – none of which would have stood a guilty test if they had stood alone. But her mistake was leaving a trail of links that formed a chain of evidence so strong that even a possibly sympathetic jury could not ignore the significance.

I suggest that had Melanie come clean from the outset...had she given evidence at her trial to say that she had been physically and mentally abused by her husband, her previous good standing would have weighed in her favour. Had she said that she was in real fear of her gambling husband taking away her kids, she might have received a legal slap on the wrist – maybe five years imprisonment or less. Had she said that she had tried to keep the family together for the well-being of her two young boys, some of the jurors might have acknowledged her plea.

As it was, she drugged her husband senseless while he was celebrating the purchase of their dream home with a glass of wine. Their two boys were asleep in their beds. The next morning, Melanie McGuire took the kids to play school. She returned, took out a revolver, placed a pillow over her sleeping husband's head, and shot him dead.

That leaves us with other questions: where was the blood spatter, and how did this tiny woman drag her large, deadweight husband into his car? Did she shoot him someplace else, and where did she dismember the body? For my part, there are a whole set of questions not paired with answers, and this is the enigma which is Melanie McGuire.

The following is a letter prosecutors received, purportedly from a Mafia mobster, explaining why Melanie McGuire could not have killed her husband. Police believe that Melanie typed the letter herself. This letter was never introduced into evidence.

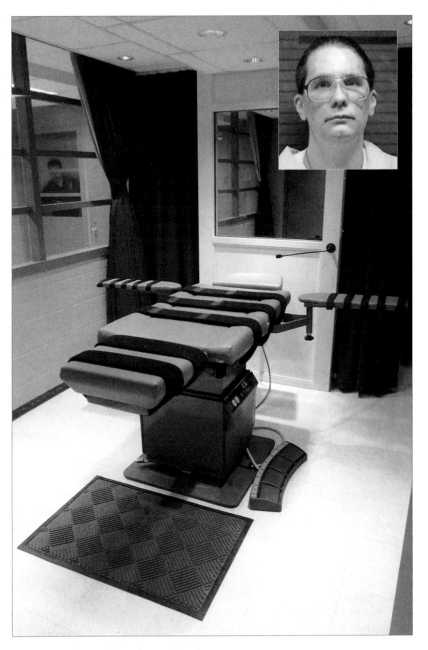

The room where serial killer Michael Ross (*inset*) was executed by lethal injection on 13 May 2005. He had raped and murdered eight girls and young women. It was the first time the death sentence had been carried out in Connecticut since 1960.

© *PA Photos*

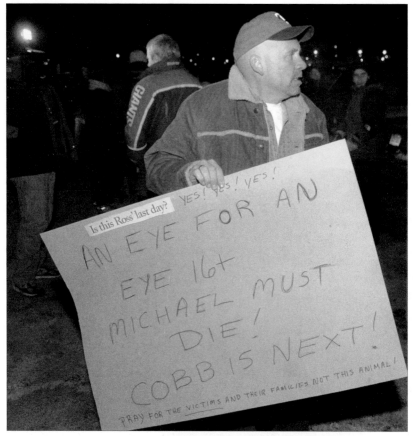

Is this Ross' last day? YES! YES! YES!

AN EYE FOR AN EYE 16+ MICHAEL MUST DIE! COBB IS NEXT!

PRAY FOR THE VICTIMS AND THEIR FAMILIES NOT THIS ANIMAL!

Above: A man demonstrates in favour of Michael Ross's execution. Capital punishment remains a highly contentious issue in the USA and Ross's 'death day' was put back numerous times. © *PA Photos*

Right: Melanie McGuire listens to her attorney during a recess in her murder trial, in the state Superior Court in New Brunswick, April 2007.

©*AP Photo/Joe McLaughlin, Pool*

Defence attorney Joseph Tacopina comforts Melanie McGuire after the verdict in her trial on 23 April 2007. McGuire was convicted of killing her husband.

A Clark County Sheriff's office booking photo of Keith Hunter Jesperson after his arrest in 1995. Jesperson is known as 'the Happy Face Killer' because of the smiley faces he drew on his letters to the police. © PA Photos

would leave me behind and the cluster behind me would catch me. Then I would just exit the road and pull into the shoulder and cut what was left of Angela away from my trailer and deposit her in the tall grass on the shoulder before the next cluster caught me. About 3 minutes to do it all. Then pull along the shoulder and come in behind that cluster of cars. It worked out in theory in my head. All I had to do is implement it and pull out into the freeway undetected by anyone.

It would take time to get it all ready to pull off. First I tied a rope around her neck with one end and made a loop in the other for a handle to pull her body out of the car and along the ground.

Next I had to tie a rope to her ankles. One end to each ankle. This would be the rope I would tie the frame rope to. It also gave me a handle to position the body under the trailer.

Left: In a letter to the author, Keith Jesperson illustrated how he disposed of Angela Subrize's body by dragging it under his trailer.
'I could feel the extra drag on the power as I applied more power. The friction was very real,' he wrote.

Below: The Happy Face Killer, Keith Hunter Jesperson, pictured with fellow inmates at 'yard time' at the Oregon prison which is now his home.

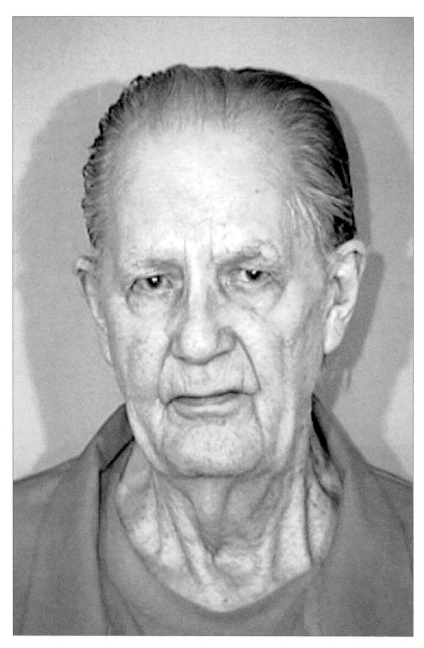

Viva LeRoy Nash, the oldest – and possibly most eccentric – man on death row. He managed to escape from prison at the age of sixty-two, only to be recaptured a few weeks later after a bungled robbery, in which he shot and killed the store's employee.

John 'JR' Robinson, the sexual deviant who lived two very different lives: that of a 'professional' businessman, and of a murdering sociopath. These two worlds eventually collided when he was arrested in June 2000.

Above: Some of the decorated envelopes containing the letters sent to the author by Phillip Jablonski (*right*), who was convicted of five horrific murders. After raping and murdering mother-of-two Fathyma Vann in 1991, he mutilated her body and carved 'I love Jesus' into her back.

Mr Harvey,

Your office and the media have reflected on the life and death of William T McGuire, and you've made it obvious that you intend to prosecute his wife. You and the media have exalted him as a decent person and a victim. He was a victim, all right. Of his greed, his big ego, and his even bigger mouth. I first met McGuire because we knew a lot of the same people. He was friendly enough at first, and loved to talk about himself along with anything and everything else he could claim to know everything about. He talked about AC [Atlantic City]. He talked about a house. About Virginia. About his wife. His sister. His ex-wife. You couldn't shut the guy up, which was part of his own undoing.

McGuire bragged about his position at NJIT [New Jersey Institute of Technology]. Said he had the placed [sic] wired and that the boss man had no idea what he was up to, which is how I imagine he got out and got away as much as he did. He talked of his connections at the local and state level, in various departments of state. How they could and would play into his consulting business. He talked of corruption at the health departments, and how it was given a pretty face by NJIT. He bragged about how he once worked two full-time jobs, at NJIT and at a local health office, and how even doing that he still had enough time to get all his side action and get home without the wife being any wiser. He talked about his scams at work, the anonymity the access to some of the technologies could give him, to do almost anything he wanted at work or outside of it. He talked about blackmailing some of the higher-ups at the state level who were doling out grant work to people collecting unemployment. He seemed to be unfazed by the stink his confrontations could raise in the office, stating it was their own fault for putting themselves in a compromised position to begin with. He talked about overthrowing his boss at the college, and about overthrowing the state level boss with the help of a guy named Roy. Did your office bother to note any of that during their thorough investigation? I think not.

He also loved to gamble, loved to flash card. I'd see him in AC, and at some private games to [sic]. The funny part is that he was a pretty good player but his ego wouldn't let him lose. He won a lot, but when he lost, he lost big and chased the money as hard as he chased some of the tail [women] that hangs around those places. He blamed everyone when he lost; the house, the dealer, even his wife, if you can imagine that. I personally find your observation that his death could have nothing to do with gambling one of the most hilarious things you've said publicly. Have you ever BEEN to AC?

Don't believe me? Ask his wife about the Steakhouse in North Jersey, and about an unfortunate accident coming home from work there later one night. What he didn't tell her was that he wasn't working, and he had lost a bundle. I heard him talk about getting pulled over on top of it that night, and how it was her [Melanie's] fault. I laughed. You can't be serious, man. She takes that from you? That and more. She likes it, is what he said and that put me off. You want to screw around on your old lady? Fine. You want to gamble away the family nut? That's fine to [sic]. But saying she likes it and seeing that he believed it blew me away. No wonder she ended up in bed with some doctor. Of course, you could say it was her own fault for marrying him, more her fault for staying.

More laughter from me when you leaked to the papers that this doctor friend of the wife's turned 'states evidence'. There was nothing that man could of said [sic] that would hurt her for the simple reason that she didn't kill him. So that either makes you a liar, or him a coward who makes up stories to save his own sorry skin. Either way, I guess she never learned her lesson about choosing men.

Also, if you haven't figured out yet that his sister knew more of what he was up to than what she ever let on, you have your head further into the sand than I imagined. He talked about her a lot, and I think they had a weird relationship, those two [Bill and his sister]. *The guys used to joke about it a lot. She* [Bill's sister] *did something with real estate – he bitched about paying for her license, and he got her to give him access to one of those agent-only sites. He could plug away on there for days at a time, looking up houses, looking up tax records of people he knew. She had a husband who owned some kind of pharmacy, and he talked a lot about all the scams there, and the cash to be had. But in the same breath he* [Bill McGuire] *would complain how selfish she was to not want to put her own ass on the line, whatever that meant. I tuned out a lot after I figured out he lacked a certain amount of follow through with some ideas. He shrugged it off, saying there were all kinds of strings that get set up around stuff like that. He wanted the cash, but didn't want to get his hands dirty where anyone could see, was more than I thought. As for the other sister, I guess the apple didn't fall for. He played us a phone message she* [Melanie] *left him, laughing at what a crazy she was. The message had said she would sue him and he wouldn't get his house he was buying. Christmas must have been something at their home.*

We kept McGuire close because he was good for certain things – obviously things you'll never find out about. But in time he developed a drug habit. He even tried dealing. Then he decided he wanted a piece [of the action] *to* [sic]. *We privately agreed against putting one in his hands. He tried Camden, Trenton, even Newark, but his problem was that he looked like a cop. No surprise the wife bought it, even if she was a damn fool for not knowing better. He always complained about how stupid she had gotten. I even asked him, wasn't she stupid when you married her? He said no way his wife was stupid but good in bed. The second he said she was a lousy lay but pretty. He claimed she had been smart but let herself go to hell after having kids. Which is why he felt completely justified in sticking it in anything that walked. Personally, I thought he was either gay or sexually bent. He said his wife was so stupid he come home high one night, and when she asked him why his eyes were bloodshot he told her he had taken Viagra. When she asked him why he got pissed and told even that couldn't help him get it up for her. Nice guy. My point being that Billy Mac* [McGuire] *liked an altered state of mind. I'll bet you twice your pension that the toxicology report showed more than a little Viagra. How about* [it] *H? Do you believe yet that I'm more than some random psycho writing to harass you? If not, you will.*

Here's a question for you, Mr Harvey. McGuire was talking about the life insurance he was going to get. A mill [million] *on the wife. Two on him. He talked about*

Virginia, and that was where he was going once he made his money here [in New Jersey]. *How his wife hated it. When I asked how he was planning on convincing her to move, he smiled and said he would be rid of her by then. Did it dawn on you that Mrs McGuire, in her 'selfish' plot to kill her husband, didn't bother to wait for him to actually purchase the insurance? Oh, she's got the boyfriend with money, she didn't need it. First, I don't know anybody who would pass on two mill, money or not. Second, even if she coaxed that boyfriend away from his happy home, how much do you think it would leave her after he paid out his old lady? I'm telling you that I don't know what he meant when he said he'd be 'rid' of her by then, but I have a couple of thoughts. And two mill on him and one on her casts a little doubt on his motivation should something tragic happen. Did any of you in the midst of your 'dogged detective work' even ask her about it? Or are you going to sit there with a straight face and tell me McGuire meant he wanted a divorce?*

Don't get me wrong. I'm not going for sainthood myself. But what got to us about him was that he eventually turned on everyone. He talked about going to the press a lot about the money the college spent on equipment for a terrorism database that no one bothered to use. He talked about getting 'rid' of his old lady. He talked about turning in the sister's husband to the pharmacy board. Even blood wasn't thicker than water with this guy. And he wouldn't shut up. Didn't matter if he liked you or didn't or even if he owed you. He feared no playback from anyone. I don't even think he wanted the piece out of fear. Not a guy like

117

this. He wanted to intimidate people with it. What intimidated people was his running mouth.

You shouldn't care that the wife bought a gun. You shouldn't care that the suitcases were hers. You shouldn't care that the garbage bags match. I'm telling you that you shouldn't care if there's video footage of her smiling and waving from the docks at Virginia Beach. Know why? Obviously you don't, so I'll make it simple. And it's not because she couldn't physically have done what it took two – and at one point three – men to do. It's because Billy Mac brought everything that was needed to do him, and more. Not on purpose of course, but it was easier than anyone could believe. And the fight with his old lady? Probably he saved her life leaving her that morning, even if all he was doing was looking to get the hell out of dodge for a few days. I'm guessing you didn't find any of his cell phones – the one's that weren't traceable, anyway. Point is if it was necessary, if she was with him, she would have been done same as him. Probably worse, if you catch my drift, even though she was a lousy lay like he said. She ended up helping us, but not in any way you or your dogged detectives think. Her bad luck was our good fortune. And Billy Mac left the door wide open.

So why write this? Well, I can tell you now to abandon the print analysis, and even analysis of the type [of this letter]. *This will be photocopied and handled in a manner you couldn't trace even if you did your job. So it's not hurting me any. And I've got nothing for the wife, or against her. But I read about those kids. The father they're better off without, but they don't need a Ma on Death Row. So now it's up to you to figure it out. She can't help you much, but did you even ask her? I know, you think this is a hoax. Well allow me to part with some facts that should finally convince you otherwise:*

- *I'm taking the liberty of sending this to the media, in case you want to close your eyes to this same as you have everything else in this case.*
- *I'm sending it to the wife's lawyer.*
- *The way the articles read last year, it made it seem like his arms were cut off. They weren't.*
- *He was wearing nothing but purple briefs when you found him.*
- *Ever figure out where the weights came from?*

NOW DO YOU BELIEVE ME????'

The police and prosecutor believed, and still do, that Melanie had written this letter, while on bail and awaiting her trial, in an attempt to blow smoke around the prosecution's case against her. And this author challenges anyone to find a similar correspondence sent to any prosecutor, in history, typed out by a Mafia mobster, whose bear-paw writing skills might stretch to 'Yeah boss', and little more.

I rest my case.

CHAPTER 3
PHILLIP CARL JABLONSKI
'I HAVE NO REMORSE'

The correspondence sent by Phillip Jablonski from Death Row, San Quentin State Prison, arrives in white envelopes upon which he draws, in crayon, rather cute cartoons. But there is nothing cute or endearing about this brown-eyed, 6ft 2in, 200lb hulk; absolutely nothing whatsoever that could induce any right-minded person to ever want to spend more than a second of their time with him, and when you have read all that follows, would you?

If JR Robinson is the homicidal Del Boy, and Melanie McGuire is brighter than we think, where does Mr Jablonski fit into the scale of things? And, if JR's IQ hits the 120 mark, with Mel's crossing the finishing line at 150, how do we rate Phillip, who now sits on Death Row, waiting for the needle?

The answers to those questions are not good, for the creature we are about to cast our eyes over is 30 degrees below trailer-park trash, and the words 'redemption' and 'mitigation' do not apply.

Line up a queue of 'rinky dink shrinks', say 'money', and they will stretch from New York to the moon. Pay these ambulance-chasing 'experts' a few bucks and they'll come up with more analyses for the character in question than you could count. The sad thing is that none, yes, not one of these psychiatrists would be able to agree with another colleague on the state of Mr Jablonski's dysfunctional mind. Why? Because this guy lives in a world where elephants fly and lead balls bounce! This human being is a living example of early man…a cave-dweller, indeed, he is sub-human, he is a hillbilly gone real bad. In summary, this is not the sort of guy you'd want your daughter to date. Mr Jablonski, you are awarded first prize for being so thumb-suckingly dumb, and you also get a second prize, too – you get to feature in a chapter in this book.

In the souls of the people the grapes of wrath are filling and growing heavy, growing heavy for the vintage.

John Steinbeck.

Born on Thursday, 3 January 1946, Jablonski has been on Death Row since August 1994. Hunting pen pals on an internet website, he describes himself thus: 'Caucasian male – seeking an open-minded male/female for unconditional correspondence on a mature and honest level that has a caring heart to create a special friendship build from the heart [sic].'

Absent, however, from the web page upon which he seeks the aforementioned relationship is the fact that Phillip is an American serial killer whose CV in this department is shocking. Nonetheless, never one to be accused of being a shrinking violet, he adds:

I am professional artists [sic], *photography* [sic], *amateur poet, writer, masseur; college educated, not a rude person,*

*like to party, travel. My home town is Joshua Tree, CA. I
am very understanding and loving. I believe in giving a
second chance. People describe me as a gentle giant. I love
cats, dogs, parrots, horses and teddy bears.*

Jablonski has been found guilty of five horrific murders. On
Monday, 22 April 1991, he killed 38-year-old Fathyma Vann, in
Indio City, located in the Coachella Valley of Southern
California's desert region. Vann was a fellow at the local
community college, which Jablonski attended to satisfy the
conditions of his parole. Fathyma, a recently widowed mother
of two teenage girls, was found shot in the head and sexually
assaulted, lying naked in a shallow ditch in the Indio desert.
The words, 'I Love Jesus' were carved in her back. Her body
had been subjected to other mutilations including removal of
her eyes and ears, which her killer had eaten.

'What do I like in a friend?' Jablonski asks. 'I like it if you like
to travel, party. Someone who is mature and wants an honest
friendship. Someone who is able to discuss personal issues on a
mature level and is not scared of Frank [sic] discussion.'

His next two killings took place the day after he had
murdered Mrs Vann, when Jablonski's 46-year-old wife, Carol
(nee Spadoni), and her mother, Eva Inge Peterson, 72, were
killed in their Burlingame home. Spadoni was shot, suffocated
with duct tape, then stabbed, while Peterson was sexually
assaulted and then shot dead. A city in San Mateo County,
California, Mateo is the second wealthiest in the state and the
fourteenth richest in the US. And Burlingame, called 'The City
of Trees' is a place where homicide is very rare.

Carol Spadoni met and married Jablonski in 1982, after
answering a newspaper ad placed while he was serving time for

having murdered his first wife, Melinda Kimball, in Palm Springs, California, 1978.

On 7 July 1978, Jablonski threatened Isobel Phals, Kimball's mother, with a knife and attempted to rape her. Phals had also been the recipient of obscene telephone calls and other malicious acts which the police believed had been committed by Jablonski. Although Phals did not file formal charges against the man, she discussed with police the possibility of his receiving psychiatric treatment. Shortly thereafter, he volunteered to undergo a psychiatric examination at the Loma Linda Veterans Administration Hospital.

The police immediately called the hospital and were informed that Jablonski would be treated by a Dr Kopiloff, however, because the doctor was unable to take the call himself, the police officer spoke to Dr Berman, the head of psychiatric services.

And it is at this point that the wheels started to fall off the wagon.

The police officer advised Berman of Jablonski's prior criminal record, the recent history of obscene telephone calls and malicious damage, and said that, in his opinion, Jablonski needed to be treated on an in-patient basis. However, although Berman promised that he would transmit this information to his colleague, Kopiloff, he failed to do so. Dr Kopiloff later said that had he received this information from the police, he would have involuntarily hospitalised the mentally disintegrating army veteran if possible. Now it was only a matter of time before Jablonski would explode.

I am very concerned about Phillip's behaviour, but I love him.

Melinda Kimball, in a private meeting with Dr Kopiloff.

On Monday, 10 July 1978, Melinda Kimball drove Jablonski to the hospital. During the interview, Kopiloff learned that his new patient had served a five-year prison term for raping his wife. He also learned that just a few days before the interview he had attempted to rape Isobel Phals. Jablonski enlightened the doctor, saying that he had undergone psychiatric treatment in the past, however, he refused to say where he had received this treatment.

Dr Kopiloff concluded that the patient was, 'vague, non-communicative, and unwilling to share his prior medical history'. He diagnosed Jablonski as an 'anti-social personality and potentially dangerous'. He recommended that Jablonski voluntarily hospitalise himself, but Jablonski declined. Kopiloff concluded that there was no real emergency and no basis for forcible hospitalisation, leaving Jablonski to return for another appointment in two weeks' time.

The result was that Melinda Kimball was killed.

The only good woman is a dead one!

Phillip Jablonski.

The hospital records of Jablonski's prior treatment reveal that in 1968 he had received 'extensive psychiatric care' at an army hospital in El Paso. The El Paso records report that Mr Jablonski had a 'homicidal ideation towards his wife... that on numerous occasions he had tried to kill her... that he probably suffered a psychotic breakdown and the possibility of future violent behaviour was a distinct possibility'. And, that he was 'demonstrating some masculine identification in beating his wife as his father did frequently to his mother'. The final diagnosis concluded in part that Jablonski had a 'schizophrenic reaction, undifferentiated type, chronic, moderate; manifested by homicidal behaviour toward his wife'.

The clock was now ticking, and the day after Jablonski's interview with Kopiloff, Mrs Phals telephoned the doctor to complain about the two-week delay in Jablonski not returning for treatment. She threatened to call the police again, but Kopiloff persuaded her not to. However, to placate her he did bring forward the date to Friday 14 July. In the interim Kimball, and her daughter, Meghan, prudently moved out of Jablonski's apartment and into Mrs Phal's home.

Perhaps somewhat unwisely, Kimball called on Jablonski, and she drove him to see Kopiloff, and his supervisor, Dr Hazle, on 14 July. Although he volunteered that he had had frequent problems all his life, Jablonski again refused to be admitted as an in-patient. This time, Kopiloff concluded that his patient was not only possessed with an anti-social personality, but also with 'explosive features'.

Dr Hazle went a step further. He believed that the man was downright dangerous, and that this case was an 'emergency'. However, despite all of this, the two doctors still believed there was no basis for involuntary hospitalisation. And, again, no effort was made to seek out prior medical records. Instead, Jablonski was scheduled for more tests and sent home holding a prescription for Valium and with another appointment booked for Monday 17 July.

During the appointment between Jablonski, Hazle and Kopiloff, Melinda Kimball had waited in the hallway outside, probably praying that the next time she saw her man he would be wearing a strait jacket and chained to a padded cell wall. However, upon hearing the quiet discussion through a partly open door, she broke down, as well she might.

Noticing that Melinda seemed distressed, a third psychiatrist, a Dr Warnell, the chief of the mental health clinic, invited her into his office, where Melinda expressed fear for her personal safety. Although compassionate, Warnell advised her in measured tones that if she was afraid of Jablonski and that if he didn't fit the criteria to be held in hospital against his wishes, that she could consider staying away from him altogether.

Apparently, Kimball took Dr Warnell's advice, for she returned to live with Mrs Phal, who was, by now, sick and tired of the whole sorry affair; reasoning that if the police were all but useless in dealing with the rages and deviancy exhibited by Jablonski, the medical profession had surpassed the cops' negligence by miles. That she hadn't filed a complaint, at least for sexual assault against Jablonski, apparently didn't enter her thinking.

On Sunday, 16 July, Kimball went to Jablonski's apartment, apparently to pick up some nappies for Meghan. He was either at his home at the time or arrived soon after. Whatever the case, he attacked and murdered her, and as murders go, this one was bottom drawer. He beat her, raped her, stripped her, slashed her, and, when death mercifully intervened, he cut off her ears, ate her eyes, and finished it all off by abusing the sexual organs and anus of the corpse.

Jablonski has since been diagnosed as suffering from post-traumatic stress disorder, 'transient' psychotic episodes triggered by 'overpowering aggressive or sexual feelings that cannot be expressed, and has a passive/aggressive personality with intense feelings of inadequacy', and that he is a sexual sadist. He also engages in 'malingering behaviour and is a schizophrenic'.

No surprises there. Nevertheless, and not one to let his

shambles of a mind get in his way of searching for a pen friend, adding to his internet page, Phillip Jablonski says: 'What I miss most? Traveling, photography, male and female company, giving massages, partying, walking in the rain, romantic walks on the beach, romantic candle light dinners, cuddling in front of a roaring fire and soft music.'

All of which Phill won't be doing anytime soon.

Mr Jablonski was also found guilty of the subsequent murder of 58-year-old Margie Rogers, in Grand County, Utah, on Saturday, 27 April 1991. The murder was in furtherance of a truck stop robbery which netted him the princely sum of $158. He was captured the next day at a rest area in Kansas. Among other evidence found in his car was a tape recording in which he described the murders and his sexual assault on Eva Peterson.

At his 1994 trial, evidence was given to show that Jablonski had a long history of violence against women that stretched right back to his first marriage in 1968. He claimed that he suffered as result of traumas he experienced in childhood and during his military service in Vietnam. However, the jury decided that he was legally sane at the time of the murders and recommended he be put to death.

In January 2006, the California Supreme Court upheld Jablonski's death sentence on appeal.

Notwithstanding all of this, Phillip wants pen pals to share: 'thoughts and feelings (good and bad) let's learn about one another freely and watch our relationship bloom like a rose and be as strong as a castle wall which cannot be broken...a loving heart is worth more than a mountain of gold. Love communicates on any subject or issue. Write me please...you won't be disappointed.'

But before you do put pen to paper you should know that Mr

Jablonski is, in his own words, an 'indigence [sic] inmate and depend on the state for postage and envelopes. I can use assistance with postage and obtain writing, etc, etc from the canteen. $50 should cover it.' He also sells his artwork through a number of web sites, so he is pretty well fixed financially, for a dead man walking.

While Jablonski claims on the internet that he has most of the virtues of a saint, he also has a fascination for John Reginald Christie: 'a famous killer in the UK, who killed his wife and prostitutes and burned their bodies,' he writes. 'A friend of mine sent me a photo of him and Christie and I look like brothers.' And balding and bespectacled Jablonski does, indeed, bear a passing resemblance to John Reginald Christie.

By the way, I have a son named Christopher, who is doing time in a Michigan prison for child rape. I guess you could say he is following in his father's footsteps.
Phillip Jablonski, letter to the author, 28 January 2008.

As a man who slits throats, sodomised and even cannibalised his victims, Jablonski is also clearly proud of his wayward son, Christopher, and this psychopath seems to have few regrets for his own actions:

I have no remorse for the murders, rapes or pimping of adolescent boys and girls. I am proud I raped my slut sister and mother. Maybe my slut mother will rot in hell – they both died in 1986. There are other unsolved murders I have committed, and few of them are over twenty years old.

Phillip Jablonski's childhood was indeed a very unhappy one. His father was a gun-toting alcoholic who constantly beat his wife, sons and daughters. What follows is his description of the sexual abuse Jablonski claims he suffered as a child; they are his own unedited words, and the reader is advised that this material is disturbing. The grammatical errors are his.

In a letter, to the author, dated 12 March 2008, headed '0-TO FIVE YEAR OLD', he writes:

My parents moved to San Bernardino, California, from Flint, Michigan, in August 1945. At the time, there were two children, Phyllis, Louie and a dog. During this stressful time of moving, my mother was pregnant with me.

The trip took two months. The trip so long because the Chevy's front end was out of alignment and so family had to constantly replace its tires and tires on their trailer. They finally had to abandon the trailer in Arizona because they could no longer afford to replace its tires. My family arrived in California with no money and had to live at a friend's house.

I was born on January 3, 1946, three months prematurely and weighed under five pounds. I was raised on goat's milk by the advice of a local doctor. I did not start walking until I was 16 months old. I was born to an abusive father who loved to beat his wife and children. My mother loved to be abused physically and sexually.

My sister, Patty, was born in 1948 and my brother born in 1949, and Nettie Jr. in 1950.

My family first house in California was on Severance Street in San Bernardino. The area was semi-rural at the time, made up of lower-middle-class of which my family were among the poorest.

My parent sleep in the one bedroom and my sisters slept in the living room. Us boys slept in the dining room, which was been converted into a bedroom for us. We didn't have a phone, and my parents raised our own chickens, pigeons, and rabbit for food. My parent would leave me and Patty with a neighbor, Oroll Crum. The neighbor was my parent best friend baby sitting us, while my parent went shopping or went pay bills.

Shortly after I turn five years old Oroll Crum and his wife Barbara was babysitting has normal. But everything was about to change be us and them. Soon has my parents step out their front door and bearly outside their, a hand was put around our mouths and I was pick up has was my sister. I was carried into the master bedroom, my sister into a share bedroom, and while Oroll carry me he whispered in my ear saying: 'Nothing to be scared of. Your sister is teaching a adult game between little girls and women. She will be a woman soon and you little boy will soon be a little man. It's normal for a man to teach a boy about being a little man.' I heard a loud slap and my sister crying.

Then Oroll Crum pulled my pants off followed by my underwear and his cold hands off over my small butt. And he made me turn over on my back and his hands spreading my butt cheeks...

I have spent hundreds of hours reading through correspondence from many of the world's most notoriously twisted serial murderers and sado-sex killers, but nothing could have prepared me for what followed next. I felt physically sick.

However, knowing Mr Jablonski as I do, one forms the opinion that what he is writing is specifically intended to shock the reader; that this sociopath is delighting in every word. Whether the account is true, or not, we will never know, nevertheless, for my part I believe that he is reliving a series of rapes he committed on his sister.

In graphic detail – and I am sparing the reader the shocking minutiae – Jablonski describes the most disgusting form of child abuse performed on himself and his sister, allegedly, how he was anally raped time and again.

'That night we told our Dad what happened. He confront them and Crum said he never touch one of us in anway. So me and my sister was seriously beaten for telling out rages lairs.'

The next time the Crums' babysat for Jablonski and his sister – and this will come as no shock to the reader that there was a next time among these two families of in-breds – Jablonski claims that he knew he and his sister were in for trouble: 'He beat us mercilessly,' he says, 'until our little butts was bright red and bleeding. And we were made to crawl and was kicked in our butts. They tied us up and around our ankles and hung us upside down and swing us back and forth. Sometimes our heads would hit together. We never mention it to our Dad again. If we mentioned it to mother she'd tell our Dad and we would get another beating. One of the Crums' favor games was making us play doctor and nurse. Making us play with each other with our hands or licking each other all over.'

According to Jablonski: 'They had their way with us for nine months then they moved to another state.' He ends this letter with a dismissive: 'I'll close for now and then start from 6 years to 8 years old. Take care. Phill.'

At the age of six, Jablonski started first grade at the Arrowhead

Elementary School, and walked a block to and from school each day. 'A rail track ran through part of the neighbourhood,' he writes, 'a water train would travel through four times a day. Neighborhood kids would lay pennies on the metal slug on the tracks and came back later to find the flattened coin or metal slug on the track and pick them up.'

Searching through Jablonski's letters for further items of interest to us regarding his early schooling, we find little that hints at a clue as to why, in later life, Jablonski went off the rails, too. He talks about these early days in an almost childlike manner, almost as if he is reliving them as a child himself today. He refers to playground and class activities. He talks about local haunts where he and his peers liked to spend their weekends and evenings. He mentions a fascination of the fire department, the flood control department, and bulldozers – but then, in a flash his mood darkens again.

'One evening a bulldozer operator ask me if I would like to take a ride with him on his bulldozer. I said sure. He gave me a hand up and had his hands on my belt and loosened it and unzipped my pants. I know if I didn't get away he was going to rape me. It was two years since I was raped the first time. I wiggle and twisted but he grab me between my legs and squeeze my balls and I screamed. He told 'Stop wiggling or I will squeeze a lot harder'. So I stop wiggling and he pulled my pants and underwear down around my ankles and position between my legs and spread my butt cheeks...' It is at this point the author ceases to quote another line from Jablonski's account; frankly, it is too disgusting even to contemplate.

There can be no doubt that Jablonski's parents were dysfunctional. His father, for the most time drunk, often driving a car at the same time, would brandish a handgun at every opportunity. He would make his children sit and listen to him haranguing them for the slightest infraction. Point the weapon at his kids, he would call the boys 'bastards' and the girls 'whores'...they were useless, worthless and that they didn't deserve to have been born or to live.

My family raised chickens, rabbits and us children were expected to help butcher the animals and during the task our dad would tease us by slinging blood on us, or pulling the tendon of a dismembered chicken's leg to make the claw move, while he chased us around the yard. We had a pig. We kept it as a pet, not to eat or sell. When it was fully grown we'd ride on it, but then my dad butchered it and forced us to eat it. Many families in the neighborhood raised chickens and killed them. In an ostentatiously sadistic way in front of us, my dad would not merely wring the neck of the chicken, but tearing off the head and watching the decapitated body run around the yard until it killed over [sic].

Phillip Jablonski, letter to the author.

Then, on the same page, Jablonski instantly reverts to a matter less upsetting. He talks about home-built scooters the kids had, playing marbles and how they all made roller skates out of wood and small wheels.

Whatever the matter, clearly the young Phillip didn't excel at school, for he was held back from entering the second grade and was joined by a sister who was younger than him. When his father learned of this, he thrashed Phillip and sent him 'straight to bed after dinner'.

Throughout all of Jablonski's letters, it is not long before yet another allegation of rape is recorded on the written page, and his teacher (named removed for the obvious reasons) was next in the firing line:

> *The teacher who lived next door would come over and set on our porch and drink beer with my dad and listen to radio and watch us kids play. My dad mention during one of their communications about my bad grade, and the teacher said all I needed was someone to set down with and take the times to explain to me and go over my class work and homework, and I would be just fine. He said that he had extra time to tutor me in his free time.*
>
> *So next night my dad told me gather up my books and any class work or homework and he was taking me to next door for the teacher.*

That evening Phillip says his assignment was reading and writing, and that the teacher promised he would walk him home.

Jablonski also says that he was brutally raped.

'The teacher said, "Now that we are alone, I've been eyeing you and like what I have seen. Special the way you fill your pants and fantastic how it would be to have you in bed with me".'

Once again, what followed in Jablonski's letter is a sickening account of the alleged abuse he suffered over the next two hours. Jablonski rounded off this account, adding: 'He said before he was done with me, I would be looking forever in pleasing any man in his bed. I would be gay forever.'

Mr Jablonski's letters ceased at this point, and the story is that the California Department of Corrections closed the guy down.

CHAPTER 4
KEITH HUNTER JESPERSON
THE HAPPY FACE KILLER

I placed my fist into her throat and locked my elbow and leaned on her neck with my upper body weight. After a little over four minutes I smelled urine as Bennett peed into her jeans. I believed she was dead and stood up over her...one good reason I had the rope around Bennett's neck was to secure her stomach contents should my moving of the body cause what she drank to move out of her... I had no idea.

Keith Jesperson, on the killing of Taunja Bennett, in a letter to the author.

I have travelled through Oregon many times whilst making documentaries and researching previous books and I always refuse to be co-opted into advertising good eating establishments by the management. I will certainly not mention that the Flying J restaurant, in Troutdale, does a fabulous prime rib and eggs breakfast, or that their strawberry shortcake alone is well worth the stop. So, in the knowledge that Keith Hunter Jesperson frequently visited this eatery, and that we did at least have one thing in common, I thought I'd write to him and tell him just that.

As the start of this hearts and minds exercise, I wrote and told him about the Flying J restaurant's fabulous breakfast and strawberry shortcake. Bearing in mind that Keith is a self-professed man's man, not a pansy, I thought that he might appreciate this no-nonsense approach, which was followed up, in short order, with an over-easy, 'Hey, buddy, you wanna work with me on a chapter for a book?'

What followed – one might call it a meal with six courses – has been quite an interesting and exhausting exercise for me, and this chapter is, but a taste, of his second autobiography. Please allow me to explain.

Jack Olsen and I have both danced with the Devil, the Devil being Keith Hunter Jesperson. Many years back, the award-winning and truly notable true crime writer, Jack Olsen, worked with Jesperson on his autobiography, *'I' – The Creation of a Serial Killer*. It was a remarkable piece of work, as is all of Jack's writing. Sadly Jack would never see his book in print as he passed away on Tuesday, 16 July 2002, shortly before its publication in the August of that year. Some may call this 'the Jesperson curse'. I have experienced working with this killer for a considerable period of time and the stress, combined with the sheer, overwhelming influence of this manipulative and highly intelligent psychopath, is enough to drive any writer – as he did his victims – to their grave.

There can be no doubt that Jack Olsen was a writer to be admired; his literary achievements are well covered elsewhere, so I will not repeat them here. His book, written with the complete cooperation of Jesperson, who had sight of the final edit, has become the empirical work on, perhaps, one of the most twisted killers of modern times. Today, however, Keith Jesperson rails against Mr Olsen, who is unable to defend himself. This chapter, in Jack's memory, hopes to redress that balance.

When I began corresponding with Keith Jesperson, I told him a little white lie: that I had never read Olsen's book. I said that I wanted to hear his life story, warts and all, from the man himself. For his part, Keith promised me that he would tell the complete truth. What followed were months and months of never-ending letters, diagrams, prison photographs, newspaper cuttings, pictures of the scores of women who wanted to marry him, and his new, second autobiography – amounting to some 2000 double-side pages. He forwarded scores of letters he has received from people around the world, most of them social misfits, some of whom must have had, 'I AM A NUT BALL' tattooed on their Neanderthal-shaped foreheads, and it appears that any scrap of paper that he didn't want in his cell, he posted to me. This deluge of frequently illegible correspondence caused me sleepless nights, a premature eyesight test, brought my postman to his knees and cost me a fortune in aspirin. To cap it all, he even sent me his prison ID card with the suggestion I might use it in this book, which resulted in him being punished by the Oregon Department of Corrections (ODOC). When Jesperson was fined $25 and suffered the loss of all privileges for ten days, he berated me for asking the ODOC for permission to use the item in this book in the first place.

This transference of blame syndrome somewhat sums up Keith Hunter Jesperson. The man is totally unable to accept responsibility for any wrongdoing whatsoever. 'Jack Olsen got his book completely wrong,' says our Happy Face Killer. Day-after-day Keith criticised me for making the smallest error, such as a comma in the wrong place, during my 'translation' of his scrawled autobiography. My own attention to detail was constantly at fault... I should 'buck up' and 'learn how to write'. 'Have you got my instructions clearly?' he heatedly penned. 'It is really quite fucking simple if you follow my instructions. Christopher, I was going to post this to you yesterday, but slept on in. Then I wake up in the middle of the night. YOU REALLY MUST pay ATTENTION to my instructions.'

Keith really does go on and on, so I wrote back, 'Fuck you, too, Keith.'

Indeed, if Jesperson is to be believed, his father, Les, was a brutal patriarch; his entire childhood was a mess; he was bullied and treated like a work-slave by him. Jesperson's own wife, Rose, was apparently less than forthcoming in any way. In his new autobiography, it was always his victims who were responsible for being murdered...they 'pissed him off', tried to 'pussy-whip' him, make unwarranted demands of his generosity. In a nutshell, Keith Jesperson is always right and everyone else is wrong. Indeed, if he were to have things his way, he should be called 'Mr Perfect'. His actions have damaged his own daughter's life and wrecked the lives of his victims' families. Is there any remorse? No!

Apart from the immeasurable loss of human lives, this former 6ft 5in trucker has cost the honest, American taxpayer millions of dollars by running rings around the judicial system. And let us not forget the tens of thousands of bucks to keep him fed, fit and well at the Oregon State Penitentiary, where he enjoys, among other things, painting (he earns a good living flogging his artwork on the internet) and attending car shows. According to the ODOC's form CD 103D 10/04, he has the following activities and perks at his disposal: 'hobby shop; canteen; card-room; picture-taking programme; telephone privileges; dayroom (movies/television); recreation, multi-purpose activities, including the gym; library, substantial visitation; and all other inmate organization meetings including AA/NA [Alcoholics Anonymous / Narcotics Anonymous]'. Indeed, the only thing he seems to lack is sex with a female, but then he freely admits to frequently masturbating to his fantasies of murdering and torturing his victims, which he says, 'keeps me with a hard-on'. In truth, it seems to me that Keith Jesperson is not being punished for his sins, he's being rewarded for heinously wiping out eight innocent lives, and that may be just the tip of the iceberg, because at one time he admitted over a hundred.

* * *

As for the smiley face on your letter, I don't really like it. Like it is rubbing it into me. Most people who write me, they make a point to put a J somewhere. And I just don't see the humor in it. SORT OF PISSES me OFF!!!
Keith Jesperson, letter to the author, 20 February 2008.

Keith Hunter Jesperson was born Wednesday, 6 April 1955, in the city of Chilliwack, British Columbia. He is known as 'the Happy Face Killer' because he sent taunting letters to the newspapers with a 'smiley' drawn on them. Not that he has much to be happy about these days; he is serving natural life sentences for murdering eight women from as far afield as Nebraska, California, Florida, Washington and Oregon, during a killing spree that started on 21 January 1990 and continued until 1995, when he was finally arrested.

The Jesperson family name originated in Sweden, where the name is not uncommon. The clan migrated to Denmark, New

Zealand, USA, and Canada. Keith's immediate ancestors left Denmark in the late 1880s, entered the USA and, apparently driving Conestoga wagons (I prefer to think it was actually in a box car), they eventually rolled onto the west coast where they took a left turn and settled in San Francisco for a short while. Deciding that the hot climate wasn't quite to their taste, the Jespersons headed north to colder climes. After months on the trail, these determined pioneers crossed into Canada and arrived in the Fraser Valley, settling just north of Chilliwack in the province of British Columbia.

Keith Jesperson devoted some 300 double-sided pages to his ancestors. His great-great-grandparents, great-grandparents, grandparents, parents, school teachers, friends, relations, workmates, and just about every person he has ever met gets a mention in his new autobiography. He recounted pretty well every movement he made during his formative years. He can recall just about every single trip he made as an interstate trucker. To give you a taste of this, instead of just saying that he drove a truck, he would come up with: 'I landed my dream job driving a massive plum-colored, dripping in chrome, Peterbilt that had a four-hundred-horsepower Cat engine, a twelve-ton cherry picker for loading heavy equipment. The tractor had twin sticks with nine forward speeds. Truck and trailer had twenty-six tires and hauled loads up to 210,000 pounds.' The only things he missed out was the tyre pressures, all 26 of them... which I considered a major oversight on Keith's behalf, and it was all I could do to prevent myself asking him, 'Did you inflate or deflate the tyres according to load and road conditions, and what happened in snow or icy conditions?' - but I didn't.

Of course Keith had blessed what must have been an

extremely patient Jack Olsen with exactly the same methodical exercise years ago. For the record, and to gain a better understanding of Mr Jesperson's penchant for writing, it is worth pointing out that in any one year he will mail out some 400 letters and will receive treble that number in return. He makes around 500 collect telephone calls a year, and he will send out *War and Peace*-length correspondence to anyone who shows the slightest interest in his life and crimes. However, with that being said, I can tell you –

in an extremely abridged form – that his family have always been hardworking, mostly prosperous, and never afraid of getting their hands dirty when he came to earning a living off the land.

Fast-forwarding several generations, we come to Keith's father, Les Jesperson. A former blacksmith who joined the Merchant Marine during the Second World War, he was a hardworking and industrious giant of a man who liked his drink. He married Gladys Lorraine Bellamy and they raised five children: Sharon, Bruce, Keith, Brad and Jill.

One could say that Les Jesperson was the pillar of any community he lived in. For example, in Chilliwack he was a 'home builder' and a local businessman. He was one of the youngest members of the city council, and the first man to join the volunteer Royal Canadian Mounted Police. He founded the Chilliwack Boxing Club, was a co-sponsor of the Chilliwack Hockey Club, and, as of 2007, was the last surviving charter member of the Lions. And, if he wasn't fully enough occupied with all of that, he started the Fraser Valley Rescue Service, which is well respected to this day.

So, with the genes of generation after generation of decent, hardworking and totally respectable parents and ancestors in his blood, how did Keith make out? Within the space of a few years, he trash-canned the historic reputation of one of British Columbia's most illustrious families.

Struggling through Keith's voluminous correspondence concerning his formative years – and we really don't have the time to go through it all here – it seems that when one sorts the wheat from the chaff, he had an idyllic childhood. He was raised in the great Canadian outdoors, he was healthy, and much loved and hand-reared by his doting parents. His schooling was normal, and with an adventurous inheritance attached to his genomic sequence. He played truant, poached for Chinook salmon and Steelheads, plagued the neighbourhood with his slingshot and BB gun, made camp by the sparking rivers, perilously swung from tree swings across deep drops and occasionally fought with his peers. The family had their own boat and went on long vacations in their camper-trailer. While Mrs Jesperson made clothes and cooked simple, decent food, Mr Jesperson worked, drank, and ruled the roost, sometimes employing a heavy hand and a leather belt to enforce domestic law. Indeed, I have come to the conclusion that Keith Jesperson was more or less graced with a run of formative years most youngsters can only dream of. But he had a fatal flaw, a fault line that ran very deep indeed.

Keith Hunter Jesperson, like so many young boys who fledge into serial killers, was a sadist. By the age of six he had started killing animals by smashing in the heads of gophers and other small creatures, a barbaric trait which he would return to when his family moved to a Washington State trailer park in the coming years. He would drag stray dogs and cats into the fields where he would beat them to death with a shovel, strangle them with his bare hands, or shoot them with his BB gun. His friends remembered that he 'enjoyed it'. In later years, when boasting to a news reporter, Jesperson had this to say:

I was Arnold Schwarzenegger. It was like I was playing war. When I looked at those dogs, they would squat and pee. They'd be so scared they would tremble. You come to the point where killing something is nothing. It's the same feeling whether I was strangling a human being or an animal. You've already felt the pressure on the throat of them trying to grab air. You're actually squeezing the life out of these animals and there isn't much difference. They're gonna fight for their lives just as a human being will.

Keith Jesperson, in a letter to the author.

It is a well-recognised fact today that those who have shown a propensity towards violence and abuse of animals during their formative years sometimes move on to more violent crimes later in life that are directed at their fellow man. Even Jesperson agrees with this: 'It's in the crime journals of all major law enforcement agencies. Abusive behavior towards animals is one of the symptoms on the road to being a murderer.'

In his prison journal, Jesperson alleges that it was in his early childhood that his aggression towards animals began when his father witnessed him throwing a cat against a pavement to finish it off. 'My father was very proud of how I dealt with the cat, and he boasted to others about how I cleared the neighborhood of any stray cats and dogs in the mobile park where we lived,' he wrote. When Les Jesperson was asked to confirm this, he categorically denied his son's allegation: 'If I had seen any of that I would have thrashed Keith until he couldn't stand up.'

More recently, Keith has said:

All this [animal torture and killing] *did was to spawn me in the urge to kill again. I began to think of what it would be like to kill a human being. The thought stayed with me for years, until one night it happened. I killed Taunja Bennett by almost beating her to death and finished her off by strangulation. No longer did I search for animals to mistreat, I now looked for people to kill. And I did. I killed over and over again until I was caught. Now I'm paying for it with the rest of my life behind bars. We should stop the cruelty to anything before it develops into a bigger problem, like ME!*

*　　*　　*

Here we now find a young man who says he was immensely proud of his family's venerable history, and although he probably didn't realise it at that time, there was a monster hiding deep inside his psyche just waiting to be unleashed. At some point he decided, either consciously, or unconsciously, that he would release the monster, ultimately leaving a trail of female bodies in his wake.

Gary C King, American author, on Keith Hunter
Jesperson

In 1967, when Keith was 12, his family upped sticks and moved to Selah, Washington State, where Les Jesperson started several business ventures, including building a mobile home park called the Silver Spur. Every one of these ventures subsequently failed but not for lack of stint for hard labour. For his part, Keith's employment history was never permanent.

He changed jobs frequently, and, on 2 August 1975 he married Rose, an 18-year-old who he had been dating. They went on to have three children before splitting up and acrimoniously divorcing in 1990.

Home Park, with him trading a wage for a place to live on-site. Thereafter, he was a backhoe operator, a welder and took work as a truck driver, until May 1989, when he started as an equipment operator with Copenhagen Construction, in Clackamas, Oregon. He hoped that this would be a permanent job, but in November, that same year, he was laid off. But here I am obliged to say that Keith Jesperson, like his father, always worked his heart out, so a lazy man he was not.

*　　*　　*

Keith and Rose separated in 1988 and he met Roberta Ellis, a somewhat scrawny woman who lived in a small, brown house at 18343 N E Everett Street, in Camas, a city in Clark County. He was now reduced to living off state benefits and, subsequently, he was at the beck and call of a woman whose legs, by all accounts, sprang open faster than a mousetrap snaps shut. And things stayed pretty calm until the night of Thursday, 11 January 1990, when Roberta failed to return home from her shift at a Burns Brothers truck stop in Troutdale, Oregon. She worked in the B-Bar-B restaurant and should have finished at 10pm. It was now almost midnight, and Jesperson was rightly worried. He drove to the restaurant to find Roberta's 1977 Ford Pinto parked close to a McDonald's, but she was nowhere to be seen.

Later I'd get a call from McDonald's telling me that Roberta's car was still there. Could I come and get it?

So, I got my neighbor to drive me there so I could bring her car home, which was just across the Columbia River. The distance was about 21 miles. It would take me about 30 minutes, but that night was icy, so maybe it took a bit longer.

So, there I was driving along, just wondering...like anyone wonders about someone you love and that someone has suddenly gone missing. Sooner or later she will call to tell me what is up. This was normal behaviour for her though. Ever since I had met her in 1988, she was flighty – off at a moment's notice and gone till she felt a need to talk to me again. So easily distracted was Roberta. I had once distracted her and we became an item. Now, it was my turn to wait to see what will happen next. That wait wasn't long.

Well, late on Friday, 12 January, I picked up the phone and heard the operator ask me: "Will you accept a collect call from Roberta Ellis?" I took the call.

Roberta told me she had found a new man. He worked for Countrywide Trucking out of Knoxville. He told her she could be his co-driver. Of course this also meant they would sleep together and enjoy sexual fulfilment all the way back to the company's main office. She was done with me. Told me she needed money. Start paying her rent for living at her home. "Bitch!" I called her, and then I hung up the phone.

I'd been drawing unemployment insurance since getting laid off work from Copenhagen Construction in Clackamas, late November 1989. Roberta begged me to go back on the road with her as a team, but I loved running heavy equipment for Copenhagen and didn't want to give it up. I reckoned that in the spring work would resume. If we were out on the road I felt we would never be able to get away from it. This sort of sealed my own fate when I refused to bow down to her wants. Now she had moved on, so I felt a need to do so myself. Around the area are several taverns and bars...it was time to check out other women who may want me in their lives.

Keith Jesperson, in a letter to the author.

Jesperson's first known murder was that of pretty 23-year-old Taunja 'Tanya' Ann Bennett, on 21 January 1990, and it was committed during the time he was still seething with rage over losing Roberta Ellis. He spotted Taunja playing pool with two men at the B&I Tavern, one of a number of similar seedy joints in Gresham, the fourth largest city in Oregon, and this is how he related what took place next. It makes for a shocking read:

The fog rolled in during that night. I would wake up about nine that Saturday morning, the 21st of January 1990. Make a pot of coffee and watch TV till about eleven. Then, locking the door behind me, I walked south towards the Fred Meyer mall, between Burnside and Stark Avenues. Like every weekend, even with Roberta at home, I went strolling through the malls just looking to look...to pass the time.

Eventually, I would go to the Jeep dealership to check out the new vehicles...then to the Fred Meyer building center and by 1pm that afternoon I walked into the B&I Tavern on Stark Avenue.

It was still early and the place was empty – void of the Saturday crowd that would soon arrive by five. Placing a quarter into a pool table, I pushed it in and released the balls and set up for the break. Staring about the Tavern there were just three customers and the lady bartender and me. Wandering over to the bar, I spotted a woman from the other table walking over to me. Without hesitation, she reached around me and pulled me close in a hug. This sort of caught me off guard. Didn't really expect this. Looking over at the bartender, I saw her twirling her index finger around her ear. I took it as the girl was nuts, so I refused her offer to join her and the two men at their pool table. From the looks of the men she was with, they didn't need more competition at their table in their attempt of bedding her. I felt better at leaving it alone...ordered a cup of coffee and went back to my game.

I guess an hour passed and I left the tavern. My mind did take in the thought of bedding her as I watched her tease those two guys she was with. A pretty girl... about ten years younger than me. But she couldn't be expected to walk home with me... and I had walked that morning, with nothing really going on, I walked home to hang around hoping Roberta would call to tell me she wanted me again. I missed her company and the sex.

By 5:00 pm, I decided to either go to the Burns Brothers truck stop to hang out with other truckers, or return to the B&I Tavern to play pool in the 1974 Chevy Nova I'd borrowed from Jerry Day six months back. It sort of steered itself over to the B&I Tavern parking lot, which was now full of afternoon customers, and to park out by Stark Avenue and walk past the fifty other cars and trucks to enter the bar.

Inside, I soon saw all six pool tables had several coins

on the side of them, meaning it could be hours before I could expect to play pool, so I turned around and left the building and walked to the car.

I could see over at the closed restaurant, east of the parking lot, the pretty young woman that had hugged me earlier that day. She was now alone and trying to open the door to the locked restaurant. She gave up and she walked back to the B&I Tavern parking lot. I watched her. Then I yelled at her: 'Remember me?' and she looked over at me.

It was at this precise moment that a thought came to me. Why not take her to dinner and possibly we could party later – maybe even end up in bed at home. Her name was Taunja Bennett, and she would become my first kill.

'How would you like to go to dinner and can find a place to play pool after?' I said. She studied me. 'Remember, you hugged me earlier in the day,' I added.

'Oh, yeah, I remember,' I heard her say. 'Okay,' she said, and I pointed to my car.

We got in and drove across Stark Avenue to the east side of the Fred Meyer mall and parked in front of small restaurant. As we sat there, I pulled out my wallet. I realized I had left the bulk of my cash at home and would have to drive home to get it. Told her my situation…that if she waited for me in the restaurant, I would be just a few minutes, or she could come with me back to my home and we could decide where to go from there. It was her choice. She told me she would ride along.

At the house we sat in the driveway and I offered her the idea of coming inside. 'Okay', she replied, 'I'll leave my Walkman and purse out here in the car.' We got out and went inside. She hung out in the living room–kitchen area, *while I went into my bedroom to retrieve a couple of $20 bills. When I came out of the hallway, Taunja was standing with her back to me in the kitchen looking at some artwork on the wall. I felt this was a good time to hug her. I slid my arm in behind her and wrapped my arms around her, kissing the back of her neck. She felt good in my arms and she responded by turning around and kissing my lips. Felt we were clicking as we kept kissing and holding each other close. Slowly, my feet moved towards the mattress on the floor a few feet away. We dropped to it and continued to make out...our hands moving to unbutton clothing or slip it off.*

Looking back, I understand how this looks. I met Taunja Bennett earlier in the day when she was with two men. Returning to the tavern later, I see her alone, searching for something to eat, and I jump on the subject and play her into coming with me to the restaurant and then my home to do what?

Taunja was now in my home and under my spell. Makes me look like a predator stalking my victim, doesn't it? She is reported by the press to be mildly retarded. What exactly does that mean? Could I have picked up on that and used it against her, or would it not be noticeable only knowing her for five minutes? It goes a long way to explain her actions in the next few moments. Her pillow talk seemed weird. It could be just her demeanor...a mild nut case not really thinking about what she is doing, like hugging a total stranger into thinking there is an attraction there.

So, there we were mugging on each other on the mattress on the floor...my hands on the buttons of her jeans and I just couldn't get them undone. I stare down at the problem. Taunja Bennett looks at me and says, 'Why don't you just hurry up and get it over with? I'm hungry.'

This just struck me as wrong, if you understand my way of thinking? Told her: 'I'm taking my time, girl.'

Taunja slapped at me, saying, 'Get the hell off me then.'

That slap struck a nerve. And, it gave me permission to hit back. Hit me – I'll hit back, and my fist hit her hard. And, one blow was not enough...I hit here again and again, over and over again and again.

Let me explain that it wasn't an angry hit. Hard to explain. I had never hit a woman before. It was like I was now allowed to hit her for all the wrongs in my life done by women. Just going through the motions of punching her face. Each time I hit her I hit her harder and harder until her voice stopped me cold...like a child crying out for help. Taunja cried not to me – but to her mother: 'Mommy, make him stop! Mommy make him stop...Mommy!'

Sitting on top of her, I stared at the bloody mess I had done. I was sick over it. My mind raced over my options; take her to the hospital, I'd go to jail. Drop her off someplace and call for help; she knows where I live and I'd go to jail. Third option; kill her and get rid of her body; hoping I'll get away with it and not go to jail or prison.

How to kill her? The television shows all depict strangulation as the cleanest and quickest way...just hold onto their necks for a minute or so and it was over. My hands went to her throat and I squeezed with all of my might. After a minute my hands were aching and turning white, and you've got to remember that I am one heck of a BIG man, with a lot of strength. At about two minutes I had to let go. When I did, she breathed in. She was still alive.

Reasoning it out, this next attempt I would place my fist into her throat and lock my elbow and lean into her neck with my upper body weight. After a little over four minutes, I smelled urine as Bennett peed into her jeans. I believed she was dead and stood up over her, staring down at her lifeless body. My thoughts went to making sure she was dead, and stayed dead.

I went into the garage to get a length of nylon rope to securely tie around her neck. This took me several minutes to do. I remember using a lighter to melt the ends of the rope to keep them from unravelling when I initially purchased the rope, so I reasoned that after I cut the rope after tying it on her, that one end was cut with a knife and burned off. What was really the case was I had cut both ends.

Remembering I had tried to unbutton her jeans, I also cut the buttons from the fly area and tossed them into the fireplace to destroy them. Didn't know if I could wipe off my fingerprints from them and feared that in the course of disposing the body I might leave my fingerprints on anything metal. That's why I cut off the fly on her jeans. It wasn't a trophy, so don't hang that dumb notion on me, okay!

Not really sure if it was before, or after I put the rope around Taunja's neck, when the phone rang, and I answered it. It was a collect call from Roberta. I accepted the call again. The trucker had got to Tennessee and went straight home to his wife. It was predictable. Me and Roberta talked awhile, and I used that time to wash and dry the blood-spattered clothes I had been wearing. Call it efficient time management.

A case in point to the evidence in this case. I never had sex with Bennett. The beating of her body would show up in the blood spatter on her clothes. Hey! The lack of blood on certain areas will also tell any crime scene investigators that the person doing it was positioned a certain way for it to happen, and death soon followed.

Was the rope the reason she died? The crime scene people and the coroner should have the cause of death as the fist to the throat. That the rope was put on Bennett after she was already dead...don't snow me. I know what happened and what you read here is the truth, period. And, any other writer, or prosecutor, or even the FBI, who says otherwise, is lying through their back teeth. Sex never played any part in the motive for killing Bennett, so I am not gonna say this again. FULL STOP!

There, on the living room floor laid the dead body of Taunja Bennett, as I talked to Roberta Ellis on the phone. One real reason I had the rope tied around Bennett's neck was to secure her stomach contents should my moving of the body cause what she drank to move out of her – like post-mortem vomit. Had no real idea on if it would, or not. You must understand that it was a precaution to it. This is why I argue with myself on when I tied the rope around her neck...before, or after the long conversation with Roberta on the phone.

After the phone call I knew I had to set up an alibi, so the people at the B&I Tavern wouldn't identify me as someone last seen with Taunja Bennett. You know, like the hug she gave me earlier in the day meant nothing at all. So, with the same clothes on when we met both times at, and near the tavern, I drove back to the place and put myself in there...to alert the staff when I left the place, I left all by myself.

In leaving the tavern, an hour or so later, I drove up to Crown point, and the Vista House, to search out a secure area to drop off Bennett's body without being seen. Being seen was my biggest worry. Transporting the body up there and placing it in a place would be nerve wracking to say the least, but it had to be done.

At the Vista House monument that night, every parking space was occupied with couples in cars making out. Why choose a popular make-out space? The answer is that lots of traffic would sort of guarantee no one would remember one car with Washington State license plates on it. A popular tourist's spot – my car would fit in nicely.

When I drove home, I stopped at the all-night deli-gas station close to my place on 181 Street. Checked out all the lights on the car: didn't want a traffic stop. Fuelled up to be sure there was enough gas in the tank to get the job done, then drove back to my driveway and backed in. Removed the dome lights and opened the passenger door against Roberta's Ford Pinto to get ready to place Bennett's body into the front seat.

In the house I examined Bennett's body. I wanted to see what I hadn't had. I exposed her breasts and vaginal area – noticed she had shaved her pubic hair to fit bikini underwear. Her flesh seemed cool to the touch. She had been dead since about 6 pm, and now it was near midnight. The house was 70 degrees inside, maybe a little warmer. The cooling of her body would be slower in these six hours than after being placed in the wet-cold leaves of the ravine, where I intended to dump her body. And, you know, this fact could also hinder the diagnosis in the precise time of death. The Crime Scene Forensics would probably not consider her lying dead in a warm home for six or seven hours before being transferred to the final resting place...just something to be considered later.

Remember the fly area? Well, with that cut away, there was nothing to hold Bennett's pants on her hips. A fact I never thought of until I moved her into the car, then drove her to the ravine. Thus, it is why when she would be found that her jeans were pulled down to her ankles...suggesting she was posed that way. So, don't hang it on me that I posed her body to offend people when I dropped her off. It just happened that way.

Before moving Bennett to my car I searched the quiet neighborhood for movement from behind the curtains in the living room with the lights all turned off. Why? So often people go for walks late at night. Cars drive through from time to time. Lots of things could still go wrong.

I decided to wear bicycle riding shoes to the area I would drop off her body. These Cannondale shoes have a rigid sole and offer a flat print. Also, lots of people bicycle the area. Hard to determine who made the tracks up there...would a cyclist drop off a body that was killed elsewhere?

I guess, about 00:30 Sunday morning, I carried Taunja Bennett's body out to the car and sat her in the front passenger seat, shut the door, and her bloodied head, with the rope still tied around her neck, slid up against the window in plain view, she would ride that way, is if asleep, as I drove to the Vista House monument, and further east down to discovering a dark-looking ravine to toss her away.

Now, you may all be thinking how cold-blooded I may seem to be. But, put yourself in my position where a woman has given me permission to hit her, and the hitting continues until death comes to her. Your options are limited, period. You go to jail for the rest of your life or you try to stay out of prison.

Once the job is done, it is all about thinking and rationalising on the way to complete the business efficiently. It makes sense to me, and anyway, Bennett was now dead and would know nothing about her body's disposal, so strip away emotions and look at the options left to me, and then think common sense.

Now, parked above the ravine, I get out of the car and looked back up the hill at the Vista House to see if any headlights were coming down the hill. None were. So, I went to the passenger door, opened it, and grabbed Bennett's arm and pulled her out into the darkness. Immediately, her jeans slid to her ankles as her body slid along the cold, wet leaves on the ground.

At this place, the ravine is really steep and her body slides faster than I can safely walk. I grab at her top and hold onto her sweater to keep the body with me. This causes me to slide over her breasts, then shit happened. I hunched over to squeeze under a bush and, at about eight-five feet down that mean ravine, we stop.

I could see headlights piercing the darkness from below. Those lights were right at me. I realize my error. Only one switchback on that road we were on and I was trying to hide a body in the middle of it. Now, with people looking up the ravine, I knew that Bennett would be found sometime soon. As for the present? I was about to be discovered and I needed to get THE HELL OUT OF THERE. No time...not a minute, not a second to waste in covering up the body. I scaled the hill, passed that bush, and ran to the car and hit first gear. Lots of things happen for a reason. You want to see a big man sweat buckets in the northwest USA in winter – watch him do what I did with Ms Bennett that night, and understand why a BIG man sweats.

When I pulled Bennett from my car, what I didn't know was that her body would drag from the car my jack knife with a red handle for the police to find. I would later miss it, but not know where it went. The switchblade really messed with my head. Over the next years I would think of how stupid I was – or just how lucky, or unlucky I was that night. You know, thoughts like this kinda eat into your head. You know, I didn't know that on the hour – every hour that passed – a Multnomah County Sheriff's car patrolled the area...and they kept a good account of the goings on along that Crown Point highway.

Anyways, in the car I drove east along the roadway towards the only switchback. Into the turn my headlights would light up the side of the car coming in the other direction...we passed like two ships in the night at sea. Neither one knowing who we were, I did read the Multnomah Sheriff's sign on the side of the car. Had I been a few minutes late, he could have caught me in the act of pulling Bennett into the ravine. Good luck on my part. Bad luck in not being able to hide her body under some old leaves.

Back on the interstate I kicked off my cycling shoes and tossed them away – one here and one there, a mile apart. Montgomery Gentry – What do you think about that?

Finding Bennett's tape player, that Walkman, with a tape by Soul to Soul in it, I tossed it into onto the bridge over the Sandy River. I knew it would soon be nothing but a pile of plastic pieces. Then I pulled into the Burns Brothers truck stop, in Troutdale. Parked my car so I could see it from a booth in the restaurant and put on my running shoes and went inside. Sat down. Ordered coffee, and relaxed – not for long.

Big man sweats when fear hit again. Three Oregon State Police cruisers pulled in and parked next to my car. One car had been working hard. A hub cap was missing and hot, sump oil dripped onto the ground. Their red/white/blue strobes were off. The law walked into the restaurant. Big men, heavily armed. Mean, confident men. They sat down in the booth next to mine. One even nodded to me a 'hello'. We knew each other, and there we were, talking to each other and these three 'super cops' had NO idea I had become a murderer that night.

This episode sort of relaxed me from being totally paranoid over what I had done to Bennett. The talk on the phone with Roberta had come at a time when I needed to slow down and think it all out. That hour of talking 'I love you's' to her had done that for me. Good luck.

I guess that you'll never understand me. Big man, trucker and used to using his hands for his work – never beating on a woman and then killing her. But, when the sun came up I returned to my car and discovered Bennett's purse under the front passenger seat. I went through it. $2 dollars plus 11 cents, thereabouts. It went into my pocket. What to do with the purse and the other contents? This is the key evidence to her existence. This is the real evidence *that could link me to the Bennett murder. Her existence, in picture form...an Oregon State identification card with her photo on it. I thought of just tossing it into a trash can. If I had, then history would have been different, today. What I did would secure in time, her existence.*

My decision is to drive up the Sandy River Road and find someplace no one would ever go to look for something. So, I drove through Troutdale, past the local police station, and crossed the Sandy River on the old bridge and turned south on the river road. Miles later, I found the road rising up and turning east away from the river. A 'Y' in the road went sharply up the hill to my left. On my right is an entanglement of blackberry bushes. I looked for a wide spot to park. About a hundred yards further south I parked on the east side of the roadway. On the river side, just twenty feet down the embankment, I saw an old stump of a cedar tree just under the telephone lines. It would serve to me as a beacon to identify the spot I'd throw away Bennett's purse and its contents. Just forty or so feet south of the stump, and forty feet down into the poison oak and blackberry entrails, I tossed all of the purse's contents and her purse. No one drove by. No one saw me do this. Time to get back home. But, today, looking back, I should have poured gas over the purse and reduced the item to ashes.

The stench of death hit me when I entered the house at 18434 NE Everett Street. It was as if Taunja Bennett was still there, in the home – her smell hung in the rooms. That was when I noticed just how much blood spatter there was on the walls and ceiling.

Opening all the windows, the cool air smelled and felt

good. Warm water and Dipsol with a rag helped to remove much of the blood. Down at Albertson's store, I'd next rent a stem-vacuum cleaner to hopefully remove the urine from the carpet. This cleaning process lasted all afternoon. After returning the cleaner, shutting the doors and windows, I finally found the bed and slept. I would have no idea that by noon Bennett's body had been found and removed from the ravine.

At about 10 am, just nine hours after I put Bennett's body down the ravine, a cyclist noticed something out of place. The woman got off her bike and went closer to see what it was. Realizing it to be a dead female, she rode to the nearest phone to call up the police, and, in doing so, she became the first suspect in the murder of Taunja Ann Bennett.

Keith Jesperson, in a letter to the author.

It might be somewhat long-winded, but is this an accurate account of the murder? No, it is not. In fact, once he had taken her inside the Jespersons' home, he locked the door and drew the curtains, imprisoning Taunja. When she refused his predatory advances, he raped her several times, which totally contradicts the story he gave to me, for elsewhere he has claimed:

I pumped another orgasm into her and then I looked down and with my dick inside her, I decided to knock her out with one punch… I smashed this girl twenty times – rights, lefts, jabs, uppercuts, hooks, I punched her till I couldn't recognise her face and then I punched her some more. When I stopped her face was squashed – broken nose, broken jaw,

162

teeth sticking through her lips...then I strangled her until my
hands turned white.

Subsequently a 57-year-old woman called Laverne Pavlinac, and her dim-witted, abusive boyfriend, John Sosnovske, 43, were arrested and found guilty of Taunja's murder. They would spend five years behind bars until Jesperson confessed the killing, but that is a story for another day.

*   *   *

Soon after killing Taunja Bennett, Jesperson found work as a long-haul truck driver working from Washington to Oregon, zigzagging to California, Montana, Nebraska, even New York and Florida, with all states in between. And we may imagine this 6ft 5in, good-looking man, hauling potatoes, steel, and aluminium across the USA, his plum-coloured Peterbilt gleaming, and his plaid shirt well pressed, all-American clean.

Shortly after murdering Taunja Bennett, Jesperson, who was seeking work in California, raped a young woman whom he met while she breastfed her baby in a bar at a shopping centre in Shasta. The woman had just argued with her husband, who had stormed off, and she was downing a few Jack Daniel's to settle her nerves when Jesperson approached her. With her drink finished, she asked him if he would walk her to a nearby Jiffy Mart to buy some beer. They carried the twelve-pack to his car, and drove out to the country, where Jesperson said they enjoyed mutual sex – at least this is what he says in his 'new' autobiography: 'Chris, I never raped this woman. She was drunk. I promise you it was a mutual thing. Then she called the cops on me and I got arrested. I would never have done that in front of a baby.'

Nevertheless, he has previously told an entirely another story, one which has been corroborated by the victim in her police statement:

I grabbed her by the hair and shoved her face down – and that made me even hotter. I was about to orgasm when a whimper came from the back seat and she pulled off. She said, 'I don't know what I'm doing here. I'm married and I don't need this. Drive me home, please.' I shoved her back on my cock as hard as I could. [...] She started screaming at me, so I put her in a headlock and yanked hard. I was trying to break her neck, but I just couldn't get the leverage. It takes a lot of leverage to break a human neck. I tried three times before the baby cried in the back seat and she yelled, 'Don't hurt my baby!' So, I dropped her off at the same place I met her. That was my big mistake. I should have killed her.

Jesperson was later charged with first-degree sexual assault (rape), and the punishment was combined with his sentences for multiple murders.

According to Keith Jesperson, he didn't kill again until the late summer of 1992, when he murdered a woman, known only as Jane Doe, and dumped her body ten miles north of Blythe, California. He was certainly in the area at the time, working for the Cheney Trucking Company, and he remembers her name being 'Claudia'.

He says that he was parked at the brake-check area on I-15 close to San Bernardino, California, 'when a girl, wearing tight bleached-out blue jeans, loose white top, big tits, called out to me. She wasn't beautiful, but pretty enough,' he said, and according to Jesperson they rode for a while, enjoyed mutual sex until she demanded money. Trapped in his 'Pete', he raped her again and again. 'At the next truck stop, I screwed her till I couldn't get it up anymore. It was supreme, it was total gratification. I'm running this show, bitch, you're mine.'

In truth, Jesperson did a lot more than rape the young hitchhiker, he tortured her:

I started to play a little death game with her, use her like a toy, an amusement. I choked her, let her wake up, choked her again, let her wake up again. That's the kind of game I should have played with Taunja Bennett....After I choked her the third time, I waited ten or fifteen minutes till she revived. I said, 'Take a deep breath. Count to ten. Now – hold your breath.' Then I choked her out again. When she woke up, I told her to count to nine and squeezed her neck again. I was playing with her like a cat with a mouse. As the game went on I'd tell her to count to eight, seven, six, five. I was breaking her mind. I wanted her to accept that one of those times she wouldn't wake up. Finally she caught on and just accepted the game.

'Claudia' gave up the will to live.

When I asked Keith to give me the details of this murder, all he would say was, 'I remember giving her a ride, we had a fuck which was nothing special, then she demanded money. That pissed me off so I just strangled her. There was no rape or torture at all.'

We can also be 100 per cent sure that Jesperson killed 32-year-old Cynthia Lynn Rose, whose body was found along US Highway 99, near Turlock, California. She had been dead for some weeks and it was originally thought that she had died of a drugs overdose, but the medical examiner determined that she had been strangled. Jesperson would later tell police that she was a hooker. He had picked her up for sex and then killed her.

*   *   *

In his new autobiography, and throughout his correspondence with me, Keith has consistently argued that he has never raped anyone, and he is adamant that he never went looking for victims. But this pathological liar, in the first week of November 1992, picked up 26-year-old Laurie Ann Pentland, whom he raped, choked to death and dumped behind a GI Joe store in Salem, Oregon. He was on the Pacific Coast, with a load of meat northbound out of Selma, California, and he went searching for a hooker – a 'lot lizard' – he knew who serviced the drivers at a Burns Brothers Truck Stop on the I-5, at Wilsonville. In a sanitised version, he told me that they had mutual sex and then she demanded more money, and because of this she had given him 'permission to kill her'. In truth, he raped, beat and tortured this victim for hours on end.

Two more Jane Doe's followed, the first in July 1993. The body was found near a truck stop on I-5, west of Santa Nella, California. The remains of a second woman, aged about 40, were discovered by a road crew on Wednesday, 14 September 1994, west of Crestview, Florida. Jesperson would later claim that her name was 'Susan'.

Victim number seven was 21-year-old Angela Subrize, who hailed from Oklahoma. She was murdered by Jesperson in January 1995. Her body would remain undiscovered until the following September, when body parts were found along a Nebraska highway.

Jesperson said that during that January, he had been hauling product for California Steel and had headed for Spokane in his Peterbilt. Due to a mechanical failure, his brakes seized and the tractor unit caught fire. The Sterling Fire Department arrived, extinguished the blaze and Keith was forced to wait while another tractor was brought in so he could continue on his way.

While hanging around in Spokane, his company put him up in Room 425 of the Ridpath Hotel, and it was then that he met Angela Subrize, who was sitting, drinking beer, in a café booth. The date was Thursday, 19 January. According to Jesperson:

She was a very beautiful woman, and she told me she was an exotic dancer, in other words a stripper. We went to my room...she went to the bathroom and came out dressed in leather. Her dance was actually rather stupid. Rubbing all over me...pushing my hand away so I couldn't touch her. Then, after she felt how hard I was, she let me kiss her and we fell into bed. The sex was great. We kept at it till nearly three in the morning.

Jesperson says that over the following days, Angela accompanied him as he drove along his route. However, the novelty of having a such available female company in his cab soon wore off, and she started to get on his nerves by asking him to drive her to visit people in towns not on his itinerary. She obviously had no money, and she asked Keith if she could use his AT&T phone card to call her father for some assistance, but her dad refused her out of hand. Shortly afterwards, Angela asked to use the phone card again; this time speaking with a former boyfriend and telling him that she was pregnant.

Business is business. Pleasure is what we make of it, some call it 'Divine Intervention'. Others call it 'the Butterfly Effect'. What goes on in order for something to materialise into something else. A meeting of souls that could never have met had the stars not been aligned properly. I call it fate. That it was bound to happen. Because of the variables at play made the two of us collide into each other's path. If it is for good, then call it a good thing. If it turns out bad, then the Devil must have been to blame. However we call it, it isn't called control. For like I have said before, it is hard to control everything that goes around us.

Keith Jerperson, in a letter to the author.

Ever the philosopher who expects that every word he utters should be chiselled into stone and passed down to the generations to follow, the hypocrite that is Jesperson writes:

I get questions all the time from people asking how is it I picked my victims…and I tell them they picked me. They chose to be with me. It was their decision to push me along to do their will. I was just a person listening to them dig their own graves. My reason for killing changed over time. At first it was to get rid of the assault charge I could have faced over Bennett. Then it was to silence Claudia from manipulating others. Then came the tongue-lashing of Cynthia that just felt wrong, and my helping Pentland not to have to deal with her miserable life. Of saving Karla's family from disappointment. Susan was just too bizarre…a true nut job that gave me clues right away when she wanted me to drive her to Miami.

I guess the real big issue here is I accepted murder into my everyday life. Normal for me to deal with – to justify it in my life. But also know that society saw it as wrong and that it was to be kept under wraps. 'Would I kill again?' I thought to myself. And I answered, 'Yes – someday. But not today, I don't have the time for it'.

These are chilling words enough from the pen of a serial murderer, but what follows sends a shiver up the spine:

I really never had enough time for killing. It seemed to present itself at the moment. A fast decision to end a life based on an inner set of requirements. And, that list seemed to be adding more things to it, to include reasons to kill. Never saw myself as God or Judge or Jury. Just someone that took care of business. Murder is a job. Something once you start, you have to see all the way through. No stopping in the middle to change your mind and say: 'I've decided to let you go today. Let this be a lesson to you. Now, scoot.' You have to end it once you start moving on them. Once you commit to it there is no going back.

Angela Subrize's last day on Earth found her trucking with Jesperson in icy conditions, leaving Wyoming and crossing into Nebraska on I-80, and 'then it happened', writes Jesperson...

I hit a patch of blade ice in a corner at mile marker 58, or so. My trailer tried to pass me and I rode the gas and steered into the skid. When I got all straightened up, my nose of the tractor pointed into the rest area and I drove into it and parked up far away from the other rigs.

This near fatal incident scared Jesperson and decided to stay where he was and catch up on his much-needed sleep. However, he says that Subrize would have none of it. Every time he nodded off she woke him up, demanding they move on. Suddenly Keith snapped:

I grabbed her by the neck and pulled her onto the bed, my weight shifted and my arm's pressure pushed her into the mattress. 'You said you weren't going to hurt me,' she said, 'why are you hurting me now?' My arm pushed down on her and she lost her voice. Her eyes – her gray, wolf-like eyes started back at me. 'I'm not going to hurt you, Angela, I'm going to kill you and save your boyfriend a lifetime of pain being with you.' Several minutes later I smelled her body release her fluids and solids. She was dead. I sat there, looking at her. 'Stupid bitch!' I yelled at her.

'Then I got to thinking as I played it all out in my head. I fucked up. I'd called her father using my AT&T calling card. Certainly Angela had a criminal record. They find her body and retrace the records and Daddy remembers two phone calls...back-track them to me and I'm in prison. There had to be a way to get rid of her identification. I would think of one. But all of a sudden I was awake and alert and hungry. I rolled Angela into a blanket and layed her against the sleeper wall and got back into the driver's seat and pulled back out onto the interstate. As luck would have it ran out of ice and snow just east of that rest area.

Keith Jesperson, in a letter to the author.

Just ahead, Jesperson saw a signs for McDonald's and Burger King. He pulled in and ordered. Now sitting in his sleeper he ate the burger as well as one he had cynically bought for the dead woman. 'You could have been eating this if you just could have left me alone. What? Cat got your tongue…nothing to say, huh?' he muttered to her. 'I laughed at the one-sided conversation.'

Jesperson hit the road again, all the while thinking how he could dispose of Angela Subrize's body. Then it came to him: 'I remembered the tale of some guy tying his dog's leash to the trailer hitch and forgetting to untie it and driving off. By the time someone had pulled him over, the dog was a pile of flesh – what was left of it.'

My plan was to put Angela under my trailer and drag her flesh along I-80 for several miles to grind away her identification.

The way the traffic flowed late at night and early that morning offered me a way to get away with doing it. The cars and trucks were gathering in clusters of vehicles. One cluster would move along at 70 mph, then nothing for about three miles and another cluster of cars and trucks would come along. Figured I could pull out onto the interstate behind a cluster of cars and rigs and cruise at my governor speed of 64 mph…that over a period of time, the cluster ahead of me would leave me behind and the cluster behind would catch me. Then, I could just exit the road and pull onto the shoulder and cut what was left of Angela away from my trailer and deposit her in the tall grass on the shoulder before the next cluster caught me. About three minutes to do it all. Then pull along the shoulder and come in behind the cluster of rigs. It worked out in theory

in my head. All I had to do was is implement it and pull
out onto the freeway undetected by anyone.

Keith Jesperson, in a letter to the author

At this point, on page 309 of his correspondence to the author, Jesperson drew three pen sketches: the first was a side view of his rig; the second was a drawing of Angela with a noose tied around her neck; the third shows how he had trussed her up.

It would take time to get it all ready to pull off. First I tied
a rope around her neck with one end and made a loop in
the other for a handle to pull her body out of the cab and
along the ground.

Next I had to tie a rope to her ankles – one end to each
ankle. This would be the rope I would tie the frame rope
to, and it also gave me a handle to position the body under
the trailer.

I needed her arms to wear off first. So, I taped them in
front of her in a cross so to sit them on the ground's surface
and they would have her weight on them. I got a length of
rope and got under the trailer and tied it to a cross-member
in front of the trailer tines. I pulled it tight as I looked to
see where the body would ride. I wanted it to lay under the
axles so the tires would shield any prying eyes should I get
a flyer flying by at mach speed. [...] I could feel the extra
drag on the power as I applied more power. The friction
was very real. I picked up speed and got to 64 mph longer
than I had hoped for. It was a waiting game. My nerves
were tight. Still a lot could go wrong. The miles clicked by.
At ten miles the cluster coming up behind were gaining
fast. At eleven miles, I turned on my turn signal to exit

onto the shoulder, then coasted up to mile marker 210,
twelve miles from the rest area.

Keith Jesperson, in a letter to the author.

After the following cluster of cars and rigs passed by, Jesperson climbed down from his cab and under his trailer where he cut the rope and pulled what was left of Angela into the grass on the shoulder, leaving it about three feet from a fence. He drove on to Grand Island, pulled off the road, parked up and went to sleep.

The following day, Keith carried on east to Lincoln, crossed Highway 2 to Interstate 29 south, and ended up in Kansas City, Missouri. But what of Angela Subrize?

Reflecting back, Jesperson says:

Her arms were gone. The front of her skull from her ears forward was gone. All of her chest cavity was gone – as well as her internal organs. The Jesperson sure-fire weight reduction plan was a success. About 60 per cent of her weight had been ground off by the rough surface of Interstate 80.

There had been a tense moment after I dropped my pliers and it took me 20 seconds to find them. Then a driver called on the radio to see if I needed help and my answer made me laugh to myself, 'No, thank you. Just getting rid of some dead weight. I need no help doing this.'

Was I worried? No one would see the birds eating her as strange. Deer die all the time and are eaten along I-80. The people in the cars and trucks would just assume it had to be a road kill...only this dead deer had only two legs. Feeling that I had gotten rid of her identity, I felt safe, but

when her body was found in late 1995, she was identified
by a pin's serial number in her hip. As a child she had
broke her hip and it was pinned together. Another ten
miles would have taken care of that.

Jesperson's final 'road kill' was that of 41-year-old Julie
Winningham, of Camas, Washington State. She was strangled
and dumped nude, like the others, along a roadside on Friday,
10 March 1995. The body had been dumped over an
embankment alongside State Highway 14, just east of the Clark
and Skamania county line. However, this time everything was
different. Keith had been dating Julie on an on-and-off basis
and Julie's friends and relatives soon suspected Jesperson as
being the killer. Here, published for the first time, is Jesperson's
account of the murder:

It was Saturday, 4 March 1995, and he was waiting over the
weekend for a new load at the Burn Brothers truck stop, in
Troutdale, Oregon. While sitting in the truck stop's restaurant,
he saw a 'cute woman who was trying to get a ride east'. He
recalls that, 'she smelled like she had worn those clothes for
several days so I offered her the use of the bathroom in my
room to clean up in. She accepted.' Keith tried his luck by
asking her if she'd like to share his bed. She politely refused and
she spent that night sitting in the restaurant.

The following morning, Jesperson checked out of the motel.
All of the rooms had been booked for a convention and they
could not spare him another night. Putting his bags in the cab,
he unhitched his load, planning to visit a few local spots he
wanted to see. He ate breakfast, and again noticed the woman,
who appeared tired and hungry. Then he left, asking the waitress
to give her what she wanted to eat and that he would pay for it

when he returned later in the day. Moments later he saw Julie Winningham talking with two other people in the hallway:

Our eyes met, but I just didn't want to see her. Had to think about this, so I sat down in the washroom and thought it through. She could be had, she had a weakness to alcohol and marijuana. Should I hook up with her? Sure I would get laid, but so would my bank account. I thought long and hard.

I had the time for at least one more night of drama. Why not? How hard could it be? Buy her a few drinks. Promise her the world and her legs flew apart. And, it is just that easy, especially if she needs something I can provide her with at the time.

'Done with business, I turned toward her when I exited the restroom. She looked hot...halter top and little white shorts...no underwear. She had to be hooking. She was advertising everything. We hugged as she said, 'Hello stranger, want to go have coffee?' I asked, and we walked to the restaurant.

After the coffee, Jesperson invited Julie to his truck for a little privacy. He watched as she strutted her ass, putting a wide swing to it, 'to give me a show of flirting,' he recalls. 'She needed something. She had not lit up a smoke yet, could it be that she was penniless? She needed me...she needed something.'

According to Jesperson, this is what took place next:

Climbing into the cab, she cocked her leg exposing her pussy. Definitely she wanted me to supply something, but right now all I cared about was to get laid. In the cab she became the aggressor...a long, hard kiss ended with her taking me by my hand to bed. The sex was rushed but good sex. My personal opinion of Julie is she hated to have sex because it was messy. No way would she ever do oral sex on me. From what she talked about, I gather she hooked and the demon for oral sex sickened her. She gave up the pussy because it worked better for her. Then we got dressed and she took me to see her car, a 1981 AMC Spirit, only it had been in a crash. I would hear all about the crash, because, like I said, she needed me.

Julie had been driving while drunk through Camas, and a traffic cop pulled her car over. He wrote her a ticket and impounded her driver's license. He knew her and gave her a break – if she had somewhere to drive her car, he would let her go. Julie found a woman to drive her car away, but several blocks away, Julie took the wheel again, ran a red light and was T-boned by another car. The same cop shows up and Julie provides him with a second driver's license. This time the cop takes her to jail and she bails out pending an upcoming trial to see if she will do some more jail times. The trial was scheduled for March 9th at 10:00 am.

From her story, I could see she was in trouble and all the help I could give her would not keep her from going to jail. So, for a while, and while I was in town, Julie would do all she could to make me think I could help her out and keep her from jail.

With Julie trying to use Jesperson to help her out, and with Keith getting all the free sex he could want, both parties were onto a winner – that was until Julie hit the bottle in a local bar and ordered scores of drinks, which she demanded Keith should pay for.

If anything, Keith Jesperson is certainly nobody's fool and he was furious, but he soon calmed down. He agreed to drive Julie over to see her mother in the morning, and to visit her lawyer in Camas; all the while, in the back of his mind was the thought that he would be railroaded into paying for her lawyer's bill and her fines.

Over the next few days, and, as Julie's court hearing loomed, Jesperson says she became even more of a drunken liability. She was conned out of her car by a woman she hardly knew, and Keith found himself being conned into signing and witnessing the bill of sale for the car. The sex between them didn't stop as she tried to make him feel good and sympathetic towards her. In fact, it got to the point where Keith says, 'I was sexually exhausted and couldn't get it up any longer.'

Crunch time came during the evening of 8th March, when Julie and Keith were naked in his cab. She said to him, 'Tomorrow I go to court. I need you to tell the judge you will be there for me. Tell him you will make sure the fines get paid. Promise me you will do this for me, Keith?'

He replied, 'Julie, I can't be there for you to pay your fines. I just don't have the money. I'll show up as moral support only.'

Apparently, Julie responded with, 'Damn you, Keith. I need you to tell the judge so I won't have to go to jail. I can't go to jail. I don't like jail.'

Jesperson was now laughing, and his laughter increased, 'Julie, you are going to jail,' he chuckled. 'Get used to it. You did it to yourself.'

'Keith, I can't go to jail. I'll die if they put me in jail. Promise me I won't go to jail!'

Jesperson's reaction was terrifying:

And there it was, my solution...she had said others things as well, like bringing my kids into it. That she would be a good mother for my kids – yes, right! A drunken, pot-smoking crazy bitch that likes to put everyone in danger after she drove a car. No way could I allow her near my kids.

She opened the door to my way of thinking. To keep her from jail, I could fulfil a promise by killing her. She faced jail, said it would kill her. I was just making sure she didn't have to face it ever. Better to have been killed by someone else than to die of your own stupidity. My mind was made up in an instant. Julie was going to die. My laughter caught her off guard. She was not happy over the developments in my demeanour. Oh, well!

The look on her face was priceless to me...total shock when I pushed her under me and held my hand to her throat to keep her from breathing. I wasn't going to kill here there, just put her under, so to make her more cooperative to deal with. A few minutes later she was unconscious and I used duct tape to secure her so she couldn't walk or use her hands or talk. Then I got dressed and drove out of the area – heading east on Highway 14 toward Stevenson and the Camas Pass.

As I drove, Julie woke up and she panicked. Leaning forward she was able to sit on the bed and when I stopped at a stop sign, she fell forward and cut herself on a piece of metal on my seat and layed there on the floor bleeding. I could smell faeces...she had shit herself and the soft diarrhoea sprayed the bottom of my sleeper. At the top of

Camas Pass, I got at several pieces of Julie's clothing and wiped up as much of the faeces as I could...placed Julie back in the bed and wiped her body clean as well...then got out of the truck and carried her soiled clothing over to the woods and tossed them down the hill.

Jesperson then returned to his rig. A police car passed by, and he realised that he couldn't finish the woman off there, so he drove back towards Camas and parked up, a few hundred yards east of the Clark County line, the county that would have had jurisdiction over the murder. This was a subtle ploy, as Jesperson explained. 'Like in the Bennett case, where the murder happened is where there is the crime. Should I really want to mess with the courts now – I could re-file to move the case to the proper county and make them do it all over again.'

Now parked up, with his engine ticking over, Jesperson lay next to Julie and explained that she was going to die. He told her that he had killed seven times before, and that she would die the next time his hands went to her throat.

Complete terror filled her eyes as she cried. Before I killed her, yes, I felt like having her again. But she was messy and I felt a need to do it quickly and throw her away before dawn broke. I said, 'I promised you, Julie, that you'll never go to jail. I'm keeping my promise with you by putting you out of your misery. Goodbye. I'll see you in the afterlife.'

My fist pressed into her neck and in about four minutes she layed there dead. I got out and pulled her naked body out if the cab. Had removed all of the tape, carried her light body over the guard rail and to the edge of a steep embankment and tossed her lifeless body some 20 feet

*down into a pile of tossed away garbage, then walked back
to the truck.*

Jesperson's thoughts at that time were that she was too close to
the road and would be found quickly. Deep down, he says he
wanted her found soon:

*I was tired of this game. I was beginning to take enjoyment
in killing them. I had to be stopped. Maybe that's why I
killed and left her body so close to home. And, I had kept
her alive for several days, I could have killed her in Eastern
Oregon or Idaho, and dragged her body under my trailer
or tractor to get rid of her. Then I could have gone on to
kill more of them, even turn into a different type of killer,
actually seek out victims to kill all of the time.*

The concern of leaving Julie's body where he had dumped it ate
at Jesperson for many days afterwards. He contemplated
returning and moving it to a more remote location, instead, he
says, 'I should have put her deeper into the woods, but I didn't.
Nope! I simply drove east.'

*   *   *

Clark County Washington Sheriff's Dept Detective Rick
Buckner was the lead investigator in the Julie Ann
Winningham case. His initial enquiries informed him that Julie
had been living in Utah for a while after breaking up with her
truck driver husband. She had returned to Camas in February
1995, hitching a ride with Keith Jesperson, who she referred to
as her fiancé.

Buckner learned from the Cheney Trucking Company that

Jesperson was en-route to Pennsylvania; his route would take him towards the West Coast, through Texas, New Mexico and eventually to Arizona.

By Wednesday, 22 March, Buckner had located Jesperson in Las Cruces, New Mexico, a city in the southern part of the state near the Mexican border. With the help of local law enforcement, Jesperson was detained and questioned for six hours about the murder of Julie Winningham. He wouldn't talk, and since the law didn't have any concrete evidence to arrest him, Buckner had no other option but to release him. With his work completed down south, Jesperson headed for Arizona, while Buckner returned to Washington. Shortly afterwards, Jesperson was arrested and charged with murder.

*   *   *

In October 1995, just before his trial was due to start, Keith pleaded guilty to the murder of Julie Winningham before Clark County Washington Superior Court Judge Robert L Harris, the same judge who had presided over the notorious Westley Allan Dodd case. Dodd was a serial murderer from Washington state, executed by hanging in 1993. This was the first legal hanging (at Dodd's own request) in the United States since 1965. Because Jesperson had pleaded guilty, he avoided the death sentence, and, in December 1995, he was sentenced to life in prison.

Risking his life, Jesperson waived extradition from Clark County and was transferred to Oregon, which also has the death sentence. On Thursday, 2 November 1995, he entered a 'No Contest Plea' before Multnomah County Presiding Judge Donald H Londer, for the murder of Taunja Bennett. He was immediately sentenced to life in prison, setting a minimum 30-year tariff before becoming eligible for parole.

This deal was a nifty piece of footwork by Keith, and it gave him exactly what he wanted. He had spent much of his time in jail studying law books and was able to run rings around most prosecutors when it came down to working a deal. With prison time in Oregon, proceedings elsewhere would require further extradition, meaning considerable expense and a lot of red tape. 'I had them by the nuts,' says Keith in a letter. And the Oregon sentence made potential death penalties in other States less likely, and he knew that too. Here was a man who had given first-rate advice to several other killers, and for which he received letters of thanks from their attorneys for spotting loopholes the 'legal eagles' never knew existed.

However, there was another Oregon case involving Jesperson that had to be dealt with in the meantime. This was the killing of 23-year-old Laurie Ann Pentland, through which he was linked by DNA. In a letter, he wrote, 'I felt so much power. I then told her she was going to die and I slowly strangled her.'

For this murder, Keith was sentenced to another life term in Oregon, with minimum 30 years to serve. If he is still alive after all of this, he'll be sent back to Washington to complete his life sentence there.

Two years later, and despite considerable legal wrangling, the state of Wyoming finally extradited Jesperson for the murder of Angela Subrize. And, if any state had the determined will to execute Jesperson, it was Wyoming. For the next few months, as prosecutors prepared for trial, he taunted the authorities and threatened to force a costly trial by changing his story regarding the jurisdiction in which he had killed Subrize. At one point he said that he had killed her in Wyoming, and at another point he said that he had killed her in Nebraska. After going back and forth for some time, and by surrounding his deliberately misleading statements in his attempts to confuse the authorities on who had jurisdiction to prosecute him, our Keith worked yet another deal – he would admit to the Subrize killing, in Wyoming, if the now 'mentally fragged' Laramie County prosecutors would agree not to seek the death penalty against him.

As the result of this 'deal', on Wednesday, 3 June 1998, district judge Nicholas Kalokathis sentenced Jesperson to life in prison, and ordered that the sentence run consecutive to the two life sentences in Oregon and the natural life sentence in Washington, leaving us all with little doubt that Keith will die in prison. It remains to be seen whether any other jurisdictions, such as the states of Florida or California, will prosecute Jesperson for the murders that he has confessed to in those states.

*　　*　　*

Keith Hunter Jesperson has admitted committing eight murders, but the author believes that this is only the tip of a homicidal iceberg. Keith has claimed responsibility for some 160 kills, and he was perfectly equipped to do so. But, as the reader will now appreciate, Keith is a 'games player'. He recanted his claims of 160 murders, which suited his purpose at the time. Nevertheless, he was an interstate trucker with a grudge, and his correspondence suggests that this man could well have been the most prolific serial killer in US history, making the number of crimes committed by Ted Bundy pale by comparison. In terms of a body count, he could wipe Henry Lee Lucas, and Harvey Carignan, off the map.

Unlike the sociopathic morons such as Bundy, Shawcross and Bianchi, Keith Jesperson stands out as being one of the most heinous, yet lucid serial killers of all time. Yet, he is also a very quiet man. A guy who thinks deep. And, if you think that the Green River killer (Gary Leon Ridgway) or the BTK killer (Dennis Rader) are bad news, you may have seen nothing yet.

At this point I had intended to close Keith's chapter – frankly, if you haven't had enough of Keith Hunter Jesperson by now, I have – but something had always bugged me about this guy. It was this: throughout all of his correspondence with me, Keith insisted that he had never raped anyone; he had never stalked a woman in his life; he had never gone out looking for a woman to kill. Guess what? I actually started to believe him. I truly, truly started to believe that maybe Jack Olsen had read Keith Hunter Jesperson all wrong. As the months passed by, I grew to accept his criticisms of me, my silly grammatical errors, the occasional misspelling of a place name, a route number. In a nutshell, and this may seem sad, I actually started to like this big guy, and his sharing with me of his life and crimes – he had almost convinced me that he had killed women just because they had pissed him off.

But it bothered me somehow, because that would mean he was the only serial killer in history who trawled for woman and killed them without any sexual motive... that just didn't sit right with me.

I pressed Keith on this issue, and then he made a fatal error. Perhaps it was a throwaway statement, or maybe he simply could not resist getting it off his chest, but in a letter, he explained that after several of his victims were dead, he completely undressed them and looked at their bodies. This statement of Jesperson's sent up a red flag, because, as we now know, he had said the same thing when he recounted the horrific murder of Taunja Bennett, which was a complete lie.

Here is what he wrote, here is that red flag:

> *The sexual element was/is, they were female and I am a*
> *male. I was curious on what I had missed out on. Much*
> *like a schoolboy trying to sneak a peek at what was up a*
> *girl's skirt. When we look at a magazine and see beautiful*
> *girls dressed up, we don't say to ourselves, 'nice dress', we*
> *stare at the breasts and that spot between their legs. We*
> *say, 'nice tits', 'great ass', 'gee – her legs go all the way*
> *up'… We undress them in our minds. When I killed them,*
> *I undressed them to check out what was really under their*
> *clothes. I was curious.*

Of course, Keith was ignorant of the fact that I had read Jack Olsen's book and that I had read all of the statements he had given to the police. He was ignorant that I already knew about the terrible pain and suffering, the torture that he had inflicted on his living victims. How he had played his sickening 'murder game', like the cat playing with a mouse, the shark circling a raft, and how he had lied and lied to me, and just about everyone who has crossed his path. In effect, Keith Jesperson, who has also admitted to being a serial arsonist, is a necrophile who enjoys sexual relations with the dead, and he even masturbated over their corpses; if the truth were known, he probably had sex with them in his cab, after they were dead.

Omitted, somewhat conveniently from his new autobiography, is any reference to his fantasies of raping his victims. This 'Mr Clean Cut Con', who sends me photos of him surrounded by the prison's 'shot-callers' during yard time. Black, white, heavily tattooed guys…mean looking 'mothers' who would stick you in a heartbeat. Here is Mr Jesperson, all-

coloured photos of him surrounded by his artwork, standing by a shiny car during a prison-sponsored auto-meet. Here is the man who viciously murdered so many innocent women.

And, it was when I received further information about Keith that I urgently called back this chapter from my publisher, a week before going to final edit. I learned that notably absent in his writings to me were any reference to the replies he sends to the women who are keen enough to want to write to and pledge their love to him. He actually draws an outline of his penis to impress them. In one letter he writes: 'When you touch and stroke the page, please get wet for me.' One woman who wrote to Keith because of her interest of serial killers, and who was studying for a Criminal Justice degree, broke off the correspondence on the insistence of her extremely agitated tutor, who went into even more grey-hair-inducing palpitations when he read: 'We can touch hands...and I will slip my fingers down to the crack of your tight ass and finger you when the guards are not looking,' he wrote. 'I will taste you for hours afterwards.' When I asked Keith about this matter, he replied: 'She [name omitted for legal reasons] wanted to marry me. She was too possessive. She was a nut case so I dumped her and she kicked up a storm.' It makes one's heart bleed, doesn't it?

Although the story of Keith Hunter Jesperson is, by its very nature, a sordid and gruesome one, I would like to end on a couple of more positive aspects of the case.

The first, and perhaps the most important, is the fact that Jesperson does have a remarkable insight into the minds of his serial killer breed and thinks outside the box, so to speak. He has provided me with perspectives on other serial killers and how their warped minds work; when one analyses Keith's mindset, one comes to the conclusion that only the serial killer himself knows what makes him tick. I have since passed all of my research, his correspondence, and my findings onto the FBI's Behavioral Science Unit, Quantico, VA. They replied saying that it was, 'of much interest, could be of immense value in the study of serial homicide. Can we move this one on?' Whether Keith will seize this opportunity to work with the professionals is a matter for his own conscience. It would be a tragedy if he didn't.

Secondly, Keith's daughter, Melissa: here we find a young woman who, for years, has been trying to come to terms with the disgrace of knowing that her father was a brutal serial killer. I make no bones about this, and I speak here for Melissa, but as a little kid she loved her dad to bits. She tells me that, from her perspective, he was generally a good father and a hard worker who, on the whole, treated his family well. When Keith had money he spoiled his kids and they were denied nothing. However, when cash was in short supply, he felt that he had let them all down and family arguments were frequent. Melissa recalls that her father did torture animals, maybe as a child she'd understandably not dwelt on that aspect of her father's life. If nothing else has come from my relationship with Keith Hunter Jesperson, at least I have gone some way to reunite him with Melissa, who had not written to Keith for years. But, of course, where they go from here is a personal matter between father and daughter.

There is something else, too: despite her struggle to comprehend how her beloved father become the Happy Face Killer, Melissa has married. She has found a quite wonderful man, and she now has children of her own. In the years to come, we will hear a lot more of her as, through the support of 'responsible' US TV, she is already an inspiration to all those who have been forced to endure the trauma of knowing that a father has become a monster.

*   *   *

This chapter is based on hundreds of letters from Keith Jesperson, documents, photos, correspondence from those close to him, and Keith's 'new' autobiography... which, I can majestically assure you, will not be published any time soon.

CHAPTER 5
VIVA LEROY NASH
THE OLDEST MAN ON
DEATH ROW

Viva LeRoy Nash is an example to us all. A total, heroic superstar. I love the guy. Even if they gas him, inject him or fry him, they can't kill the man.

Charles Bronson, Britain's most dangerous prisoner.

As my regular readers will already know, I speak as I find, so I make no exception here, and pushing the boat out even more, I love the old rascal to bits. Sure, LeRoy (as he likes to be called) is a silly old fool these days, and a tad inventive when the mood takes him, but decades on Death Row will only serve to further unhinge even the most fragmented of minds, as I am sure you would agree.

Sadly, the door to LeRoy's mind has long fallen from its rusty hinges and his sanity has all but bolted. It is absolute fact that he killed a cop, and shot to death a jewellery store clerk during a bungled robbery, and it is a tragedy that two lives were lost, with the pain and suffering heaped upon the next of kin, a sin. However, Mr Nash should never be on Death Row...he has done his time in spades, and if there is any forgiveness and compassion left in this world, LeRoy should be at the front of the queue when it is handed out.

Maybe I am being presumptuous here, but compared with JR Robinson, or the British sex-killer Ian Huntley, LeRoy is saintly. Actually, when you have read his story, you might want to write to him...even have him home for tea and give the old codger a big hug.

> *You could say that I'm on the Green Mile. This is my home, and it's kinda like a downmarket condo unit bordered not by flowers and the fancy trimmings of upscale USA. Hey, no! I shit you not, for the address is Death Row, Eyman Complex, ADC. My house is small, like a concrete box, all of 8 feet long, 6 feet wide, and maybe, at a guess, 8 feet high. Three concrete walls, ceiling and floor. My front door? Solid steel with a food hatch. Outside is another door enclosed by a brick wall. Like a submarine hatch, only my inner door can be opened when the outer door is locked. They built the cell especially for me.*
>
> LeRoy Nash, to the author.

Born as long ago as 1915, only five years later than Bonnie Parker of Bonnie and Clyde, Nash was already serving two consecutive life sentences for murder and robbery in Utah, when, at the astonishing age of sixty-seven, he escaped from prison in October 1982. Three weeks later, on Wednesday, 3 November, he entered a coin shop in north Phoenix, Arizona, and demanded money from store employee, Gregory West. Mr West bravely refused and pulled a gun, firing off a shot at the elderly robber. West's bullet missed Nash, who returned his fire and shot him with a .357 calibre Colt Trooper revolver, killing him.

In a letter to the author, dated 25 December 2001, the lively old jailbird gives his own account of the gunfight. He says: 'I saw the flash from his gun and instantly jerked my torso aside so his bullet would not hit me. It went past me and ploughed through the wall into a beauty salon next door. Four women ran aside and watched. But my bullet not only knocked his gun aside, so he couldn't shoot a second time, but the damned bullet bounced off his gun, entered his flank and went through his body, killing him.'

As LeRoy fled the scene, the proprietor of a nearby shop pointed a gun at him. The veteran hoodlum, despite his age, grabbed the weapon and struggled with the younger man. Police officers soon arrived and arrested LeRoy Nash.

Offering nothing in mitigation, Nash pleaded guilty at his trial, which was over in one day. Now, 26 years on, at the ripe old age of 93, he is seeing his days out on Death Row, Arizona State Prison at Eyman. One thing is certain, Nash, a survivor from a bygone era who has no sense of fear, will go to his execution – if that day ever happens – without a whimper. Having said that, the author nurses the hope that common sense will prevail and that he will be allowed to see out his days in better surroundings than 'the green mile'.

Correspondence between the author and Mr Nash has shown him to be an intelligent and articulate man. Despite a heart condition and a partially crippled right hand, he produces copious amounts of carefully worded information, using just the refill of a biro – the condemned are not allowed the plastic outers for fear of them being used as weapons – he reveals that he has led a full and interesting life. His account of his beginnings as a bank robber during the Great Depression is a wonderful piece of social history, but are all of his accounts of his days on the lam and his crimes really true?

This six-foot-tall, life's-chewed-upon-faced Nordic man describes himself as 'a natural explorer who has travelled both the American continents, looking at everything, especially Mexico City'. He says that he was formerly 'an Olympic-class athlete in the disciplines of swimming, tennis and running'.

For some reason, best known to the authorities, Viva Le Roy Nash, disabled and elderly with a heart condition, more recently enduring a major hip operation, is considered to be so dangerous that he lives in an escape-proof cell within a cell. Under lockdown, he is not allowed exercise privileges, media interviews or any visitors such as other inmates might have – or, that's what he says.

In his own words, he says, 'I am in solitary confinement 24 hours a day, every day,' adding, almost humorously, 'and I am partially hard of hearing.'

My pa went to war when I was six. He went off to fight the Russians, and he came home when I was twelve. Walked straight in and beat the shit outa me. See, you can take it from me what people want now's a good time, and they want it with a vengeance.

LeRoy Nash to the author.

On an overcast Friday, 10 September 1915, three months before Francis 'Frank' Albert Sinatra came into this world, Mrs Nash had a breech birth, on the outskirts of Salt Lake City, producing a howling son whom she named 'Viva' on account of her release from the suffering. 'That was me,' says Nash.

LeRoy's father was Wilbur Roy Nash, an uneducated man, but a professional auto mechanic and amateur home-builder. His mother, LeRoy describes as: 'Marie K. Nash, a beautiful, brainwashed control-freak, who had two children from a previous marriage; a son, Fred, born 1907, and a daughter: Elva, born 1905. LeRoy also had a true sister in Louise M. Nash, who was born in 1917. 'All of these people,' LeRoy adds, 'died of natural causes years ago. I married, had a son, and was divorced in 1960. She does not want to be mentioned in this book. Her privacy should not be violated or mentioned.'

The area where LeRoy was born and raised was in a 'wooded or farm area three or four miles south of Salt Lake City. That area is now overgrown with miles of new neighborhoods – about four suburbs,' he writes.

Reminiscing about those early days, LeRoy says almost with Country & Western music ringing in his ears:

I was about five years old. The big wagons that brought all the lumber and other building materials had, at the direction of my control-freak mother, who was there alone when it arrived, the men dump the loads on the side of the road, rather than down near where the house was to be built, because she didn't want the wagon wheels making deep furrows, and hundreds of horse hoof prints in her intended garden area.

The address of that old home, which is still there, and occupied today, was so well built it seems able to last forever. A five-room home with a full attic and half basement, at: 2847 South 5th East Street, South Salt Lake. Several other newly built homes were in that same area. At least twelve families where there when our dads went off to war, all of them from that area.

To put this period into perspective, time-wise, gun-toting John Dillinger was twelve years old. Alphonse 'Scarface' Capone, soon to become 'the Bootleg Emperor' was 16 years old and Bonnie and Clyde were still eating cookies and vanilla ice cream. In 1915, Pluto was photographed for the first time, Albert Einstein published his theory of relativity, George V was King of England, and Woodrow Wilson was President. The Mafia boss, John 'The eflon Don' Gotti – so named because very few criminal charges stuck – would not be born for another 26 years.

'Hey, you guys. I was fourteen at the time of the St. Valentine's Day Massacre [Thursday, 14 February 1929]' says LeRoy, and this was the time of the Great Depression; the era of bootlegging, moonshine, speakeasies and Eliot Ness of *The Untouchables* fame. Joe 'The Boss' Masseria was the most powerful gangster in New York; buried in a $15,000 casket, he had a cortege of 40 Cadillacs.

'But, names such as these were always front-page news, when I was young,' says LeRoy. 'I was one of the original "Angels with Dirty Faces",' he recalls. Reeling off a list of infamous criminals as if they were imprinted on his mind: Vito Genovese, Salvatore 'Lucky' Luciano; Paul Kelly's 'The Five Points Gang'; 'The Black Hand'; Benny 'Bugsy' Siegal; Peter 'The Clutching Hand' Morella; Ignazio 'The Wolf' Saietta, who ran 'The Murder Stable', where he systematically tortured and murdered his victims, were characters that everyone back then knew well.

'These were not cowardly, bottom-feeding guttersnipes who steal for small change and a mobile telephone, who pass themselves off as criminals today,' rails LeRoy. 'All of these names and many more were familiar to me. Then there were the enforcers such as Little Davie Betillo, the beautiful dolls and molls, beautiful, voluptuous sirens, Polly Adler, the raven-haired Virginia Hill, Igea Lissoni (an Italian ballet dancer at La Scala Opera), and countless more "CLASS A" acts that fell at the feet of the organised crime figures.'

By the age of twelve, LeRoy was already robbing stores. His father was overseas in the army. 'My family was destitute, along with about seven other families whose men were drafted into the army,' he says. 'None of us got any welfare or any other subsistence from the government. So, we boys joined forces when our families began starving and decided that, one way or another, our families were going to be fed. We all learned to be burglars, thieves, liars and sneaky people. There was no thought about our group violating the law. It was merely a matter of survival and to hell with anyone who didn't like it. Careering along in a stolen Model T Ford, me and my pals were so small we could hardly see over the steering wheel, and because we committed crime to help feed our families, we were called "The Angels with Dirty Faces".' The exploits of these kids inspired the 1938 Warner Brothers' movie of the same name, starring James Cagney and Pat O'Brien.

'That attitude carried over for years,' remembers LeRoy. 'Even after our fathers came home, got jobs and were supporting their families. By that time I was nearly twelve years of age and despised local cops and anyone else who disliked we kids, especially after word got round about our illegal proclivities. That led, eventually to my leaving home, completely ignorant of civilised social patterns of working for wages and knowing nothing about how people used electoral or commercial methods as natural rights that everybody was presumed to know.'

*   *   *

In those days, the Depression had crippled the country. After the worldwide flu epidemic had devastated the country along with most of Europe, there were millions of Americans out of work and hundreds of thousands of unemployed people, mostly men and boys, either living in the hundreds of hobo camps, spread across the USA, or riding the rails from town to town.

'There was a rule, at the time,' says LeRoy, 'that, if a father, or any breadwinner in a family had lost his job and had deserted his family, then that family was entitled to welfare, especially if children were involved.'

LeRoy is at pains to point out that they knew nothing at all about the US Constitution, or its attached Bill of Rights, back then, 'nor that we had as many legal rights as anyone else'. He adds: 'So, it should be no surprise that at least eight of the twelve boys in our "kid group" eventually were known convicts. Most of them became hobos or tramps, experienced at being down and out, homeless predators, rouges, vagabonds, common beggars, who felt complete contempt for the law, because of the brutality that many had experienced, or witnessed, while in various prisons.

'So, when a breadwinner lost his job and couldn't find employment, he deserted his family so that they could at least get welfare. That was one of the main reasons that thousands of men and boys were on the road. Every one of the major cities in America at that time had one or more "hobo jungles"'.

And many of those hobo jungles were of such a nature that the activities within them, seldom regulated by police, made them into some of the most degraded and lawless places in America.

Wishing to dispel any myths surrounding the hobo camps, LeRoy has this to say: 'The general public, at that time, and many still do, even today, had the romantic notion that there hobo jungles were places where impoverished men would share and share alike, in some fraternal style. Disenfranchised men who share equally? Wow! Not true. The only ones who shared were those who gathered together, in small groups, mostly for protection from crazed hopheads, mentally ill people or brutes of one kind or another. Many were sick dope addicts, many of whom were also active homosexuals. Hoboing, at that time, was considered by many people to be a marginally viable lifestyle for the intermittently employed. Towards the end of the Depression thousands of ignorant American youngsters joined the hobo life. Few recovered.

'However, the same wasn't true for the majority of Americans and tens-of-thousands starved to death during this era, many disappearing without trace, having perished from despair, hunger and exhaustion, separated by hundreds of miles from their homes and families. Homelessness was at epidemic proportions with banks foreclosing on mortgages and loans and repossessing houses and farms across wide swathes of the country. This was the era in which bank robbers, such as Bonnie and Clyde, and Pretty Boy Floyd were, for a time, regarded as folk heroes by much of rural America, enjoying the sort of status generally afforded to legendary figures such as Robin Hood.'

Thanks to his upbringing, if it could be called that, LeRoy was better able than most to adapt to living and surviving in the teeth of such adversity.

Some time during 1929, LeRoy returned home to his family on the outskirts of Salt Lake City. He was fourteen, but had already experienced life in a way that would have seemed daunting to men thirty or forty years older. There was little or no conventional work available at the time so he earned a living by becoming a bounty hunter, shooting mountain lions and other predators, in return for which the cattle ranchers of Utah paid good money. Eventually, however, after about a year, the wanderlust proved to be too strong and, when circumstances presented themselves, he embarked on another odyssey. This time, he headed out for the tents and shanties of the construction camps on the Colorado River: camps that housed the thousands of men who sought to work building the Hoover Dam.

LeRoy writes:

In 1930, I had gotten an old Model T Ford that had been rolled over and the body wrecked. I had just been paid bounties for two mountain lion skins, by the cattle ranchers association, up in central Utah, so I felt rich enough to buy that wrecked Ford and put a second body on it from another wreck. And then the good news came.

The 1929 Great Depression was sweeping across America. Everybody was broke. Thousands of men were heading out West toward the huge new dam that was being built, where Arizona and Nevada meet. They said it was to be the highest dam in the world, so they needed a lot of workers.

I had had a fight with my dad, and as a result, I packed my ragged clothes, my small box of tools and my 'lion gun', a model 98 Winchester 30-30 rifle, into the trunk of my 1928 Ford coupe and headed south, toward Black Canyon and the proposed Boulder Dam, later renamed the Hoover Dam. Six construction companies had joined forces to get the dam built, after Congress had authorized starter funds.

The nearest town was Las Vegas, 23 miles west of the dam site. But, the tent-town on the eastern side of Vegas was rapidly expanding, toward the river dam site. Then, another shack, tent and makeshift camp sprang up, much closer to the dam site, and rapidly became populated. They named this new settlement 'Boulder', and soon most of the 2,000 new dam workers were finding lodgings and meals there.

LeRoy was still only fifteen, and the employment manager called him 'Hurry up Crow', and refused to hire him, even at the lowest rate of two dollars a day, and told him to go back home.

I was so pissed off. I momentarily thought about shooting the big bastard. But, by the time I'd gotten back to Boulder and my little pup tent, I got another surprise. A fairly large shack had been erected near my little spot and the font of this shack had a sign on it, saying 'CAFÉ – Three Meals a Day $1.35', then 'In ADVANCE'. Beneath that sign was another, which said, 'No Niggers!!' I walked in. It looked like a saloon, but, instead of a bar, he had a long table with benches. I asked the man with the apron: 'How much for just one meal?' 'Fifty cents in advance,' came the brusque reply. I put two quarters on the table. The coffee was 5 cents extra. He bought me a good-sized bowl of stew. I finished half of it, then asked, 'How come there's no meat *in it?' He says, 'If I had meat I'd charge more.' The light came on in my head. 'How much would you pay, in cash, for fresh-killed venison?'*

From that day onward, the young Nash shot deer, earning 10 cents a pound of meat from Big Tom.

Although he says that he has no wish to glorify his crimes, he says that his 'history is most certainly the stuff of legends. By the age of eighteen I had already robbed two banks, lived the life of a juvenile hobo and killed my first man. I shot a hobo for squashing my pal's watermelon.'

This first murder took place when LeRoy says he was sixteen. (in much earlier letters he says was eight). He was riding in a boxcar with a friend, a fifteen-year-old kid. The train, which was proceeding slowly through Kansas, stopped momentarily to take on water next to a farm where many small, but ripe melons were growing. 'So, we both leapt down, grabbed a watermelon, and climbed back into the boxcar,' says LeRoy. 'I ate mine right there and then, being hungry, but my pal saved his.'

According to LeRoy, about an hour later, after passing through another town, where again the train stopped.

My friend cut open his watermelon and was greedily eating it, when a tall negro climbed into the boxcar. He stared and gruffly demanded a share of the melon. The tone of the big man's voice irritated my companion, who promptly told him, 'Go fuck yourself. Jump off the train and steal your own melon.' The negro blew up. Without a word, he kicked the melon so hard that it flew out of the boxcar. I was sitting on the other side of the boxcar, my feet dangling outa the doorway. Realising that a second kick, that hard, could send my friend, who only weighed about a hundred pounds, flying to his death, I pulled out my pistol that was under my belt, hidden by my jacket, and turned to defend my friend. But to my surprise, he had his own gun out. And he continued firing it into the body of the big man until he collapsed – all in all six shots. Then I fired my gun because life was cheap. I went through his pockets, found photos of his wife an' his young daughter in a ragged old pocket book. There was no address to send the stuff to…felt bad at first, then thought, 'FUCK IT'.

We kids at the time were all dead shots with either a pistol or a rifle. My favorite guns were a .45 Colt Auto and a 30-30 Winchester saddle gun, the barrel was four inches shorter than the regular rifle.

LeRoy Nash's adventures would fill a book on their own; in later years he escaped from two prison facilities. Aged 67, he says while serving two consecutive life sentences for murder and robbery, in Utah, he made a desperate dash for freedom. 'I scaled a twenty-foot prison wall, crossed no-man's land, and went through the razor wire perimeter as if it didn't exist,' he says. 'Yep! Got cut really bad, but never felt a thing.'

Dodging the marksmen's bullets and although badly injured by the steel barbs, he evaded bloodhounds and hundreds of police during one of America's largest manhunts.

Living off the land and what I could five-finger from the locals, I was physically and mentally well equipped for life on the lam. During my second week, I came across the

Highway Patrol. Casually strolling up to an officer, who was half asleep in his car, I disarmed him and tied him up. I stole his money and a .357 Colt Trooper revolver, and then drove off leaving the man sitting in a cloud of dust.

The cop just handed over his gun. It was as easy as picking up a warm pie from a stoop. He was just a fresh kid and had no right to be wearing a badge. Sure, I could have killed him right there and then. But I never killed nobody who never threatened me. That's the Gospel truth, I doubt that any bigoted Bible-thumpers will believe that.

Three weeks after my escape, on Wednesday, 3 November 1982, I entered a coin shop in north Phoenix. I demanded money from an employee called Gregory West, and then I shot the man three times with the cop's stolen gun. Another employee was in the line of fire but was not hit. As I fled, the proprietor of a nearby store pointed a gun at me and told me to stop. I grabbed his weapon and we struggled over it. Police soon arrived, and today I am on Death Row, and the system has finally closed me down.

At my trial, which lasted a day on 25 June 1983, before Judge Rufus Coulter, prosecutor, Gregg Thurston stated: 'Mr Nash presents a grave risk to others, shows no remorse and only the death sentence would be appropriate.'

Bank robber, jewel thief, I was once as fit as an Olympic class athlete. Sure, I have a face etched by the wrong side of the tracks. I am still a big, powerful man for my age. Once out of my cell, broad-shouldered, I stand tall. Fuck the guards, I rarely smile, but sometimes a cynical smile spreads across my face. Fuck them and fuck you, too.

*　　*　　*

But, who is the real Viva LeRoy Nash – is he really the true stuff of legends, or is he something else?

> *Petitioner* [Nash] *described himself as 'one of the most tenacious, jailhouse lawyers in the country' and recounted the '20-year span of constant and unwavering, and to some extent devastating, legal activities' upon which he had embarked as a prisoner in Connecticut.*
>
> US Supreme Court.

LeRoy has written over a hundred letters to me, and they are long, long, long letters. And, to be fair to this elderly man maybe we can forgive him for being vague about firm dates, and maybe his imagination does get the better of him from time to time, nonetheless, his history is the stuff Hollywood movie producer would die for.

He has no time for religion, and says that at one time he was an 'unknown millionaire' who helped many people who were far less well off than he at those times. He, like most incarcerated criminals, has no time for the American judicial system, claiming: 'In open court, both state and federal, I have politely but definitely kicked the verbal shit out of at least four of the perjuring bastards. But, I also admit, that in the long-run they got the best of me, judicially.'

When I took LeRoy to task over the shooting of Gregory West, which to me seemed a cold-blooded affair at best, he had this to say:

> *First, I did not kill him deliberately, which would have, if the killing would have been, a first-degree killing It was an accidental killing, and even under those circumstances,*

would have been second degree murder, or manslaughter, under our law, prohibiting the imposition of the death penalty.

The fact that Mr Nash shot and killed a man in the furtherance of a robbery, and that is a capital crime in Arizona, passes LeRoy by. He wrote nineteen pages, in a letter dated 9 March 2006, explaining how the judicial system was all wrong, that the cops and prosecutor fitted him up, and the judge was a crook, and it was all West's fault for trying to defend himself, despite conveniently overlooking another fact: he pleaded guilty in court, the reason for the one-day trial.

In a letter that followed days later, LeRoy tries to distance himself from responsibility even further. Itemising what he needs to say:

Note 1. That the clerk [West] might have fired directly toward my heart legally is contrary to American law.

Note 2. I had no intention of allowing the store clerk to murder me in an effort to save his boss some money.

Note 3. If a store clerk has already fired his gun aimed at my heart, I would be very stupid to let him take another shot.

Conveniently forgetting that the threat of deadly force may be met by the use of deadly force, LeRoy goes on, while at once pointing a handgun at Mr West:

Note 4. One of the known reasons of the standard prohibiting store clerks from shooting a suspect to death without any warning is that, if allowed to shoot first if a potential enemy had a gun, was because then any feuding store clerk could point a gun over the store counter, then promptly shoot him before he could ask, 'Why?'

Note 5. It is rather far-fetched for any store owner to hand a loaded gun to an untrained amateur employee, and to then consider he will only kill in order to save the boss some money.

Note 6. Mr West was not trying to merely get the better of me, he was deliberately trying to murder me so he would be a hero. I'd bet his wife thought that was kind of stupid, as well as suicidal.

Note 7. It should be illegal for any store manager to give a clerk a loaded gun and not send him to a class to learn to shoot it correctly and lawfully.

Having now admitted to the murder, LeRoy soon backtracked, saying that he didn't want to kill West, but that he nudged his arm and his gun fired, the bullet 'accidentally' hitting the clerk in the chest. LeRoy could not account for the other two shots that he fired into the man – going to write another fourteen pages explaining why it was an accident.

I also questioned LeRoy about his alleged daring escape over the high prison wall, through the razor wire, dodging the bullets and evading the police in one of America's largest manhunts. He had previously told me that he had been serving two life sentences for murder, however, the truth later emerged that, in reality, he was serving two five-years-to-life concurrent sentences for a 1947 conviction for assaulting a Connecticut police officer with intent to kill. The escape? He was working, unshackled, on a forestry crew, and made a run for it.

All of this information now puts LeRoy in an entirely different light. He is not the cold-blooded cop-killer he once portrayed himself as. His only murder was that of Gregory West, which he argues was an accident. Indeed this extremely successful jailhouse lawyer has managed to tie the Arizona judicial system up in knots for years – just as he did in Connecticut, a talent even acknowledged by the Supreme Court.

On Death Row, LeRoy says this:

I have never heard a death row inmate discussing his crimes. Everyone knows about me, but not the details. When I was acting as a paralegal, decades ago, I encountered mostly a bunch of sad people who were nervous and neurotic, afraid to discuss their case, for fear that other cons would hate them, often because their trial transcripts exposed them as gutless rats.

Yet there actually are a few good people in death row. But prison officials seldom know much about the prisoner's actual character.

On the other hand, alert prisoners hear a lot about prison psychiatrists, or psychologists; but most such professionals are used by prison officials for only one purpose: to learn if the prisoner is a danger to the prison administration in any way.

Most prison guards, the same as most prisoners, are uneducated, low-level people, incapable of worthwhile sociobiological cogitation; followers and freeloaders.'

So, what about his hunting adventures around the Hoover Dam? Sadly, this all seems to be the invention of our man's over-active imagination. At the age of fifteen, when he was supposed to be hunting deer around the Hoover Dam

construction project, his rap sheet shows that he was arrested
for riding in a stolen car and started serving a one-year plus six-
day prison term at the Ohio Federal Reform School, at
Chillicothe, from which he promptly escaped. A woman, living
nearby, heard the prison escape siren, spotted him, and he was
recaptured about four miles away.

LeRoy now found himself resentenced to a further one year
and a day, which he served at the Federal Prison at
Leavenworth, thirty miles from Kansas City. Here, under the
name of Roy Taylor, he says that he 'knocked a Mexican on his
ass because he groped my ass'. He adds: 'That brief action, in
the observable presence of four elderly prisoners who promptly
ordered a watching group of "Spanish gentleman" to stay out
of it, which they did. Courage-plus! So, to my delight, those
four old-timers were four of the most respected ex-professional
thieves in the whole prison. So I hung out during recreation
with them because they were educated in thieving on a
professional level, and I knew (I soon learned all the basics).'

But, according to Leroy, during the same sentence he was
placed in solitary confinement for 'knocking out four blacks
who tried to rape me. I put them in hospital', he writes,
adding, once again with more than a hint of invention, 'and
the fight turned into a full-bore riot involving at least 40 cons.
I served my whole sentence (his prison record says eight
months) in solitary.'

Whatever the case, he was released, aged seventeen, in 1932,
but was soon back serving a further four years for parole
violations.

And, the truth of shooting the hobo who stole LeRoy's pal's
melon, when he was aged eighteen? In later letters LeRoy seems
to have forgotten about the 'melon shooting' altogether. He

says he had learned all about jewellery and diamonds; teaming up with the Mafia he was 'making his bones' selling gems to jewellers. His first sale earned him $24,000 in cash. 'I bought a legal-size briefcase, second hand, big enough to hold my money, a clean shirt and my .357 Magnum, and a box of bullets.'

He then says he went out and robbed a jewellery store.

* * *

So, what do we make of Viva LeRoy Nash? Well, for all of his sins, and when we compare him with seriously heinous killers, this is a man who most certainly does not deserve to be living out his last days on the Green Mile. He is highly intelligent (his IQ is measured at 150), he is articulate, and a first-rate story-teller, therefore, after reading and re-reading his countless letters, it is almost impossible to sort the wheat from the chaff, the facts from the fiction.

This old rascal has an eye for a pretty girl. He hates the US judicial system with a vengeance, an institution which he's bamboozled for decades. As far as he is concerned the internet is 'full of shit'. That most authors 'especially American ones, are assholes who never get their facts straight'. And, what we read in newspapers is 'erroneous crap'. All cops are 'crooked', and judges and prosecutors are 'perjuring bastards'.

As for television? He reserves a special disgust for TV, and gives us the benefit of his thoughts, while at once complaining about news coverage of the New Orleans hurricane Katrina disaster of 29 August 2005:

There is a lot of fraud and blatant criminals, illegal information, plus degeneracy, on today's TV junk. Especially by those freaky religious scam artists. For example: last week, after watching a few camera shots of the wreckage, flooding, fires and destruction of the Katrina hurricane damage of New Orleans, especially the many dead bodies in the flood waters, our main TV station then allowed a goofy Christian minister to take over the microphone in New Orleans, and he began in a loud voice, waving his fists and yelling: 'God has destroyed New Orleans because of its habit of wanton sin, and bawdy houses and dens of corruption. He has smitten the evil city because of their indecent parades by the corrupt elements of their vile French Quarter. The hundreds of bodies floating in the flooded streets, or rotting in the ruined buildings attest to the power of our God we have dishonoured.' That ranting and raving of an obviously insane nature was by a famous southern preacher who is the son of a famed deceased preacher. After he had ranted and raved, he begged listeners softly to send donations to his church, giving their address, with the soft promise that 'our Christian group need help to do life-saving work at once'.

Yes, sir, God doesn't sit well with LeRoy at all. Referring to Iraq, he writes:

When our combined Forces in Iraq had won a series of battles, and many of the local military enemy holdouts had acted as if they had quit the war, and thousands of Iraq people were actually seriously considering adopting a new Constitution of their own making, God got into it again, supposedly loudly.

One of our regular TV ministers was seen loudly, and with happy exclamations with both hands reaching high, he screamed: 'Praise the Lord! At Last! God is at last going to have his way. The people of Iraq are finally going to adopt an honourable Christian-type of Constitution for their own country as a whole'.

Having got that bit off his chest, LeRoy slipped into top gear:

Even I, a supposedly vile convict on death row, recoiled in shock to hear such an idiotic scream by a famous Christian minister on our Sunday morning nationwide television. Muttering to myself: 'Damn! Doesn't that idiot realize there are thousands of devoted Muslims right here in our country?' And at least a few of them, respecting their own, will promptly report that idiotic statement to the Muslim Mullahs in Iraq. So what are we in America going to do about our own supposed Christian big-mouthed own ministers, and their satanic habits as dangerous as the idiotic and vile as the 'shaken baby' syndrome? Or other religious ideologies?

On 12 February 2010, just over a year before the second version of this book went to press, LeRoy Nash died of natural causes at the ripe old age of 94.

For my part, I was very fond of the old fella... Death Row inmate or not. Although one should not appear to be glorifying a man who commits murder, Nash had an endearing, never-say-die quality which marked him out from the spineless guttersnipes who knock over convenience stores and kill women and children indiscriminately for a handful of loose change. Compared to the other killers in this book, I found LeRoy Nash to be a breath of fresh air.

CHAPTER 6
MICHAEL BRUCE ROSS
THE ROADSIDE STRANGLER

There was nothing they could have said or done. They were dead as soon as I saw them. I used them. I abused them. I treated them like so much garbage. What more do you want me to fucking say?

Michael Ross, in a Death Row interview with the author,
26 September 1994.

It had taken years of lengthy correspondence, and Ross had written countless letters to me in his neat hand, then suddenly there he was, in person – Connecticut's only convicted serial killer.

Surrounded by three immaculately uniformed correctional officers, wearing starched light-khaki shirts, knife-edge creased trousers, and spit-and-polished boots, Ross, who looked almost antiseptically clean, was in full body restraints – handcuffs chained to a heavy belt, chains down to ankle chains – he shuffled along, his loose-fitting prison garb covering a plumpish physique. In life, Michael stood around 5ft 10in, and weighed about 140lb. In life he appeared bookish, which indeed he was, with his thin-rimmed spectacles perched high on the bridge of his nose. A well-read young man and polite too. But that was in life. Now he is long dead. He was executed by lethal injection on Friday 13 May, 2005, and that's the way he wanted it to be.

Michael was no dummy. He had the intellect. He enjoyed a bright intelligence and with an IQ of 150, became an Ivy League student at Cornell University. With a fresh complexion, a chubby face, a cheeky smile and mischievous eyes, he gave the impression of a stereotypical 'All-American' homespun boy. At face value, Michael was very much the boy next door; the type a girl's father might approve of his daughter dating. But, as all parents know, appearances can be deceptive. Michael was a sexual sadist who had raped six precious daughters before killing them.

During the course of my relationship with him for the purposes of writing this chapter and the making of a TV documentary, Mike added to this tally, by confessing, for the first time, to raping and killing two other girls, and having anal intercourse with the dead body of another.

*   *   *

Michael Bruce Ross was born in Brooklyn, Connecticut, on Wednesday, 26 July 1961, a Leo. He was the first of Daniel 'Dan' Graeme Ross and Patricia Hilda's (nee Laine) four children, the others being Donna, Kenneth and Tina. By all accounts, the marriage was a stormy one, and Patricia, a borderline schizophrenic, who would later twice run away from her husband, never hid the fact that she had been forced to get married because she had fallen pregnant with Michael. From the outset, her first baby was an unwanted child.

Family and friends have described Patricia as a woman who could be charming one minute and cold and calculating the next. She had spent time in the state's Connecticut Valley Hospital (CVH), at Middletown, and at another hospital in Norwich. A number of people who knew her had witnessed at first hand a volatile, manipulative woman who would takeout her resentment on her family, especially Michael, whom she blamed for ruining her life.

Mike remembered his mother's mood swings, which all of the children feared. For example, they couldn't understand how she could laugh after making them ill by feeding them bad meat. Or why she would ruin her two daughters' clothes with a box of dye. Spiteful, vicious and sadistic, bordering upon pathologically unstable, it was Patricia who tried to trick young Michael into shooting his pet dog, after convincing him that it was suffering, after a short illness. It transpired that she had tried to poison the dog too. She even set Michael's mattress on fire on the front lawn because she once caught him masturbating. So, by all accounts, Patricia Ross was 'the Mother from Hell'.

Yet, the four kids loved their mother, simply because she was their 'mom'. They grew to accept her mood swings, and learned to keep out of her way when she blew her top. Like unwanted pets, which return even meagre scraps of affection with devotion and loyalty, the children had to love her just to survive. As Keith Hunter Jesperson astutely points out: 'We cannot pick our parents, so we accept our situation as being normal. Only when we venture out in later life do we question our upbringing.'

Michael Ross explained this in an audio-taped interview with the author, and the authenticity of his account has been verified by one of his sisters:

We had what we called 'Mom Drills'. The first person up in the morning would go downstairs while the rest of us kids would wait and be real quiet and listen to what type of reception we'd get from our mother. And, if we got one kind of reception, we'd know how to act. An' I'll give you an example.

See, one day my sister, Tina, was setting the table, and, uh, there was six of us in the family, you know. So, she opened up the dishwasher to get six glasses, three in each hand. You know how you do it. You know, the glasses clink together. My mother went off. She was screaming and yellin', so we knew that was a bad day coming. You just knew how she was but we loved her.

The Ross children had little time for fun and games, and they were even discouraged from having any friends, or participating in after-school activities. With these restrictions in place, they had bonded into a tight-knit group for self-preservation and mutual support, although Michael was alienated because his brother and sisters erroneously believed that he was favoured as a 'mommy's boy'.

For his part, young Michael was very proud of his father, and the family egg farm business in Brooklyn, a town of some 7,500 residents in Windham County, Connecticut. 'Eggs Incorporated' would become the most important part of Mike's formative years. Indeed, by the age of ten, he had his own set of chores, which included wringing the necks of sick and deformed chicks. He was a hard worker, a mixed-up kid who desperately wanted to live up to his father's high expectations of him, while, at the same time, he was very much seeking the approval of his schizoid mother, and constantly vying for her rare affection.

And, when the author asked him if he was physically abused as a child, he had this to say:

> *It's hard for me to tell you what was wrong with my family because I don't know anything different. That's how I was raised. I was beaten sometimes but I don't think that was it. It was more emotional abuse, an' like I mean with my dad when we were beaten, we would have to go out an' pick up a stick out of the garage where we had a woodpile. An' what you would do was to go out and you couldn't pick one that broke 'cos if it broke he'd get pretty mad. But, you didn't pick yourself a club. You know, you didn't want to get the hell beaten outa you. An' so I had my own stick put away, hidden away in the back so that people coming in to get firewood wouldn't inadvertently take it. But, I mean there is something wrong there when a kid goes to the wood house and picks up his stick; his own stick for getting beaten. And, he hides it so no one accidentally takes it. And, you know if you got beat you didn't scream because my father just got madder.*

So, it now seems that Mr Ross was no great shakes, either!

Michael loved his parents despite the physical and psychological abuse they handed out in spades, but the effects of such treatment on the developing mind are often irreparable unless drastic countermeasures are taken to remedy the problems.

Many psychiatrists and psychologists now generally agree that if contact and interaction with others in a peer group are restricted during the early stages of infant development, the ability to interact successfully at a later stage in life is retarded. That is, the limbic nuclei in the brain will not develop normally and gross mental abnormalities may result. Children will lose the ability to form emotional attachments with others, or any attachment that does come about may only be superficial, and this abnormality may last for the rest of their lives.

Michael Ross certainly had this problem. During an FBI study of serial sexual murderers, 53 per cent of the subjects' families had a history of psychiatric problems, 42 per cent of the subjects had been subjected to physical abuse, and 74 per cent had a psychological abuse history.

*　　　*　　　*

In September 1977, after a period of schooling, at the ironically named Killingly High School, about 3.5 miles west of Brooklyn, Michael's future looked decidedly bright as he drove his car on to the Cornell University campus in Ithaca, New York. The 16-year-old had overcome long odds, and was justifiably proud of himself, as only 10 per cent of Killingly High's vocational agricultural students went to college. Fewer still attended Ivy League schools.

At Cornell, Ross enrolled as an Animal-Science major, and he started a course of study that would well suit his ambition to become the third generation to run the family poultry business. This was an obsession with Michael and, for a short time, his fraternity brothers even called him 'The Egg King'.

Michael joined the Agricultural Student Union Council (AgPAC), and attended the Collegiate Future Farmers of America (FFA). He became a student teacher, counsellor, researcher, teaching assistant, and a study group leader around this time. Alpha Zeta, one of the two campus fraternities dedicated to agricultural activity, recruited Ross, and he pledged to them. He lived in the fraternity house throughout his sophomore and junior years with his 'brothers', who were mostly young men with small town farming backgrounds. He rarely cut class, and was known as an 'all-nighter' because often he swotted all night.

Since his incarceration for multiple murders, however, a number of Michael's former Cornell friends said that while he enjoyed the house, its social life, and the chance to share common interests, they also recall that he could be a loner, aloof and somewhat arrogant at times.

The student body of Cornell (today it stands at around 20,000) was almost three times larger than the entire population of his hometown of Brooklyn, subsequently, the campus became an expansive playground for Michael Ross. Now free from his mother's unpredictable influence, he could do whatever he wanted, without fear of reprisal. He literally went crazy with all the fun he was having, plunging headlong into the party life to the extent that he started taking Ritalin three times a day to control his hyperactivity. He would continue to use this drug for a further six years. He now drank heavily and he started to experiment with sex, often sleeping with different girls four nights a week (which Keith Hunter Jesperson suggests is 'normal college behaviour').

During his first junior year at Cornell, Mike met his first true love, the pretty Connie Young. They always say that 'love is blind' and 'beauty is in the eyes of the beholder', and if Ross was somewhat of an unattractive, lanky, thin and bespectacled youth, he must have considered Connie a 'real catch' when they met at a party. She was window-display CoCo Chanel, while he was Fred Myer. He walked her home through the moonlight, and according to Michael, they 'kissed as we watched a team of divers swimming in the shimmering silver water of Beebe Lake'.

According to campus lore, if a couple walks the entire mile-long footpath around Beebe Lake holding hands, they are destined for marriage. They strolled to the statues of the college's founding fathers, and he explained how they were supposed to move together and shake hands when a virgin passed between them. On this occasion, the statues apparently did not move, for 'Connie was hotter than a kitchen stove', Michael recalled.

Connie remembers Michael as a 'go-getter', and a guy who always liked to be 'the centre of attention'. At first she accommodated this behaviour because he seemed a worthwhile prospect for a permanent relationship, even marriage, if the legend surround Beebe Lake had anything to do with it. She certainly overlooked his arrogance and constant boasting about his father's egg farm. In Connie's eyes, he was handsome, if just a little nerdy. He was articulate, took her dancing and dined her out. She recalls that he always had money when he needed it and, for his part, he enjoyed taking her places to show her off. To everyone who knew them, they seemed the perfect couple, and most were thrilled when they became engaged to be married. Maybe the legend of Beebe Lake wasn't hogwash after all?

For a short period Connie shared Mike's bed... then the arguments started. His fraternity brothers threw him out of the house because he was breaking the rules by sharing his room with a female. As a result of this, the couple rented a small apartment where Michael withdrew into himself. The schooling pressure and the demands made by the close relationship with Connie had started to take their effect. Added to this were his parents' escalating marital problems, and these were clouding his judgement over the future, as home issues were never far from his mind.

Connie's distress over her lover's change of attitude came to a head when he started to miss classes. She was a dedicated student, trying to cram four years of education into three, but Michael Ross seemed to have lost interest, and he started to hang around their apartment all day, watching television and reading pornographic magazines. He changed his major, to Agricultural Economics, and his grades plummeted. He became bone idle, expecting Connie to do all the housework and cooking and, despite the fact that she was exhausted after studying, he demanded sex with her at least four times a day.

Initially, Connie complied with Michael's priapic demands, for fear of rejection. She loved him deeply, and even allowed him to have rough sex with her, although it was very painful and hurt her badly. Then, as the day-to-day events became even more unpleasant, she now started to wonder if marrying Mike was such a good idea after all. He was, she now believed, sex mad and getting worse. With his graduation approaching in the spring of 1981, Michael could not face the prospect of leaving Connie behind at Cornell, and he became even more restless and agitated, withdrawing for much longer period into a fantasy dream world of his own.

Michael has admitted to me, in correspondence, that even as a pre-teen, he had experienced constant fantasies about women when he would take them to what he called 'a special underground place', where he hid them, and kept them so that they could fall in love with him. From juvenile records, it is known that, at the age of fifteen, he molested several neighbourhood girls. Now an adult, his fantasies grew even more sexually extreme and progressively more violent. During these fantasies, he says that he was always the assailant and, by the time of his graduation, Connie had joined his faceless dream victims. He terrorised his fantasy girls and humiliated them by forcing them to undress and drop to their knees in front of him. He said that he gained enormous sexual pleasure and relief from raping his fantasy victims. He savoured the sense of domination that accompanied their fear, and he reasoned that he had control over real women, too, even though these bizarre thoughts were still locked away inside his mind.

Whatever dreadful though patterns were developing inside Michael's head during that period in his life, it seemed that there was a meeting between his distorted subconscious thinking and the bland reality of everyday life. He had now reached a crossroads, where two roads met, for not only did Ross overlay the beautiful face, and body, of Connie onto his fantasy victims, his demands for kinkier sex from her began to spiral out of all control. And, despite sex with her four times a day, he masturbated himself raw. Although he did not know it, he was suffering from satyriasis, an abnormally intense and persistent desire in a man for sexual intercourse. In women, the compulsion is called nymphomania.

More and more, Michael found himself wandering aimlessly around the campus. He became titillated by stalking female co-eds, staying just far enough behind them to remain undetected. He explained, 'This turned me on so much I always had a hard-on.' To release this almost uncontrollable compulsion, he had to masturbate ever more frequently, or else tip right over the edge, and act out his fantasies in reality.

Aged 20, Ross crossed that threshold in April 1981, when he found himself running up behind a co-ed, grabbing her and dragging her into a small copse where he forced her to act out his fantasy of stripping naked before him and giving him oral sex. After he ejaculated, he said that he ran off into the night, swearing to himself that he would never do such a terrible thing again.

Just three nights later, he was revisited by the same uncontrollable demon and, overcome with sexual compulsion, and now unsatisfied by masturbation, he attacked a second co-ed. During this assault, for which he was better prepared, he slipped a rope around the student's neck, enjoying the heightened power this form of restraint bestowed on him. The terrified girl was an animal he could control with a quick tug of his hand. Fortunately, someone approached the scene before he raped her and he fled into the shadows, his sexual frustrations still boiling inside him.

Michael has said that he firmly believed that these outrageous acts would cease after he left Cornell, and that he prayed that he could last out the final month without attacking anyone else. At the same time, he says he also felt, 'cheated of the ultimate sexual satisfaction', which had been denied him. Weighing up all the pros and cons of his distorted mental balance sheet, he said he was 'compelled' to satisfy himself 'fully', at least once before he graduated, but he promised himself that would have to be the final attack, after which he would never hurt a woman again.

But there is an important factor to be considered here, and it is this. The observation raised by serial killer Keith Hunter Jesperson is, basically: 'Did Mr Ross tell you that he really promised himself that he would never attack a woman again, or is he saying this to blow smoke in your yard, Chris? Ross was now hooked on rape and control over women. The guy was a fuckin' control freak, so this is all bullshit from him. It's BULLSHIT!'

Maybe this is not exactly a professional appraisal, but it does kind of make sense.

*   *   *

On Tuesday, 12 May 1981, Ross stalked a pretty 25-year-old student called Dzung Ngoc Tu. He followed the young woman from her class. She was petite, slim, even tiny, with perfect white porcelain features and long, glossy back hair cascading down to her waist. As she walked through a secluded area of the campus, he approached her, and then raped her. However, during the attack, she recognised him and, when she told him this, she effectively signed her own death warrant. To avoid arrest, Ross had no option other than to kill her, so he put his hands around her neck and strangled her before throwing her body over a stone-arch bridge and into Beebe Lake.

A chilling fact of this homicide was that, during the autopsy, the medical examiner determined that the cause of death was by drowning, indicating that Dzung had been alive when she plunged into the water. Although Ross had always been suspected of committing this murder, he never allowed himself to be interviewed by police. The case was finally cleared up when he admitted the crime to the author during a filmed interview for a TV documentary in Somers Prison, Monday, 26 September 1994.

Michael believed that his parents attended his graduation ceremony only for appearance's sake and he decided, from that moment, not to return to the family farm. However, when I put it to him that his parents had financially supported him at Cornell, he failed to comment! Nevertheless, by a stroke of good fortune, despite his poor grades, he managed to land an enviable job, in June 1981, with Cargill Inc.

According to the company's website, Cargill, whose byword is 'Nourishing Ideas, Nourishing People', is an, 'International provider of food, agriculture and risk management products'. They are 'committed' to using their 'knowledge and experience to collaborate with customers to help them succeed'. The firm is best known for grain sales, and Ross found himself employed at one of the company's more modest operations, in Louisburg, a country town about thirty miles north-east of Raleigh, North Carolina. As a production-management trainee in the poultry products division, Michael was taught how to supervise the 'care and management' of a quarter of a million laying hens. It was a plumb job, well-suited to him, his career prospects with Cargill were excellent. But he soon managed to ruin it.

During the transitional period between graduation and full-time employment with Cargill, Michael tried to convince Connie to transfer to the North Carolina University, where, he suggested, she could complete her studies. Over the preceding months, their relationship had so deteriorated that he was now paranoid about the looming separation and feared that she would soon be gone for good. Nevertheless, he was secretly hopeful they would marry one day. But Connie had ideas of her own, and marriage was no longer one of them; besides, unbeknown to Michael, she was now dating someone else.

Then a thermonuclear bomb dropped on Michael's world when he learned over the phone that his mother and father had separated for the third time, with Mr Ross leaving the family home, and business, to its own devices. The mentally unstable Patricia flew to Louisburg, and Michael was pleased, if not surprised, to see his mother so quickly after learning the bad news. Mistakenly, he thought this visit was a belated sign that his relationship with his mother might improve. At the very least, he wanted to believe that she would keep Eggs Inc going until he returned home to take charge, if only for his father's sake. This thought, however, was the furthest thing from Mrs Ross's devious mind, for she had, in fact, come to visit her son for one reason only. She needed Michael to sign over his shares in Eggs Inc so that she could dispose of the company, while becoming rich into the bargain.

Michael was suckered. He was duped into signing the share transfer, and soon after learning of the true reason behind his mother's impromptu visit, he felt he had betrayed not only his father but himself; added to which were his dreams of becoming the third generation of Ross's to run the family egg farm – something he had dreamt, and boasted about for years – now lay in ruin. Mike was mad, and justifiably so.

That wasn't the end of it by a long chalk.

Life for Michael was made even worse when Connie flew to North Carolina with more bad news. Of course she never could, in her wildest nightmares, have known that Mike was now a serial rapist and killer; a young man whose life's dreams about running Eggs Inc lay in shattered fragments. For her, the trip was to be short and not so sweet. She explained that she didn't like his parents one bit, and even if he did end up running the family egg business, this wasn't exactly her idea of a future. The finality of the relationship hit home on Tuesday, 25 August 1981 when, at Raleigh Durham Airport, the couple fell into each other's arms, sobbing their farewells. Mike could not bring himself to believe that his relationship with Connie was finished, so he was understandably distraught as he drove back along Highway 410 to Louisburg.

*   *   *

Location: Rolesville, a small town with a bright future in Wake County, North Carolina. Population: circa 900, in 1981. It is a place where decent people live and are very proud of their close-knit community. It is a place which is simply proud to be Rolesville. That is the 'American way'. And it is a community where serious crime does not exist: that was until around 6.30pm, when Ross passed through Rolesville where he spotted a young woman pushing her seven-month-old child in a buggy along Main Street, which sits on Highway 401.

Within milliseconds of spotting the woman – whose name has been withheld for obvious reasons – the demon inside Ross's head surfaced again and, after parking his car, he ran up to the woman and offered to carry her groceries. The young mother, used to such a secure environment, did not hesitate when this helpful and seemingly decent chap approached her. She thanked him for his offer and passed over her heavy carrier bags. They walked to her home several blocks away and, as they entered the backyard, and out of sight or prying eyes, Ross suddenly metamorphosed from helper into monster. He dropped the groceries...whipped off his leather belt...threw it over the woman's head...dragged her into a nearby soya bean field, while threatening to smash the baby's head against a tree if it didn't stop crying.

The woman now became an innocent depository for the months of Ross's pent-up anger and sexual frustration. He smashed his fists into her face...he choked her with his belt, forcing her to her knees to beg for mercy. Then with his hands tightly grasped around her neck, he ejaculated.

After regaining his breath, Ross sat back on the ground with his victim squirming around in front of him. Somehow he felt cheated again, for he had wanted to satisfy his perversions by ejaculating as she died...just like he had played out in his previous fantasy moments back in his teens and at Cornell.

Enraged, acting like a wild animal, he ripped off this young mother's clothes, beating her again and again before reapplying his grip around her throat while the baby screamed close by.

And, as suddenly as he had appeared, Michael Ross vanished.

It was over an hour before his victim regained consciousness. Painfully, she crawled across the dirt to a street, where a neighbour summoned the local police chief, Nelson S Ross. Officers arrived almost immediately and roadblocks were set up to the Wake County lines. But Ross was long gone. He was not charged with this offence until he was arrested in Connecticut, three years later.

When asked by the author if he recalled the Rolesville attack, Michael said:

I don't really remember her, or any of my victims for that matter. It's like an old black and white movie; a collage of strange faces, that's all. Nope, I couldn't remember this woman if you had showed me her photograph the next day. There was nothing she, or any of them, could have done when I zeroed in on them. They were dead. All over. This one that lived [the Rolesville victim] *ain't got nothing to do with me. That she lived? Well, that was purely an act of God.*

When I asked Ross if the Rolesville woman fought back, and tried to escape, he replied:

Nothing. She could have got away or something, but it never happened. I can't remember. I can't remember any kind of struggling with her or anything like that. I can't remember, uh, any kind of fighting at all. I do recall, with the Rolesville victim, saying that I would smash the baby's

*head into a tree or a wall. So, I would imagine I probably
said things equally horrible to, uh, the other ones that
would make them stop and think not to do anything.*

Ross simply carried on with his daily existence as if nothing
untoward had happened in Rolesville. Then, on Tuesday, 17
September 1981, his parents filed divorce papers at Windham
County Superior Court. A week later, Michael's employer,
Cargill, sent him on a field trip to Illinois, where he would visit
the Chicago Commodities Exchange. Before this trip was over,
Ross would be arrested for the first time.

He decided on Monday, 28 September, to look over the
Cargill operation in La Salle, which is about eleven miles south-
west of Chicago. He rented a car at Chicago's O'Hare
International Airport, and headed west across the flat, central
Illinois farm country.

Just before 11.00pm, an attractive sixteen-year-old La Salle
girl was walking along a road that threaded through a cluster
of houses, when she noticed a car creeping slowly past her. She
had noted the vehicle several times beforehand, and she was
now becoming frightened for her safety.

Without warning, the teenager was suddenly grabbed from
behind and a handkerchief was stuffed into her mouth. She was
dragged into nearby woods where the attacker wrapped a belt
around her neck and asked her for her money. She gave him the
22 cents she had and, when he loosened his belt, she screamed.
She was now moments from a terrifying rape when salvation
arrived. A woman living nearby had just switched off her
television, with the intention of going to bed when she heard a
noise that made her blood chill. Opening the kitchen window,
she heard a gurgling sound and rustling in nearby bushes, so she

called the police. Luck was on the teenager's side, even more so because a patrol car was only 100 yards away, and it arrived on the scene in a flash. When Ross saw the beams of police Mag-Lites illuminating the woods, he hurried back to his car but, this time his luck deserted him.

Sergeant Lewis of the La Salle Police explained how Ross got himself arrested: 'What happened is, when we took the girl home, Ross had his car parked on the same street where she lived on. And, on the way home, she saw the car, and said, "That's the car, that's the car." And, so pretty soon we were looking at the car, and he comes up and says, "What's the problem?"'

After Michael's arrest, for 'unlawful restraint', Sergeant Lewis said that he was puzzled by the contradiction between Ross's demeanour and what he had done:

He was real humble. He wouldn't look you in the eyes when you talked to him. He was a very educated and a talented kid. He didn't appear to be the kind of guy who would go out to other towns and do this kind of stuff. He more or less kept his mouth shut, and he was subdued and spiritless when we took him in.

The downside of the La Salle attack was that Ross was fined $500 after pleading guilty and, on Tuesday, 8 October, he was fired from his job. On the upside, and with no alternative, he returned to Brooklyn where he attempted reconciliation with Connie. Indeed, he was very pleased when she invited him to spend Christmas with her at her parents' home in Vermont. He was even more delighted that they had also been invited to share the New Year with his mother in Brooklyn.

Unfortunately, the visit to Mrs Ross was an unmitigated disaster. His mother couldn't stand the sight of such a beautiful young woman in her house, and Mike was very upset by the fact that his father had been reduced to living in a rundown shed nearby. The hoped-for rekindling of his relationship with Connie failed, for the second time, and she took off for Ithaca, New York, to visit a 'friend', and this proved to be the catalyst that precipitated Ross into rape and murder again.

*   *   *

Brunette, seventeen-year-old Tammy Lee Williams lived with her family in an expansive property on Prince Hill Road, Brooklyn, which was only a mile or so from the Rosses' egg farm. That Christmas, among the presents she received from her parents, was a pocketbook. A free-spirited young woman, who had quit high school, she came and went more or less as she pleased, and it wasn't unusual for her to walk east along Route 6, to visit her boyfriend who lived in Danielson, about three miles away.

At 10.15am, on Monday, 4 January 1982, Tammy left her boyfriend's apartment and started to walk home, after first promising him that she would telephone him to let him know that she had arrived safely. She did not fulfil this promise because she encountered Michael Ross on her journey. He was surprised to see the young woman walking along a busy road on such a bitterly cold day. Seizing the moment, which distinguishes the opportunist serial killer, he parked his car and ran up to Tammy offering her a lift. When she declined, he dragged her screaming and struggling into nearby woods, where he forced her to strip and get to her knees. He raped and strangled her before hiding the body, under a pile of rocks, in a swamp. He said it took him all of eight minutes to throttle her to death, because he kept getting cramp in his hands. Each time this happened, he had to release his grip and massage his fingers before finally throttling the life out of her.

Tammy's father reported his daughter as missing the next day and, on 6 January, a motorist found Tammy's pocketbook, lying along Route 6, at the junction of Brickyard Road, and exactly one mile from Tammy's home. He explained that he had thrown the item out of the car before arriving at his mother's place shortly after the murder.

On Saturday, 30 June 1984, Ross guided police officers to the decomposed corpse of Tammy Williams, and said later that she had recognised him and that she pretended to enjoy the violent rape to avoid being killed. He also said that he returned to the corpse several times, during the weeks following the murder, in order to masturbate over the body.

During January and February, 1982, Ross's thoughts continually returned to Connie. Acting on impulse, he decided to drive to Ithaca to visit her, without prior warning of his intentions. On arrival, he found Connie in bed with another man. He stormed out in a rage and headed south in search of a victim to kill.

May Day fell on a Monday in 1982 and Paula Perrera left Valley Central High School early because she didn't feel well. With no money for a bus fare, she started hitchhiking, and she was last seen alive near Montgomery Auto Shop, on Route 211, during the early afternoon. Paula's mother, Christine Canavan, reported her sixteen-year-old daughter as missing to the Crystal Run Police later than day.

Those in Orange County, New York, who knew Paula couldn't help but like her. She had short, blonde hair, was a bubbly, confident, carefree girl who performed well in school, enjoyed the company of her tight-knit group of friends as much as a good book and was active in the church youth group. According to a November 2000 article in *The Times Herald-Record* by Oliver Mackson, Paula 'never complained' even though she was known to have had an unhappy home life.

Despite her normally cheerful demeanor, Paula's problems at home peaked in 1981 leading to her unsuccessful attempt at suicide by overdosing on pills. From that moment on, while on the bus en route to school the kids mockingly called Paula 'Tylenol' but she refused to let the comments get to her. On many occasions she chose to bypass the school bus altogether and instead hitchhiked to classes, and even though Paula's boyfriend begged her not to hitchhike because of the inherent dangers, she ignored his pleas claiming that 'Only nice people pick me up.'

Although Ross had always been the prime suspect in Paula's killing, there had never been enough evidence available to charge him with her murder, a situation exacerbated by the fact that Ross point-blank refused to be interviewed by police investigators while he was on Death Row. This changed when Ross was subsequently interviewed by the author, on camera, for a TV documentary and the chapter in this book. Confronted by me with police documents, he revealed information that only Paula's killer would know. He made a full and frank confession, and the case is now classified as solved.

He said that he had seen her walking along Route 211, and had offered her a ride home. At a spot near a marshy wooded area, and close to a rest stop, he pulled over and raped his victim before strangling her. He hid her body near a low stone wall, and close to a large willow tree, and then drove home. Asked during the interview what Paula had been wearing, he said that he could not recall the details and tossed the documents to the floor, saying, 'Well, it's just another murder, isn't it?'

* * *

Ross started work at Croton Egg Farms on Friday, 5 March 1982. The world's largest poultry operation, based in the small town of Croton, north-east of Columbus, Ohio, hired him as a co-supervisor for thirty employees. He was also responsible for fourteen hen houses and over one million birds.

A fellow supervisor, Donald Harvey, remembered Ross, saying:

He was a disaster in the job, and we were planning to fire the guy pretty soon. He was very bossy. And he just didn't relate to you in giving an order. He just didn't know how to come across. He wanted everyone to know that his education was higher then theirs and they were hourly workers and high school drop outs.

On Sunday, 25 April 1982, Ross spotted Susan Aldrich in a laundromat in Johnstown, a small town six miles south of Croton, and followed her home. She was completely unaware that she was being stalked; he was completely unaware that she was an off-duty police officer. He knocked on her door and told her that his car had broken down and asked if he could use her telephone. As soon as Susan turned her back, he reached over her shoulder, cupped his hand over her mouth to prevent her screaming, and forced her to the floor. She struggled and managed to shout out, saying that her husband was a policeman, and that he would be home at any minute. After giving her a severe beating, Ross ran back to his car, ripped a parking ticket from the windscreen and drove off.

Ross's car had been parked close to the laundromat, and it was there that he got the ticket. Police also found a witness who saw him running from the direction of Susan's home towards his vehicle, so they put two and two together and traced the owner through the Vehicle Licensing Office. In an act of poetic justice, it was Susan's husband who arrested her attacker.

Ross was sacked from Croton Egg Farms on 3 May, and bailed to his mother's home before sentencing. While there, he visited a psychiatrist at the Learning Clinic at 473 Pomfret Road, Brooklyn. He was trying to win a little sympathy from the doctor, who might have influence with the Ohio court.

The following month was another disaster for Michael Ross, for, although he had returned a number of photographs to Connie, she still had his engagement ring and he wanted it back. However, the day before he turned up to collect it, she set off across country to marry her new boyfriend. When Ross learned of this, he went crazy with anger. But, if that slap across the face was hard to take, a family development enraged him even further.

Financially, his mother's divorce had paid off handsomely. When Patricia flaunted her new lover before speeding off in her flashy new Cadillac, it was too much for Michael. These emotional setbacks coming so close together were sufficient to set him off on the murder trail again.

*   *   *

The last time anyone could recollect seeing 23-year-old Debra Smith Taylor alive was around midnight on Tuesday, 15 June 1982. The vivacious, dark-haired brunette was driving home with her husband when their car ran out of fuel on Highway 6, near Hampton, just 6.5 miles east of Mrs Ross's home. A State Trooper came across the stationary car and drove the couple to a service station in Danielson, where the boyfriend of one of Ross's earlier victims, Tammy Williams, had lived. The Trooper recalled that the Taylors were arguing, and that Debra was so annoyed that she said that she would find her own way home. After leaving her husband to his own devices, she walked across Danielson Town Green, to the bandstand, where she gratefully accepted the offer of a ride home from a bespectacled young man who had walked up and spoken to her.

Two hunters discovered Debra's skeleton on Saturday, 30 October, in one of the largest tracts of woodland east of Route 169, in Canterbury, ten miles south of Danielson. The body was so decomposed that identification was only possible by means of dental records and items of jewellery.

During the first week of August 1982, Ross returned to Ohio for sentencing over the assault he had committed four months previously. The psychiatrist who had examined him earlier said that Mike was an 'over-achiever', and had 'too much spare time on his hands'. In his report, the psychiatrist also suggested that he should find a hobby, such as learning how to fly an aeroplane. The judge nevertheless packed Ross off to the Licking County Jail, Newark, where he would serve a six-month jail term for the attack on Susan Aldrich. He was ordered to pay a $1,000 fine. Daniel Ross collected his son from prison on Wednesday, 22 December, drove him back to Connecticut, where he offered him a place to stay.

Michael Ross had misrepresented when he applied for work with Croton Egg Farms by declaring that he had never been in trouble with the police, and he did exactly the same thing again in May 1983, when he applied for a job with the Prudential Insurance Company of America. He would become one of the 40 agents selling health, life, automotive, property, casualty insurance and securities, from the company's office, at 115 Lafayette Street, Norwich. With steady money in his pocket, Ross rented a ground-floor apartment at 58 North Main Street, in Jewett City, some nine miles south-east of Norwich. He settled in, and his former landlady remembers him as a 'decent, smart and extremely affable young man', whom she enjoyed having around her large, Victorian-style, white-painted house.

Ross's female work colleagues also took an immediate liking to him. They thought of him as, 'kinda sweet, and inexperienced in romance'. He dated when the opportunity arose, and when he met recently divorced Debbie Wallace, while out canvassing for business, he reasoned that his past problems were well behind him.

During this relationship, Ross said that he spent a great deal of time masturbating, fantasising and stalking women. Some he followed at random. With others he set out to learn their daily schedules. He slipped into apartments, just to watch women undress and get into bed. On one of these occasions, he raped a 21-year-old Plainfield woman called Vivian Dobson, but allowed her to run away. In later years, the compassionate and devoutly Christian Vivian became a vocal opponent of the death penalty in an effort to save his life – despite a 22-year ordeal of psychiatric wards, medical bills, and emotional trauma following her rape. However, the Plainfield police rejected the possibility that Ross had been Vivian Dobson's rapist. They did not press charges and Ross made no confession.

Although he was often out until all hours of the morning,

Debbie Wallace was totally ignorant of Michael's perverted behaviour. She believed that he would make a good father for her three children; however, like Connie, Debbie was stubborn, independent and strong-willed. She was a spitfire, full of energy, and sex with Mike was excellent. Their relationship was volatile, too, and their frequent arguments often ended in physical violence. During Thanksgiving 1983, the couple had a furious fight over dinner arrangements.

From the outset, Patricia Ross had never liked Connie, and she didn't approve of Debbie either, so she invited her son for a meal and refused to extend the invitation to Debbie. Ross did not know what to do. He felt torn between the two women, so he and Debbie fought and the outcome was that he spent the holiday alone.

Around the time Ross was learning the insurance business, nineteen-year-old Robin Dawn Stavinsky was moving from Columbia to Norwich, where the attractive blonde hoped to find a job that paid enough to allow her to go to college.

In August 1983, she had taken up employment as a switchboard operator at Direct Part Marketing Enterprises (DPM), a company that specialised in bar code technology. At 9.30pm on Wednesday, 16 November 1982, she disappeared after apparently arguing with her boss. Although it was cold and dark, Robin refused a ride from a workmate and, in what proved to be a fatal mistake, decided to walk to her boyfriend's house.

That evening, Ross was driving along Route 52 between New London and Norwich, when he saw Robin storming along the roadside. He stopped, climbed out of his car and approached her with the offer of a lift. When she rebuffed him, he became angry and dragged her struggling into a patch of dense woodland just a few hundred yards from the office of the Connecticut State Police Major Crime Squad. Ross had started to strangle Robin as soon as he grabbed her, and by the time he was ready to rape the young woman, she was barely conscious. Ross recalled that by now he was no longer excited by the idea of sex, and his satisfaction came about only from the act of killing, and by reliving the moment, occasionally driving by the murder scene and masturbating, until the body was discovered eight days later.

A jogger, running through the grounds of the Uncas-on-Thames Hospital in Norwich, found the partially clothed corpse of Robin Stavinsky under a pile of leaves. Police retrieved the remainder of the dead woman's clothing from the Thames River, after Michael's arrest.

The brutal murder of Robin Stavinsky was to prove a dreadful watershed in Ross's killing career. Previously, he had murdered out of the fear of recognition if his victims survived. However, he had always hoped that one day he would achieve his ultimate sexual thrill: that of ejaculation as his victim's death supervened. So far, the murders had provided him with only part-realisation of this fantasy. The overwhelming emotions, topped up with feelings of power, domination and the act of murder were there, but he reasoned that Robin Stavinsky had short-changed him. She had provided him with none of the sickening criteria because she had collapsed limp and helpless as he dragged her into the scrub. Nevertheless, he strangled her and raped her after death. He told me later, 'I was surprised, ya know. It was a pretty good thrill, but not the best.'

*   *   *

Two schoolchildren, both fourteen, and from Griswold, disappeared in eastern Connecticut on Easter Sunday 1984. Leslie Shelley and April Brunais, inseparable friends and neighbours, had decided to walk into Jewett City, 2.6 miles from where they lived. For the girls, it would have taken them around an hour to walk this distance, with stops and starts, at best. Both girls were aware that their parents would not have permitted them to walk back during the hours of darkness, so each said that the other's parents had agreed to drive them home. It was a childish deception that would cost them their innocent lives.

As darkness fell, the girls phoned their parents; both were ordered to walk back as punishment. At 10.30pm, when neither girl had returned, their parents called the police who listed the kids as 'runaways'.

The exact time Ross stopped and offered the girls a lift is unknown. It is known, however, that April, who was the more assertive of the two, climbed into the front passenger seat, while the petite and fragile Leslie sat behind. Both were understandably startled when Ross drove right past the end of their street, and despite their protests that he had missed their turning, he wouldn't stop. April pulled out a small pocket knife with which to threaten their abductor, but Ross easily disarmed her. Driving east out on Highway 165, he headed for Voluntown, and nearby Beach Pond, a vast expanse of water holding back the Pachaus River, which separates the states of Rhode Island and Connecticut.

After the nine-minute drive, and parking up at a still undetermined location, Ross tore off April's jeans, cutting them into strips which he used to bind his victims' hand and feet. He shut Leslie into the truck of his car and then dragged April a few yards and forced her to her knees. There can be no doubt that the terrified Leslie overheard her friend arguing with Ross. April put up a spirited fight for her life before he raped her and strangled her to death.

Ross now turned his attention to Leslie. He said that the girl made a great impact on him:

She [Leslie Shelley] was delicate with wispy blonde hair. She was calm as I talked to her in the car. I told her that I didn't want to kill her, and she cried when she found out that her friend was already dead. Yes, I suppose she started shaking and appeared resigned to her fate when I rolled her over. This is the murder that bothers me. I can't remember how I strangled her, but her death was the most real and hardest to deny. With the others, it was like someone else did it, and I watched from afar through a fog of unreality. This was real but somehow not real. It was fantasy but not really fantasy. Her death? Leslie? It wasn't someone else and for the first time I saw it was me. I watched myself do those things and I couldn't stop. It was like an invisible barrier between us. I didn't want to kill her.

At this point during his interview with me, Ross showed the first signs of stress and remorse. He stopped talking, lowered his head, and sucked in a lungful of stale prison air. His three burly prison guards almost stopped breathing. When he resumed his sickening account of the murder of Leslie Shelley, there were tears in his eyes – maybe crocodile tears.

I couldn't do anything but watch as I murdered her, and

you want to know something outrageous? Well, I cried afterwards. You know something else? Well, ah, I wanted to have sex with her straight after I raped and killed April, but I couldn't get it up. So, I had to sit back with Leslie for an hour, just talkin' and stuff. Then, because she started crying, saying that she would be in trouble for being late home, I had to kill her. But, I anally raped her, after death, to release the tension. You see, nobody has been told this before.

You know, they call me a serial killer, right? Well, I've only killed eight women. Big deal! There are a lot more guys you could meet and they've killed dozens more than me. An' in that context, I'm a nice guy. I'm such a nice guy really.

With that, Ross burst into an uncontrollable fit of laughter, before explaining that he had dumped the bodies of April and Leslie at another location near Beach Pond, and over the state line into Rhode Island, occasionally revisiting the site to masturbate over their remains. 'I'd just sit there, just to look at their decomposing bodies. Like my childhood fantasies, they were there for me and they gave me pleasure when I needed it.'

Ross took police to the bodies of April Brunais and Leslie Shelley shortly after his arrest on Tuesday, 28 June 1984, although the precise location of the murder scene was never established. This was put down as an 'oversight' by the Connecticut State Police, and later proved in court enquiry to be a deliberate attempt by them to avoid a jurisdictional boundary dispute between Connecticut and Rhode Island – the latter now having to pay millions of dollars to foot the bill for the murder enquiry. The issue of moving bodies over state, or county lines, or from one law enforcement jurisdiction into another, is endemic throughout the United States, especially in the poorer counties where the cost of a murder enquiry and the subsequent trial can all but bankrupt a local authority.

The enquiry judge gave several officers from the Connecticut State Police a severe roasting; the implication being that they had actually shifted the two bodies over the state line, into Rhode Island, leaving the RI police to pick up the tab. But the question was, however: if the CST had moved the bodies, how was it that Michael Ross knew where they were in Rhode Island? Ross had the answer. The police had found the bodies, and, working a deal with Rhode Island law enforcement, that he would not face further charges in that state for their murders, he would say that the Rhode Island police had described the place where they lay.

It was an awful mess, one that would take this author weeks to figure out, and the real truth came from Ross in correspondence:

I thought it would be great fun to play games with the police. I murdered the girls in Connecticut, then I moved their bodies into Rhode Island. Actually, I did tell the Connecticut police where I killed the girls, and they went there and found several strips of Brunais's jeans, which I used to bind the girls. That, with other stuff, proved where I murdered them. I said that I left them in Connecticut, an' the Rhode Island police claimed that the Connecticut State Police moved the bodies, and this kinda fucked everyone up. I think it was very funny.

Michael was now nearing the end of his run; he was mentally out of control, and his work at the Prudential Insurance

Company was suffering as a result. Faced with the prospect of dismissal, as he was failing to bring in new business, Mike was also coping with his turbulent relationship with Debbie Wallace which had taken a more active turn. Her father had died while she and Michael were on vacation and, after the funeral, on the return journey home, they had argued. A major rift followed and, once again, he felt alone and rejected.

* * *

For seventeen-year-old Wendy, the daughter of Roger and Cindy Baribeault, Wednesday, 13 June 1984 was the final day of examinations at Norwich Free University where she was a junior student. She was well liked by her fellow students and friends, who described her as 'a caring and sensitive person who enjoyed life'. She liked going to the movies and hanging out at the beach. She loved music and would sit in jam sessions with a local band that played some of her favourite tunes. She had stopped at her parents' home, in Lisbon, after studies; leaving a note to say that she was catching a bus back the 2.3 miles to Jewett City to visit a convenience store. It was a fine afternoon, so she decided to walk back and, at around 4.30pm, she was seen, by a passing motorist, walking along the fairly busy Route 12. But she was not alone, for other witnesses later came forward to say that she was being followed rapidly by a man on foot. He was about 6ft tall, white, clean-shaven, of medium build and had dark hair. Other witnesses saw this man get out of a blue, compact car with a rear window wiper, and they recalled that he walked briskly off in the direction of the young woman who answered Wendy's description.

When Wendy failed to return home, Cindy reported her as missing the following day. Hundreds of police and local residents launched an immediate search of the area, and, two days later, her body was found by a fireman. The corpse was about 100 yards from the road – just a quarter of a mile from her home – in dense woods, and an attempt to hide the body in an ancient stone wall was evident. She had been raped and strangled.

Ross later told me that he had intended to go to work that day, but had cut himself while shaving and blood seeped on to the collar of his only clean shirt. After phoning in with the excuse that he was ill, he dressed himself in smart, casual clothes, and hung around his apartment, reading pornographic material and masturbating. At around 2.00pm, he went for a drive, and later on he saw Wendy walking along the road towards her home.

After swinging his car around and parking up at the entrance of a gravel track, he dashed across the road and asked Wendy if she would like to go to a barbecue that night. When she turned him down, Ross dragged her into a clearing in the woodland bordering the highway. Here, in a dappled, sunlit clearing, he rolled her over on to her stomach before strangling her. He said that he ejaculated almost immediately, so he throttled her again. She struggled and kicked, and her body twitched. Michael had cramp in his hands as he fought to strangle the life out of his victim. When he stopped to massage his hands, she heaved and squirmed under him until he re-applied his grip. Finally, a kick of her legs told him she was dead.

*　　　*　　　*

Known for disarming suspected criminals with his boyish smile and supportive 'good-cop' manner, Connecticut State Police

Detective Mike Malchik has used his investigative skills to crack even the toughest of homicide enquiries, including 40 or more which were considered 'unsolvable' by his colleagues. A legendary figure in Connecticut law enforcement, the fair-haired, blue-eyed cop often worked alone and unpaid on these jobs, such was his dedication to policing. The case of Wendy Baribeault was no exception.

The Ross investigation is obviously one of the high points of Mike Malchik's career, and this becomes all too apparent when one visits his spacious, up scale home, set in lush, green grounds. Photos of him, with Ross, hang on the wall, and, despite the horrific nature of Ross's crimes, Mike Malchik still refers to Ross as 'Michael'.

Most US cops seem to love being in front of a camera, and Mike Malchik is no exception. Wearing a tight, white T-shirt, and stone-washed blue jeans and white running shoes, he accompanied me, and my film crew, to several of the most important locations in the Ross story. He explained that he had already formed solid links between the murders of Debra Smith Taylor and Tammy Williams, and when he placed Robin Stavinsky and Wendy Baribeault into the equation, he knew that he was hunting a sexual psychopathic serial killer who would not stop murdering until he was arrested and brought to justice.

Indeed, Mike Malchik's experience in homicide cases was such that he didn't need to consult the FBI for advice, but, to confirm his belief, he did speak to a colleague at the National Center for the Analysis of Violent Crime, Quantico, Virginia. Malchik already knew what type of suspect he was looking for. 'He would be a young, dark-haired Caucasian male in his later twenties or early thirties. He would be of the "white-collar" type, who worked in Norwich, yet lived further south, and this man would frequently travel along Route 12, between his place of work and his home.' To Malchik, Griswold seemed a good bet for the suspect's locus and now there was the extra bonus knowing that the man drove a blue, foreign make of car.

Using what Malchik calls 'basic common sense', he reasoned that whoever murdered Wendy who would want to flee the crime scene as quickly as possible, and he reasoned that his target was a local man. He telephoned the Vehicle Licensing Department and asked them for a print-out of all vehicles, and their owners, in the locality. For this service, the VLD charged the Connecticut State Police $12 per car, which, as it turned out, proved to be a cheap investigative tool. When the list rolled out of his teleprinter, Malchik started looking for a blue, foreign make of car. At number 27 on the list was a vehicle owned by one Michael Bruce Ross who lived in Jewett City.

Ross seemed intrigued when Malchik arrived on his doorstep on Thursday, 28 June, to question him. He invited the detective in for a cup of coffee and enjoyed the attention of the police. For his part, Mike Malchik actually felt that the personable Ross could not have been a serial killer. As he was about to leave to rejoin his colleague, Detective Fran Griffen, outside in their car, Malchik was asked a question. Ross wondered if such a murderer would be declared insane, and escape the electric chair, if he was convicted. It was such a pointed question that it prompted Malchik to return to Ross's sitting room. As Keith Hunter Jesperson observes: 'Ross must have been questioning his own sanity ever since he started his perversions. Now he wanted a professional's opinion from a detective looking into one of his murders…not a very smart move.'

The sleuth knew that the description of a blue car didn't

exactly match that of Ross's vehicle, which was parked outside. The cop was looking for a hatchback with rear wipers and, while Ross certainly had a blue Toyota, it was a sedan and had no rear wiper blade. After a few more minutes of general conversation, Malchik got up to leave, for the second time. He had only walked a few yards before a gut instinct prompted him to turn around and ask Ross a question of his own.

In the manner of Peter Falk in his role as Columbo, Malchik asked, 'What were your movements on Wednesday, 13 June, the day Miss Baribeault went missing?'

Amazingly, thought Malchik, Ross immediately reeled off his movements for that day almost to the minute, with the exception of the hour encompassing 4.30pm. This was the time when the witnesses had seen Wendy walking along the road, with a man answering Ross's description following her. The detective thought it remarkable that anyone could so rapidly recall his or her exact whereabouts, along with solid timings, two weeks after an event, without at least considerable thought, or reference to a well-kept diary, so he reckoned that 13 June must have been a special day for Ross. Malchik them asked him what he had been doing on the two days either side of this crucial date. Ross couldn't remember a thing and the detective was stunned, for the implication was now obvious. Ross had tried to alibi himself for the day of the murder and in doing so had been too clever for his own good.

Malchik then asked his suspect to accompany him to the murder incident room, which had been set up in the nearby Lisbon Town Hall on Newent Road. Ross thought that a ride in an unmarked police car would be 'fun', so he changed into a white, short-sleeved shirt, and dark, lightweight slacks for the five-minute journey, the very same clothes that he had worn when he killed Wendy Baribeault.

Once seated in the police interview room, Ross was soon rambling about his life to the amiable cop. By now, Malchik had learned about Ross's criminal history, and he was privately convinced that he had a serial killer sitting in front of him. But in the bustling confines of the command post, obtaining a full confession was another matter entirely. At one point, just as Ross was about to make some serious admissions, a cleaner burst into the room and started to mop the floor. This unexpected intrusion broke the spell and Malchik had to begin coaxing his suspect again.

Suddenly, Ross asked: 'Mike, do you think I killed Wendy?'

Malchik said that he believed so, and with that, Ross admitted eleven sexual assaults and six murders.

Recalling that first meeting, during a subsequent prison interview, Ross told me:

I remember the detective coming to the door. He was looking for a blue hatchback with wipers, and I didn't have a blue hatchback. I had a blue sedan with no wipers. And, uh, he was getting ready to leave, and I told him something. I don't remember exactly what I said, but something that made him pause. And he said he had better ask me a few more questions and then afterwards he was getting ready to go. An' I said something else, so I guess I didn't really want him to leave.

Remembering the interview with Mike Malchik, Ross explained:
You know, it's not exactly the easiest thing in the world

to do. You know, 'Hello Mr Police Officer, I killed a load
of people.' You know, it was hard for me. If you actually
listened to the audiotape confessions, ah, it was very
difficult for me to admit that I did it, and then I had got
one out. Then he would have to kinda get the next one
out. Then I could talk about that one. Yes, it was hard
at first saying I killed this one, or that one. I mean I told
'em about two they didn't know about… I mean they
didn't even question me about them 'cos they thought
they were runaways.

When I asked Ross why he had confessed to the murders of
Leslie Shelley and April Brunais, when he hadn't even been
asked about them, the killer complained:

Well, the police said that there was something wrong
with me, and there was a place at Whiting Corner for
insane criminals. Yeah, I fell for that one, an' I thought I
was going to get the help I needed and that's what I
wanted to hear. 'Hey, you know you have got something
wrong with you and we are going to do something about
it 'cos the murders have stopped.' Yeah, Malchik said all
the right things, so I thought, what the hell, and I gave
'em everything.

To be fair to Mike Malchik, he did honour his promise to Ross,
for the murders did stop, and the law eventually did do
something about Ross's problem: they would execute him.

*   *   *

Wyndham County Prosecutor, Harry Gaucher, only charged

Ross with the 1982 murders of Tammy Williams and Debra Smith Taylor. Whether it was because of lack of physical evidence to support the rape portion of an aggravated capital felony charge, which carried the death sentence, or Gaucher's anxiety about losing his case at trial, he allowed Ross to plead guilty solely to murder.

Sitting on Saturday, 13 December 1986, the trial judge sentenced Ross to two consecutive life terms. He would serve no less than 120 years behind bars. However, the murders of Wendy Baribeault, Robin Stavinsky, April Brunais and Leslie Shelley fell under the jurisdiction of a more tenacious prosecutor. New London County State's Attorney, C Robert 'Bulldog' Satti, of the 'hang 'em and flog 'em brigade', wanted to be the first prosecutor for decades to send a murderer to Connecticut's electric chair.

Satti also knew that he was up against a death penalty statute that tipped the balance in favour of life imprisonment. But the formidable counsel stuck to his guns, for he strongly believed that if ever there was a man worthy of the chair, it had to be Michael Bruce Ross. Apart from the morality of executing a man in the liberal 'Nutmeg State' of Connecticut, there was another cost to consider. 'Old Sparky' had not been used since Joseph 'Mad Dog' Taborsky had been electrocuted in it on Tuesday, 17 May 1960, since which time it had fallen into disrepair. If they wanted to kill Michael Ross, the state would have to fork out at least $30,000 to refurbish the old oak chair, upgrade the wiring, renew the restraints, redecorate the witness viewing area and death house suite.

For their part, the defence attorney had to convince a jury that Ross was not legally responsible for the crimes to which he had confessed. Making their job tougher was the fact that Ross didn't qualify for an insanity defence. Moreover, the case had received so much pre-trial publicity that, in the summer of 1987, the venue was moved to Bridgeport, where the prosecution would argue that Ross was a rapist, a cold-blooded, calculating monster, who had planned his assaults and murdered his victims simply to stay out of prison.

In June 1987, after four weeks of testimony, the eight men and four women jurors took just 87 minutes to convict Ross of capital felony murder. At the penalty phase, three weeks later, it took them under four hours to prove that Connecticut's death sentence could be imposed. On Monday, 6 July, 20 days before his 28th birthday, Ross was condemned to death. Under Connecticut law, he would have been spared this sentence if the court had found even one redeeming factor or quality that the jurors believed to indicate remorse or mitigation. They could not, for Ross, it seemed, did not have a conscience and didn't give a damn.

During and after the trials, Michael became angered because he felt that the judge and jury were biased and the testimonies of some of the witnesses were grossly inaccurate. Yet, probably his greatest source of irritation was that he felt the court failed to recognise his alleged mental illness. Michael suggested that this was most evident when the judge disallowed testimony by his psychiatrist, Dr Robert Miller. The defence team claimed that had Dr Miller been allowed to submit his testimony concerning Michael's psychological state, the jury would likely have been more lenient during the penalty phase. Moreover, his 'mental illness' might have even been considered a mitigating factor, which could have spared him the death penalty altogether.

Ross had told me that he wasn't afraid of dying in the

electric chair. He said that living was too good for him, but he was worried that, if that fateful moment did arrive, he might say the wrong thing or show weakness in the face of death. He was also afraid of something he said was far worse then death:

I've always felt that I had to be in control of myself and, even to this day, I feel the need to be in control. What scares me the most isn't life in prison, or the death penalty, but insanity. I'm scared of losing touch with reality. Sometimes I feel I'm slipping away and I'm losing control. If you're in control you can handle anything, but if you lose it, you are nothing.

When asked if he had feelings or remorse for his crimes, he replied bluntly:

Nope! I don't feel anything for them. I really wish I did. I don't feel anything. I feel really bad for the families. I mean, I feel lots of times. Like I can see Mrs Shelley, the mother of one of them girls I killed, on the witness stand crying. And, then there's Mrs, ah, I can't remember her name, but I can think of another one on the stand describing her daughter. She went to the morgue and saw her at the morgue. But the girls themselves I feel nothing for, and I never have.

Ross then explained why he hadn't turned himself in to the police when he started to commit his earlier offences, way back at Cornell University, when he knew he needed help:

I made myself believe that it would never happen again. And, I know it sounds hard, but looking back, I can't understand how I did it. It was a fluke because I really didn't do those things. Even sitting here now, I know if I was released I'd kill again. There's no reason to think otherwise. But, I can't, as I sit here now, picture myself wanting to do that. I can't really see myself doing it. I mean, it's like being on different levels.

When asked if he had any detailed memories of the murders, Ross chuckled, and then said:

Yes and no. I used to fantasise over the crimes every day and every night. I would masturbate to the point of, um, actually having raw spots on myself from the masturbation. I would bleed. It's weird. I get a lot of pleasure from it. It is really a pleasurable experience. But, when it's all over, it's a very short-term thing. I guess it's like getting high. You know I've never used drugs, but you can get high, then you come down and crash. That's almost how it is. It's just not an easy thing to live with.

An inevitable question was to ask him what had been going through his mind when he was raping and killing his tragic victims. His reply was:

Nothin'! That's what so weird about this thing. Everybody seems to think, you know, the state's theory that I'm a rapist and I kill them so they can't identify me. Look, most of the time it's broad daylight. I mean, I'm not a stupid person. As sure as hell, if I was going to do

*something like that, I sure as hell wouldn't do it that way.
There was nothing going through my mind until they were
already dead.*

*And then it was like stepping through a doorway. And,
uh, I remember the very first feeling I had, was my heart
beating. I mean really pounding. The second feeling I had
was that my hands hurt where I always strangled them
with my hands. And, the third feeling was, I guess, fear,
and the kind of reality set in that there was this dead body
in front of me.*

*And, again, I don't want to mislead you because I knew
what was going on, but it was like a different level. I mean
it was like watching it* [on TV]. *And, after it was all over,
you know, it kind of sets in, an' that's when I would get
frightened and stuff. I would hide the bodies and cover
them up, or something.*

*I abused them, I used them and I murdered them, what
else do you need?*

The Osborn Correctional Institution, formerly known as the
Connecticut Correctional Institution-Somers, was opened in
November 1963 as a replacement for the Old Wethersfield State
Prison. It served as the state's maximum-security prison and as
the Reception/Diagnostic Center for incoming male inmates
state-wide. When I first met Michael Ross, before Death Row
inmates were transferred to the newly opened Northern
Correctional Institution, in 1995, he was incarcerated at CCI-
S, and his 'house' on 'The Row' was a truly ancient dungeon
painted a muddy-brown colour. 'Death Row' was stencilled in
white on the brown-painted steel door leading to the tier which
housed Connecticut's seven 'Dead Men Walking'. Indeed, there

will be few readers who have not seen the 1999 movie *The Green Mile*, starring Tom Hanks, as Officer Paul Edgecomb, but I can assure you that the squalid conditions on Death Row at Somers made the Louisiana's imaginary Cold Mountain Penitentiary seem like a first-rate hotel.

On my final visit to Death Row, only Michael Ross and Robert Breton were 'at home'. Sedrick Cobb, Ivo Colon, Richard Reynolds, Todd Rizzo and Daniel Webb were enjoying fresh air in the yard and taking in a little sun.

*   *   *

Robert Breton, Sr was sentenced to death in 1989. He was convicted of two counts of murder and one count of capital felony for the 13 December, 1987, beating and stabbing deaths of his 38-year-old ex-wife, JoAnn Breton, and their sixteen-year-old son, Robert Breton, Jr. In the early morning of 13 December 13, 1987, Breton entered the Waterbury apartment that his ex-wife rented after their divorce eleven months earlier. Surprising her while she slept, he slashed at her with a sharp five-inch knife and pounded her with his fists. JoAnn Breton scrambled across the room. Her ex-husband followed and killed her by thrusting the knife through her neck, opening a major artery. Robert Breton, Jr heard his mother's screams and ran into her room, where his father attacked him. Bleeding from his arms, hands, and fingers, the younger Breton tried to escape down a flight of stairs. His father pursued him, overtaking his son at the bottom of the staircase and continuing the attack. Robert, Jr. bled to death from a wound that severed his carotid artery. Police found him, clad only in his underwear, at the bottom of the stairs, his head propped against a wall.

Sedrick Cobb was sentenced to death in 1991. The former

deliveryman from Naugatuck was convicted of the rape and murder of 23-year-old Julia Ashe of Watertown, whom he kidnapped from a Waterbury department store parking lot on 16 December, 1989. Cobb flattened one tyre of Ashe's car using a valve stem remover and, when she returned, offered to help her change the tyre. When he asked her for a ride to his car, she obliged. He then forced her at knifepoint to drive to a secluded road and raped her. Cobb then bound and gagged Ashe with fibreglass tape and carried her to a concrete dam. He pushed her, and she fell 23 feet into the shallow, icy water below. She managed to free her hands by rubbing the tape across wire mesh protruding from the concrete and gouged her face trying in vain to remove the tape across her mouth. When she tried to crawl up the bank to freedom, Cobb forced her, face down, back into the water. Her ice-encrusted body was found on Christmas Day, 1989.

Ivo Colon beat two-year-old Keriana Tellado to death. He was the mother's live-in boyfriend. He was also beating another child called Crystal, as well. He would hit the girls with his hands and a belt because they were slow in potty training. Two days before she died, he picked up Keriana by the arm after she wet herself and, 'heard something go pop'. He refused to let the mother take the girl to the hospital to treat the broken arm, because he feared the doctors would see the cuts, bruises and burn marks that covered her little body. He began beating Keriana again, kicking this poor baby and cutting her with his rings. When she threw up after dinner, he took her to the bathroom and began banging her head against the shower wall. Little Keriana could not stand up, so he kept on picking her up by the hair, He picked her up a couple of times and her hair was coming out in his hands. The medical examiner ruled that little

Keriana died of blunt force trauma to the head. As of December 17, 2004, the death sentence of Ivo Colon was overturned by the State Supreme Court. The prosecuting attorney has indicated that he will move towards a second death sentence.

Richard Reynolds, a Brooklyn, New York, crack dealer, was convicted for the murder of 34-year-old Waterbury Police Officer Walter T. Williams, on 18 December, 1992. While being searched by Williams, Reynolds bumped against him to determine if the officer was wearing a bullet-proof vest. Reynolds then shot Williams point-blank in the head with a handgun.

Todd Rizzo confessed to, and was convicted of the 1997 murder of thirteen-year-old Stanley Edwards of Waterbury. He lured Edwards into his backyard under the guise of hunting snakes and then hit him thirteen times with a three-pound sledgehammer. As of October 6. 2003, the death sentence of Todd Rizzo was overturned by the State Supreme Court. The prosecuting attorney has indicated that he will move towards a second death sentence.

Daniel Webb was convicted of kidnapping and murder for the 1989 slaying in Hartford of Diane Gellenbeck, a 37-year-old Connecticut National Bank vice-president. Prior to this, Webb already had an extensive criminal record including a 1983 robbery conviction, 1984 rape and kidnapping conviction and an arrest in 1987 for rape. While out on bail after the 1987 arrest he raped one woman, robbed and assaulted another and murdered Gellenbeck.

*   *   *

When I visited Ross, it was obvious that he was proud of his cell. It was piled high with books and writing materials; indeed he boasted about the fact that he was allocated a second cell next to his own where even more of his books were stored. He also bragged about the dozens of pretty young women who courted his attentions, one of whom was as pretty as a starlet and had even signed her photograph, 'With Love'. Her letters contained promises that she would marry him in a heartbeat. It would have probably been the last heartbeat she would have ever had, for he would have killed her in an instant.

And, while he was not busy writing letters, or studying the law, he was learning how to transcribe Braille. The pompous and self-opinionated Michael Ross was a very busy Death Row inmate indeed.

Michael Ross is not unique among the serial killer breed but, to his credit, he did try to understand why he had been driven to commit such terrible crimes on young women. In fact, he was striving to understand the forces that propelled him into such severe anti-social behaviour in the first place. To this end, he had volunteered for a series of treatments, which included chemical and surgical castration, the latter being refused by the state.

Many acknowledged experts seemed to believe that this treatment could separate the beast from the decent Michael Ross and, for an extended period, he was treated as a human guinea pig, and prescribed the female contraceptive Depo-Provera to reduce his enormous sex drive. At the same time as he was taking this drug, he was being prescribed Prozac – a powerful anti-depressant – and this cocktail certainly reduced his abnormal sexual cravings. Unfortunately, the excessive use of Depo-Provera ballooned his weight by several stone and, as a result, he suffered pathological changes in liver function and hormone levels. He was troubled by abdominal pains, headaches, asthenia (weakness or fatigue), and nervousness, and his depression reappeared, as one might well expect.

Before these drugs were prescribed, Ross claimed he masturbated constantly. Occasionally, when in the company of a female correctional officer, he experienced an overwhelming desire to kill her. The Depo-Provera reduced his sex drive, and Michael said:

You know that everybody has had a tune playing over and over again inside their heads. And if you have this tune that plays all day, over and over, it can drive you nuts. An' just imagine having thoughts of rape an' murder, an' you can't get rid of it. Well, just like the tune, it'll be driving you nuts. No matter what you do to get rid of that tune, it's going to stay in your head. And that's how I am. I don't want these thoughts.

Asked if he thought this tune was, in reality, the monster, he replied with one of the most chilling statements I have ever heard from any serial murderer:

No, I think he's separate. He goes to sleep for a while and, uh, you never know where he's gone, and that's very true. I mean, sometimes he's there, and especially with the Depo-Provera, I can feel him back here [Ross touched the back of his head]. *I don't know how anybody is going to understand this, but he used to be always in front of my mind, and was always intruding, like an obnoxious roommate, always butting into your business and you can't get rid of him.*

In a letter to the author, Ross described what happened to him when he became used to the drugs:

> *I would do anything to clear my mind. The medication gave me some relief but my body has adjusted to it now, and the thoughts and urges have returned. Now, my obnoxious roommate has moved back in and things seem worse because now I saw what it was like without him. Today, I feel like a blind man from birth who was given eyesight as a gift, but was taken away a month later. It's really hard to understand what is normal for everybody else if you've never had it yourself.*

Excluding the two years he spent in prison before his first trial, for the better part of fourteen years, Michael Ross lived in a state of limbo, volunteering for execution, while at once thinking that the State would never execute a man who was 'mad enough' to want to die using a method known as 'State-sponsored suicide'. When I interviewed Mike, in 1984, he was the very picture of health, but after he was transferred to the newly opened Northern Correctional Institution, in 1995, his physical and mental well-being deteriorated to the point that I would have hardly recognised him. To those who came into contact with him he came across as a man literally begging to die.

Following years of legal wrangling, and after nine days of deliberation, the Superior Court jury finally reached a verdict. On Thursday, 6 April 2000, he once again received the death penalty for the murders of April Brunais, Wendy Baribeault and Leslie Shelley. He stood impassively as the verdicts were read, whereas the families of the victims wept or sat with bowed heads. It had taken the state a total of sixteen years to secure a death sentence against him and they were determined to make it stick this time around, despite the fact that he had an automatic right to appeal.

'It's over until the first appeal,' Edwin Shelley said. 'But I don't think any appeal will hold up now.' Sixteen years of court proceedings, the Shelleys said, have taken their toll emotionally. 'We did all of the 1987 trial. We did all of this trial,' Lera Shelley added. 'If we have to go through it again we will, for our daughter.'

In August 2001, while his death penalty appeal was pending, Ross was extradited to the Sullivan Correction Facility, Fallsburg, New York – the same prison that holds Arthur Shawcross. From there he was transferred to Orange County to face arraignment in the rape and murder of Paula Perrera. The filmed admission he had given to the author during the making of the TV documentary series, *The Serial Killers*, was incontestable. On Monday, 24 September 2001, this killer stood before Judge Nicholas DeRosa and pleaded guilty to the first-degree murder charge, and the following month he was sentenced to eight to 25 years in prison for killing Paula. Michael expressed relief when the sentence was handed down, and was quoted as saying: 'I regret that this has taken so long to be taken care of,' reported Timothy O'Connor for *The Times Herald-Record*.

Despite his filmed admission to the rape and murder of Dzung Ngoc Tu in 1981, Tompkins County District Attorney said that it was pointless to seek a conviction against Ross because he had already been sentenced to death in Connecticut. Besides, Dzung's family in Vietnam had no interest in pursuing the case and had no wish to relive the pain.

Ross's last few days were spent back in his old cell at the Osborn Correctional Institution in Somers. Two last-minute appeals from his father and his aunt, Ann L Rich, were rejected by the 2nd US Circuit Court of Appeals in New York. Then the US Supreme Court rejected a final 11.00pm appeal on Thursday, 12 May 2005. The ruling was that Ross was mentally competent to choose death. He opted not to have a special last meal, choosing from the standard menu Ross lunched on a cheeseburger and hash browns, at 3.00 pm. Then he spent much of that Thursday afternoon talking with visitors. For his last meal, he ate the regular prison meal of the day, which was turkey a la king with rice, mixed vegetables, white bread, fruit and a beverage.

Michael was escorted to the death chamber around 2.00 am, Friday, 13 May. He could have stopped his execution right up until the moment the lethal drugs started to flow. Now, strapped down onto the gurney, he offered no final words, and was given a lethal injection. Nine members of his victims' families witnessed his final moments, and he coughed once and fell silent, being pronounced dead at 2.25am.

I am against the death penalty. I would have rather seen Ross sit in jail. That was more mental torture for him. I believe Connecticut assisted him with his plan of suicide. It's a shame! I truly pray that he really did become a Christian. I wrote a letter to him but I don't know if he got it. Well, God is his final judge. I have no feelings of 'justice has been served', or 'he got what he deserved'. State-assisted suicide is just wrong!

Barbara Emery-Willard, Paula Perrera's best friend.

*   *   *

Michael Ross was the boy-next-door who turned into a monster, and his own words to the author leave an indelible mark:

> *You know, they* [the medical examiners] *found strangulation marks around the neck of Wendy Baribeault. They called them 'multiple strangulation marks', 'cos they were kinda all around her throat. An' they got confused. I knew that she was struggling and my hands kept cramping up. I kinda laughed at them for that. I thought that was funny.*

Yet Michael's chilling sense of priorities was masked by the impression he gave to outsiders. Karen B. Clark, an experienced New York journalist, who visited him in Somers, said, 'Michael Ross looks so normal he could be the guy next door. If I was walking down a dark alley at night, heard footsteps behind me, and turned around, well, I would have been relieved to see Michael Ross. That's how normal the guy looks.'

Michael Ross is buried at the Benedictine Grange Cemetery, Redding, Fairfield County, Connecticut.

*   *   *

This chapter is based on video and audiotape Death Row interviews between the author and Michael Bruce Ross on 26 September, 1994, within the Osborn Correctional Institute, Connecticut, and several years' correspondence.

SUMMARY

Each and every one of the killers featured throughout this book has been, or still is, bombarded with letters and photographs (often sexual in nature) from men and women wishing to strike up relationships, and even marry them and have their children. For the most part, serial killers – or any type of incarcerated killer – are only after funding. One only has to browse the internet pen-pal sites to confirm that these monsters are only after one thing: your money.

This book highlights just two examples: Mr Robinson and Mr Jablonski, while LeRoy Nash, Melanie McGuire, and Keith Hunter Jesperson don't ask for a penny. For that matter, neither did Michael Ross, when he was alive.

I recall Kenneth Bianchi, with whom I corresponded for many years, culminating in me interviewing him for a TV documentary years back. He married several times in prison, and he had the gall to send me his wedding photos, after he had fleeced these women hook, line and sinker. This animal became an 'ordained priest', for a short while, and also a member of the American Bar Association.

I recall another moron, called Ronald DeFeo Jr ('the Amityville Horror'). This old punk ended up marrying a woman who runs a website for him, while he continues to milk her for money for small prison luxuries. As God is my witness, how can any woman fall in love and marry a man who has blasted to death his family of six, including four of his younger, terrified siblings, in their beds? It defies belief.

It goes on and on, specifically from somewhat deranged women who write to Keith Jesperson. Flashing their photogenic attributes, they pledge their love to a serial killer, who, if they, themselves, had 'pissed him off', would have beat them to death in a second.

My book *Murder.com*, also published by John Blake Publishing, highlights the very real dangers of trawling for love and sex over the internet, specifically the final chapter, 'Men and Women Behind Bars: Internet Lovebirds'.

*   *   *

For every convicted control freak of a serial killer, man or woman, there must be at least fifty misguided souls who want a serious relationship with them. In some cases this twisted form of morality runs so deep that a woman will kill another person, by proxy, to please her loved one.

This was the case with Veronica 'Verlyn' Wallace Compton; an incredibly beautiful creature with looks and a body most men and women would die for, and she almost did die, thanks to sexual-sado serial killer, Kenneth Alessio Bianchi. In attempt to prove that he was not one of the notorious 'Hillside Stranglers', Ken smuggled his semen out of prison secreted into the finger of a rubber kitchen glove which he hid in the spine of a book, which his dominatrix pen friend, and lover, took out of jail after a visit.

The plan was that she would travel to Bellingham, Washington State (where Bianchi had murdered two co-eds – Karen Mandic and Diane Wilder – and lure a woman called Kim Breed to a motel room. Here, Verlyn would kill Kim, and drip Ken's semen into the dead woman's vagina, to make it appear that the true killer was still at large, thus it could not have been Mr Bianchi.

Kim Breed, however, was a martial arts expert, and the result being that Verlyn was soon arrested to spend 15 years in prison. I actually met and interviewed Verlyn at the Washington Corrections Center for Women (WCCW). By this time, she had been writing to one of the subjects in this book. She and Douglas Clark talked about love, and opening up a mortuary and having sex with the dead, if he were to be released.

Ronald DeFeo, of Amityville infamy, Richard Ramirez, 'The Night Stalker', Kenneth Bianchi, and Arthur Shawcross, are among hundreds of serial killers who have married while in prison. Thousands more killers, including Michael Ross, Aileen Wuornos, in fact every serial killer alive or dead, is, or has been inundated by people seeking love with a monster. Thousands more write as pen friends to the 'Legion of the Damned', and among them are the apple-pie-making, sweater-knitters and Bible-readers who believe that God has ordered them to save these killers' souls.

It makes one want to weep!

And, I can tell you that Keith Hunter Jesperson has more than his fair share of blue-chip fruit cakes writing and pledging their love to him, too. Around 80 plus. Take it from me, 50 per cent of these women are drop-dead gorgeous. A small percentage are gay, while the remainder, as far as I can determine, are of undeterminable gender. Some of these social strays can read and write; some struggle with simple words like, 'common sense'. Some have a brain, others half a brain; while others obviously have a 'To Let' sign inside their skulls. A minority can actually think, and one of them is 'Laci' (name changed to protect her identity).

Astute, street-wise, drop-dead gorgeous, with a figure to die for, erotic and into 'stuff' that will make the older reader's hair fall out, part-time entertainer of gentlemen with the discreet use of a pole, Laci has also been writing to serial killers since she was 18. At the time of writing she is 29. Indeed, she has some 84 of the most heinous killers in her little 'black book', and the correspondence from them amounts to over a thousand pages.

Laci fell in love with Keith Hunter Jesperson, then, somewhat predictably, six years later, she fell out of love. Below is her completely unedited story, and if Keith had been executed he would turn in his grave. Her story is disturbing yet insightful, all providing food-for-thought for anyone seeking love with a monster behind bars:

It was 1995. I was 18, and in high school, when I first heard of Keith Hunter Jesperson, and that he'd been arrested for multiple murders. Initially I was attracted to the fact that he had killed so many people for no good reason. I also thought he was good looking and that was a huge plus for me. I remember watching him on TV and reading about him in my many true crime books and thinking, 'I would love to know him'. At the time, I had no way of knowing that in a few years I would know him as a person and not just a vicious killer. I would be his friend and eventually be his lover.

My attraction to killers and extreme violence goes as far

266

back as I can remember. When I was a little girl, I loved seeing killers on TV, watching horror movies and even got enjoyment from looking at car wrecks. I have been this way for so long that it is a natural, normal thing to me. I always knew that I had a love for deviant things, but it did not come full circle until I reached high school. When I was 14 years old, I bought my first crime book. In high school I was known as 'the girl that knows everything about serial killers'. It was a title that I did not mind having. Most people thought it was just a phase, but I knew it was no phase. It is part of who I am. It started with my crime books, and then I started to watch 'shockumentaries' - actual death caught on tape. Films like Faces of Death, Traces of Death, World of Death, *became my favorite type of films.*

Fantasizing about serial killers and mass murderers became part of my daily life. I wrote about them in my diary. I was obsessed with them to say the least. These feelings would not come and go, they were constant. I feel that I have a lot in common with them. I can understand why they kill people. I am a lot like them in some ways. I consider myself to be a mean, cold-hearted bitch. I have no feelings or sympathy for other people. I have more consideration for a dead animal on the side of the road than I do to suffering people. I do have a lot of friends but the majority of them mean nothing to me. I have a few that I do love and care about. These people are my lifelong friends. I don't allow myself to get close to people. In the end, everyone will screw you over. I have been married twice and I walked away from both of them without a second thought. The marriages were meaningless to me.

They were something to do at the time. I have no compassion for people at all. So, in this way, I have a lot in common with the serial killer. The only difference between them and me is that I have not killed anyone – yet!

I put myself into dangerous situations hoping to meet a serial killer. When I was a teenager, I would hang out with a bad crowd. I ran away from home often. I would hitchhike a lot hoping to run into one. I wanted to die and I thought the best way to do that is to find me a serial killer. I tried. In the beginning, my dream was to meet a serial killer that would kill me. A serial killer is a professional at killing and he would get the job done. When this did not happen as I hoped it would, I began to have a longing for wanting to know them as human beings. I knew there was another side to them than being a monster. I knew this is who I was and there was no way to ever escape from it. I do have two distinct aspects of my personality. One side of me is a country girl that loves animals and cartoons. The other side of me loves everything that is dark and sadistic. This is where I feel at home.

When I was 18 years old, I wrote to my first serial killer. He wrote me back. And that is how it all got started. Soon, I was corresponding with all the people that I had read and studied about for so long. I was writing to killers all over the USA and in other countries. I was stunned at the number of them that did write back to me. I was only 18 years old and they still wrote to me, and I was just a lonely kid. Sure, I had a job, a boyfriend and friends but I preferred to be locked in my room writing to my killers. It became a natural part of my life and I stay in touch with them till this day. Sharing with them things that I had never shared with anyone before. I felt comfortable and safe with my killers. They understood me in a way that no one ever had. They accepted me the way I was, and they liked who I was. These killers actually understood everything that I had went through in my life. It felt good to know someone that is just like me in a lot of ways.

As I got older, I realized that I was into even more extreme things than serial killers. I love things that most people would never think of. I enjoy a variety of sexual fetishes. I am a hybristophiliac, which means that I am sexually aroused by outrageous or extreme violence. I literally get off on it. If I see a murdered victim, or a rotting corpse I will get aroused. Even hearing about violence will turn me on. I want to see the gruesome crime photos, and hear all the grisly details of murder because it will turn me on. I am also into sexual things like vincilaginia, BDSM, bondage, chains, rope, gags, role play, rape, porn, group sex, bisexuality, rough sex, ECT. The most extreme thing I am into sexually is necrophilia. I have never tried this, but I did go to Mortuary College and have worked at funeral homes just to be close to dead bodies. I do have a respect for the dead and that is the only reason why I did not perform any indecencies on them. I have other fetishes that many would not consider to be sexual but I do because I get turned on by it. Things like cannibalism, vampirism, bloodletting, self-mutilation, torture, gore, graveyards, decomposition of a corpse, senseless murder, violence; it all drives me into a sexual frenzy.

While I was discovering all of this about myself, I was also discovering things about my serial killers. Of course, I loved all their details of rape, murder, necrophilia and cannibalism. I would often masturbate to their words. But I was also learning about who they are as people. They soon started to call me on the phone. I have even visited a few of them in prison. Many of them asked me to be their girlfriend and to marry them. I have only been with a few of them romantically. I treat them as I would any other boyfriend. They receive no special treatment from me just because they have killed people. They know that I get off on what they did and that is all they get. Honestly, being with a killer is no different than having any other guy doing a life sentence. There are a few of them that I love as people and I will always love them. I wrote to one infamous killer when I was 23 years old. He is a necrophile and killed many. I did not even think he would respond back to me but he did. He is not one of my very best friends in the world. I love him and I adore him. He is the real Hannibal Lecter. He is a brilliant man, but yet he killed many people to satisfy his needs. He is a lot like me; he has two sides to him. We have never been together as a couple. We love each other and that is all we need. I know that he is the one for me, but we can never be together and I accept that because I do truly love him as a person.

In January of 2002 I wrote my first letter to Keith Jesperson. I wrote to him because I remember seeing him back when I was 16 years old. I wanted to know him as a person. I read a book on him titled, 'I' - The Creation of a Serial Killer, by Jack Olsen. I felt sorry for Keith. I thought he had a bad childhood, like me and that women took advantage of him. I did not know if he would write me back, but he did. A week later I received a great, long letter.

That is how it started with me and Keith. We wrote on

a regular basis for six years and I considered him to be a good friend. Out of all my killers, he really was one of my favorites. Eventually he asked for my phone number and he would call me on the phone. He called a lot. So much that I had to start hanging up on him when he called. I was not trying to be rude but he was calling multiple times a day trying to reach me.

The first couple of years we basically talked about everyday things. I told him about the jobs I had, my fiancé at the time, the travelling I did. He told me about his job at the prison, his family, his art work, and his cell mates. He did tell me several times that he was in the 'hole' for fighting. Most of the time it was because some inmate wanted to be known as the guy that hit 'the Happy Face Killer', some nobody trying to make a name for himself had hit him. In one letter of June 2005 he said to me, 'I'm in the hole, a guy attacked me out in the yard and I had to protect myself. Ruled a mutual fight. So, I get 60 days.' It seems like Keith was in the hole often. He did not talk about his case much with me, and I did not ask him anything. He would tell me little things in passing. When I did ask him something he would always tell me what I asked of him and he never held back.

When we were engaged, I began to ask him about the murders. I figured if I am going to marry the guy then I want to know why he did it. I asked him, 'Did you really do what you're accused of', and he wrote back to me and said, 'Yes! I killed them all.' From the way he wrote it, I got the image of him dancing with glee: 'Yes I did it, I killed them all.' I also asked him why he killed them. He told me it is because these women did something to make him angry. He also blamed the killings on stress and lack of sleep. I did like the fact that Keith did not sugar coat things, he said it like it was. He did talk a lot about the media and all the book deals and interviews that he had lined up. I swear if every book that Keith talked about got published there would be an entire shelf of Keith Jesperson at the book store. Keith truly is a media hound. He will talk to anyone that will listen.

I also recall that he tried to reach out to other serial killers with not much luck. He wants to be known as a serial killer. At this point, that is all he has going for him. That made me nervous about him. I am a very private person. I don't want my life out there for everyone to know. I prefer to keep things to myself, and live my quiet country life. I asked Keith more than once NOT to give my information to the media and he promised me that he would not. Obviously he lied because here I am writing about him. I see now that friendship and loyalty mean nothing to him. He only cares for himself and no one else. He wants the world to see him as a violent serial killer no matter what the cost is.

In the six years that I knew him, Keith and I got along great. Only one time did he express anger toward me. He had sent me some of his art work for my birthday as a gift. I was extremely busy travelling at the time with my fiancé and working so I didn't write him back right away. Perhaps that was wrong of me. I received a letter from him in June 2005 telling me: 'It's been a while. I have called and the phone goes dead when I hear your voice. What gives? So you didn't like the art I sent? Or were you just waiting for it to come so you didn't have to pretend any more. Did I do something wrong? Say something wrong? Suggest something wrong?'

I wrote him right away to explain that I had just been busy. When he wrote back he said it was ok and he told me that he is moody at times. No kidding. That is the only problem that we ever had.

After a couple years he started to say that he loved me and asking me to be his girlfriend. He would draw little hearts on his letters to me. At the time I did not know if he was serious or just being cute. I would always thank him for the compliments but turned him down for love. My main reason was because he is so attention, and media hungry. I always trust people until they give me a reason not to but it is the way he craved the attention that made me nervous. I thought I was safe as long as I was his friend and nothing else.

During the time that things were good he always gave me good advice. In 2006, I had a violent ex that just went to jail for various things he did to me. I told Keith what happened. I tried to defend my love at the time saying, 'He [my ex] is not a bad person, he just has mental problems.' I will never forget Keith's reply to what I said. In my opinion it will go down as one of the best quotes ever from a serial killer. He told me: 'You said it yourself, he is not a bad person he just has some mental issues. The same could be said about me, but will they let me go after a couple years for each murder? Hell no. Why? Because they believe that I cannot be cured of my head problems.'

A couple years later, what he said is still in my head because it makes so much sense. In the same letter he told me: 'I have done eleven years in prison so far and I can say ten years tells me how much my actions have hurt everyone around me. And I am just a murderer. Not a rapist or a kidnapper or worse. My victims died never to feel a long drawn out pain of surviving and living with the questions of why and how and did I do something wrong. Guilt for not knowing who they were messing with. I admit my guilt and I'll get seven life sentences in a row to think of what I have done.'

In a strange way this made sense to me to. Keith was always there for me, to listen to me and give me good advice. On a few occasions, I asked him for advice or help with assignments I had from college and he always gave it to me.

My romantic relationship with Keith started in January 2008. I was married at the time but going through a messy divorce. I told Keith about it and his response to me was, 'If you had married me then you would not be in this mess. You know that I have always loved you.' He has told me things like this for almost six years. He would tell me that I represent his ideal woman because I am so independent and I don't need a man to make me happy. I thought, 'Why not, this guy has been pursuing me for years now. He is a good friend and I like him. The fact that he killed people is a huge turn on for me, so why not, I will give him chance.' I asked Keith what he would expect from me as his girlfriend. He told me he would expect me to love him for whom he is, and he hoped that I would help him out with things. He wanted me to sell his art work, and he said he would even help me financially if his art work would sell. So, there it was. I was the Happy Face Killer's steady girlfriend.

When we became a couple we would write sexually

explicit letters to each other, and I won't lie, that was fun. It was not long after that we became engaged. He asked me on the phone to marry him and I said yes. Things went downhill after that. He got very moody and mouthy with me. Something that I don't tolerate from any man. He told me to write him often and when I did he griped that I was writing too much. I stopped writing him. When he called he asked why he had not got any mail from me, I told him, 'You told me not to write so much,' and he yells at me, 'You better start writing me more.' Geez, someone woke up on the wrong side of the bed.

The point is I felt like I was damned if I do and damned if I don't with him. There was no earthly way to please him. He also started to get jealous of my friends. I don't know why, they were only friends. On the phone he would make comments about me staying out too late or goofing off at work. He never had a problem with that stuff until we got engaged. While we were engaged he told me about a woman, 'a serial killer groupie', as he described her was coming to visit him but he didn't know if he wanted to see her. He saw her and then told me about it. I got the feeling he was testing me to see if I would get upset or jealous. I just told him, 'Oh! Glad you had a good time, hope you get to see her again.'

Sorry Keith, no jealousy here. When we were together, I asked him if he was ok with me telling my closest friends about us, and he said he did not mind. The only people that ever knew of my relationship with Keith were a couple of my dearest friends. Keith said that he told his friends and family about us. I told him I didn't mind for that but to never give out my information to the media. We had a few little ups and downs like that.

I would tell Keith about my life, my friends, etc. I suggested that he get to know my best friend, John. Since Keith was going to be my husband, I felt he needed the seal of approval from my best friend first. Keith wrote John a letter in April 2008. The letter was both hilarious and a disturbing look inside his head. John called me that night to read me the letter word for word. The funny part is that Keith continues to get my best friend John confused with another friend I have named Ken. Keith wrote the letter to John, but for some reason thought he was writing to Ken.

Ken is a different story all together. He has been in love with me since I was 14 years old and since he is such a character I would tell Keith about him. Keith wrote to John, 'I know you love her, just tell me. I am not the enemy. I understand more than you know.' At this point John is thinking, 'What the hell is he talking about?' Keith then goes on to ask things about me like he is trying to get information about me in a sneaky way. That is what made me mad. I felt like he was trying to spy on me or something. Of course, John was shocked and outraged. He told me, 'Who the hell does he think he is? Does he really think I would betray an 11-year friendship for him, I don't even know him. What an asshole.' I told John to send me the letter and he did. Keith called me that Monday. Everything was all happy and rosy at first. He thanked me for the books I had sent him for his birthday. I say, 'Keith, I want to talk to you about something. John read me the letter you wrote to him.' Keith says in a quiet tone, 'Oh, he did.' I reply with 'Yes he did and he sent it to me... I'll have it in a couple of days. What were you thinking, oh and for the record you keep getting John and Ken mixed up.' Keith said, 'Oh! Ok. I'll see you later.' And he hung up on me!

Can you believe the nerve of some people? That same day, I changed my telephone number. He did send me a letter that week and I sent it back to him. That was the end of me and Keith Jesperson.

I learned a few things about him in that moment. He really is a coward. When confronted and cornered he ran away like a scared little boy. He did not like the fact that he got caught red-handed, not one bit! I believe he was in shock that John would not bow down to his serial killer status and do what he asked. The way he tried to get information behind my back tells me that he is a very deceitful and deceiving man. Not to mention being very arrogant. I learned from being with him that he is very arrogant and controlling. He wants things done his way and when they are not he will act like a child. When things don't go according to his plan he will get angry and yell at you. I can only imagine the way he yelled at his victims. There is no way to make him happy. There is nothing you can ever to do please him. I don't believe that he has any remorse for what he did. I think he only regrets being caught. He did tell me if he had the chance to do it all over again that he would make a run for Canada. There he goes again, running away when he gets caught in something. He has the attitude of, 'I am an infamous serial killer so everyone should just do as I ask with no questions and no complaining.' Well I guess he met his match with me.

When we were together he did send me a bunch of his art work to sell for him and I still have it all. I will not make money off of him like that. I am a better person than he is in that way. I do not feel bad that we broke up, it is for the best. I am sad over the loss of our friendship. I did love and trust him as a friend. He was a wonderful friend but a horrible boyfriend. If we had just stayed friends, we would still be in touch. One of the last things I ever asked Keith was, 'Do you think you would ever kill again?' His answer was, 'Will I ever kill again? I hope not. But I do know how to kill and if faced with it in here I will if I have to.' It was one of those questions that I already knew the answer to but wanted to ask anyway just to hear it from him.

I know there are a lot of woman out there that claim to love serial killers. I believe that it is 50/50. I believe that everyone is different so women are attracted to serial killers for different reasons. In my opinion, some are just looking for their 15 minutes of fame. Society has turned serial killers into celebrities in a way. These women want the notoriety of it. They want to be known as the woman of a serial killer. It is very easy to achieve this. All you have to do is write a letter to a serial killer, form a relationship and there ya go. Of course to meet a celebrity in Hollywood, it is not that easy. These women know this is the easiest way for them to get their few minutes of camera time.

I also believe that some of these women are naturally submissive and want to say that they have dominated a serial killer. If you really think about it, the woman does have all control in the relationship. She decides when she will write to him, visit him, accept his phone calls, send him money, etc. She can do anything that she wants and there is nothing the killer can do about it since he is in prison. I am sure if the role was reversed and these killers were out and about these women would be too afraid to be with them.

Some woman have this, 'Oh, I can save him; I want to help him attitude'.They want to save the world and think they will start by changing a serial killer from a monster to a productive member of society. I am sorry to be the one to break it to them but that is not going to happen. Once someone has crossed the line to multiple murders there is no going back. Killers are what they are and there is no rhyme or reason for what they do. I believe that even some killers themselves don't know why they have killed over and over again. To them it is like second nature. But some women still feel that love will conquer all and they will be the one to save him.

Some women are looking to be abused. They have had an abusive childhood or an abusive spouse so that is all they know. Some women just want the thrill of being with a killer. It is a rush to be in the room alone with someone that has killed so many times in cold blood.

Some women want to be with a notorious killer because it is the 'cool thing' to be doing these days. These women are posers of the worst kind. They pretend to like these killers just because it is the cool thing to do. In reality they don't know the difference between Jeffrey Dahmer and Charles Manson. They don't even have enough sense to educate themselves about killers before getting involved. They jump into it to be liked and accepted by their 'gothic' peers.

Then there are woman like me that just get off on that type of violence. They are few and far between but they are some out there. They are sincerely sick and sadistic themselves and have no problem with the fact that their man is a killer, in fact they like it. Women like me don't want any fame from it, they don't care what others think of them. All that does matter is the killer they are in love with. They simply want to live in their own little world with their killer and not be bothered by anyone else. The women that are sincerely into it and love these people for who they are and for what they did are usually very strong and independent woman that don't need anything from anyone. They are the exception to the rule. Of course everyone is different and who am I to judge. One of my favorite quotes of all time is a quote by French critic, essayist and novelist André Paul Guillaume Gide: It is better to be hated for what you are than to be loved for what you are not.

Laci's first book containing hundreds of explicit letters written by scores of the most heinous serial killers alive, and since executed, is to be published in 2009.

*   *   *

This book is all about letters to and from serial killers. There are thousands of men and women who are determined to find love with those convicted of the most serious of crimes. I guess I must close now, but I shall leave you with a letter, one most recently received from a 22-year-old woman, who wrote to Keith Hunter Jesperson. I have omitted her name and Oregon SID number, but she is serving time for serious offences in Lincoln County Jail:

I am a fan of yours. I need to know all about every detail of all your murders...Did you enjoy it all...did you get sex

*pleasure, cum? I want to know. I need to know everything
about all of your murders. It turns me on. I am a strange
woman with weird tastes. Send me a signed photo, please?*

Do I need to say any more? Write these killers letters if you will.
But check out their true histories before doing just that. Indeed,
if you are so inclined, ask for the person's criminal antecedents,
from the jurisdiction involved, before you 'fall in love' with any
offender behind bars. The authorities will always send you a
current 'rap sheet' and a photo if you ask them.

Now check out all of the web sites concerned with prisoners
seeking love and 'personal relationships', with criminals behind
bars... and think again.